THE READER'S VOICE

THE READER'S VOICE

DEVELOPING YOUR UNDERSTANDING AND ENJOYMENT OF COLLEGE READING

DEBORAH SILVEY
DIABLO VALLEY COLLEGE

PEARSON
Longman

New York • San Francisco • Boston
London • Toronto • Sydney • Tokyo • Singapore • Madrid
Mexico City • Munich • Paris • Cape Town • Hong Kong • Montreal

Vice President and Editor-in-Chief: Joseph Terry
Senior Acquisitions Editor: Susan Kunchandy
Development Manager: Janet Lanphier
Development Editor: Ann Hofstra Grogg
Senior Marketing Manager: Melanie Craig
Senior Supplements Editor: Donna Campion
Managing Editor: Bob Ginsberg
Production Manager: Joseph Vella
Project Coordination, Text Design, and Electronic Page Makeup: Thompson Steele, Inc.
Cover Designer/Manager: John Callahan
Cover Photo: Courtesy of Getty Images, Inc.
Photo Researcher: Photosearch, Inc.
Manufacturing Manager: Mary Fischer
Manufacturing Buyer: Roy L. Pickering, Jr.
Printer and Binder: Courier Corporation—Westford
Cover Printer: The Lehigh Press

For permission to use copyrighted material, grateful acknowledgment is made to the copyright holders on pp. 395–398, which are hereby made part of this copyright page.

Library of Congress Cataloging-in-Publication Data
Silvey, Deborah.
  The reader's voice : developing your understanding and enjoyment of college reading / Deborah Silvey.
    p. cm.
  Includes bibliographical references and index.
  ISBN 0-321-08575-2
  1. Reading (Higher education) 2. Reading comprehension. I. Title.

  LB2395.3.S53   2005
  428.4'071'1—dc22   2004018598

Please visit our website at http://www.ablongman.com.

ISBN 0–321–08575–2

1 2 3 4 5 6 7 8 9 10—CRW—07 06 05 04

To my students at Diablo Valley College

Their voices are part of this book.

BRIEF CONTENTS

DETAILED CONTENTS

✳ ✳ ✳

TO THE INSTRUCTOR

The Reader's Voice places special emphasis on helping students discover their role in the reading process. By experiencing themselves as active, engaged readers, students are motivated to learn the systematic instruction in basic reading skills provided in the book. As the first-level college reading text in a two-book series, *The Reader's Voice* uses the same approach as its companion text, *Reading from the Inside Out*. Both texts focus on the reading process as an interaction between reader and writer that allows for self-discovery as well as for gaining information. In both texts a thematic arrangement of readings helps students become personally involved with many different types of readings, and reading instruction is integrated with these thematically linked readings. However, *The Reader's Voice* focuses instruction on more basic reading strategies, such as finding main ideas and supporting details, while providing appropriate reading selections for first-level college reading students.

The book presents a sequence of reading strategies—starting with ways of connecting to the writer's ideas, and then moving through a logical but flexible progression for comprehending and interpreting. Each strategy is introduced as a way to find meaning in a complete reading on a theme. This integration of instruction with thematically linked readings increases students' interest in learning the strategy. Several choices of readings are available for practice with many readings linked to more than one theme.

Follow-up activities for each reading help students expand their ways of interacting with a writer's ideas. By talking with other students and collaborating on activities, students experience the connection between reading and talking. By writing personal responses, answering questions, and asking and answering their own questions, they learn to refine their thinking through writing.

Organization: Reading Strategies and Themes

Each of the 11 chapters in *The Reader's Voice* introduces a new reading strategy and provides one or two appropriate readings to practice the strategy. Additional readings are provided at the end of each part, and you can choose from among them for supplementary or substitute material. In addition, an optional study skills supplement called "Time Out for You" follows each of the book's chapters. You may assign any or all of these supplements, but students can also use them on their own.

Each part of the book deals with an overall category of reading strategies as well as its own theme.

- In Part I, "Discovering the Reader's Voice," students learn to check in and respond, using readings on the theme of "learning for yourself."

- In Part II, "Predicting and Questioning," the strategies taught are working with new words, both by using context clues and by finding the right definition, and asking questions, using readings about "popular culture."

- In Part III, "Understanding Main Ideas," students learn to find topics and main ideas, find support, and look for patterns of thought, using readings about "men and women, boys and girls."

- In Part IV, "Remembering and Interpreting," the strategies taught are writing to remember, making inferences, and analyzing the information, using readings about "working in America."

Special Features

The foundation for instruction in *The Reader's Voice* is developing the student's role as an active, engaged reader. The book contains several features to emphasize this student-centered approach:

- Focus on the reader as an active participant responding to a writer's ideas

- Thematic arrangement of readings, to enhance student interest and develop the ability to see relationships among ideas

- Complete readings to accompany each reading strategy

- Strategies for developing vocabulary, along with vocabulary exercises as an integral part of each reading

- Consistent presentation of each strategy, with an introductory outline, step-by-step demonstration, and follow-up practice

- Clear, flexible sequence of reading strategies that support development of metacognitive processes

- Choice of readings for teaching each strategy

- Writing activities for each reading

- Collaborative activities

- "Time Out for You" study skills supplements

- Additional questions in a multiple-choice format for assessing comprehension and vocabulary

Teaching and Learning Package

For Instructors

Instructor's Manual.   A complete Instructor's Manual is available to accompany *The Reader's Voice*. The manual gives a wide range of general guidelines for reinforcing the central concepts and practices of the text, along with sample syllabi, transparency masters, and other teaching resources. In addition, detailed answers and suggestions for teaching and testing are provided for each chapter (Instructor: ISBN 0-321-08576-0).

The Longman Instructor's Planner.   This planner includes weekly and monthly calendars, student attendance and grading rosters, space for contact information, Web references, an almanac, and blank pages for notes (Instructor: ISBN 0-321-09247-3).

Printed Test Bank for Developmental Reading.   This test bank offers more than 3,000 questions in all areas of reading, including vocabulary, main idea, supporting detail, patterns of organization, critical thinking, analytical reasoning, inference, point of view, visual aids, and textbook reading (Instructor: ISBN 0-321-08596-5). An electronic version is also available.

Electronic Test Bank for Developmental Reading.   This electronic test bank offers more than 3,000 questions in all areas of reading, including vocabulary, main idea, supporting detail, patterns of organization, critical thinking, analytical reasoning, point of view, visual aids, and textbook reading. Instructors simply choose questions, then print out the completed test for distribution *or* offer the test online (Instructor CD: ISBN 0-321-08179-X).

For Students

MySkillsLab 2.0 (www.ablongman.com/myskillslab). MySkillsLab 2.0 offers the best online resources for developing readers and writers, all in one easy-to-use site. Here, students can improve their reading skills with the newly updated **Reading Roadtrip 4.0** and sharpen their writing skills using **Writing Voyage.** In Reading Roadtrip 4.0, each of the 16 cities and landmarks on this tour throughout the United States corresponds to a reading or study skill (for example, finding a main idea, understanding patterns of organization, thinking critically, etc.). This new release of the most popular and exciting reading tool available offers even more practice exercises and test questions in all areas of reading skills. Students can now begin by taking a diagnostic test that helps them determine areas of weakness and offers feedback that directs them to key topics for skill improvement. An Instructor's Manual for MySkillsLab is available. Please contact your Longman Sales Representative for more information.

The Longman Textbook Reader, **Revised Edition.**   This supplement offers five complete chapters from our textbooks covering computer science, biology, psychology, communications, and business. Each chapter includes additional comprehension quizzes, critical thinking questions, and group activities. (Student: ISBN 0-321-11895-2 [with answers]; ISBN 0-321-12223-2 [without answers]).

The Longman Reader's Journal **by Kathleen McWhorter.**   The first journal for readers, *The Longman Reader's Journal* offers a place for students to record their reactions to and questions about any reading. (Student: ISBN 0-321-08843-3).

The Longman Reader's Portfolio and Student Planner.   This unique portfolio/planner supplement provides students with a space to plan, think about, and present their work, as well as a calendar to schedule their semester and keep key instructor information. The portfolio includes a diagnostic area including a learning style questionnaire, a working area including a personal reading log, suggested readings, textbook reading response sheet, and more, and a display area including a progress chart and a final assessment.

10 Practices of Highly Effective Students. This study skills supplement includes topics such as time management, test taking, reading critically, stress, and motivation (Student: ISBN 0-205-30769-8).

Newsweek **Discount Subscription Coupon (12 weeks).** *Newsweek* gets students reading, writing, and thinking about what's going on in the world around them. The price of the subscription is added to the cost of the book. Instructors receive weekly lesson plans, quizzes, and curriculum guides as well as a complimentary *Newsweek* subscription. The price of the subscription is 59 cents per issue (a total of $7.08 for the subscription) (Student: ISBN 0-321-08895-6).

Interactive Guide to *Newsweek*. Available with the 12-week subscription to *Newsweek*, this guide serves as a workbook for students who are using the magazine. FREE with the adoption of a Longman textbook (Student: ISBN 0-321-05528-4. Value Pack Item Only).

Research Navigator Guide for English **by H. Eric Branscomb and Linda R. Barr.** Designed to teach students how to conduct high-quality online research and to document it properly, Research Navigator guides provide discipline-specific academic resources, in addition to helpful tips on the writing process, online research, and finding and citing valid sources. Research Navigator guides include an access code to Research Navigator™—providing access to thousands of academic journals and periodicals, the *New York Times* Search by Subject Archive, Link Library, Library Guides, and more (Student: ISBN 0-321-20277-5).

Penguin Discount Novel Program. In cooperation with Penguin Putnam, Inc., Longman is proud to offer a variety of Penguin paperbacks at a significant discount when packaged with any Longman title. Excellent additions to any Developmental Reading or English course, Penguin titles give students the opportunity to explore contemporary and classical fiction and drama. The available titles include works by authors as diverse as Toni Morrison, Julia Alvarez, Mary Shelley, and Shakespeare. To review the complete list of titles available, visit the Longman-Penguin-Putnam website: http://www.ablongman.com/penguin.

The New American Webster Handy College Dictionary.   This paperback reference text offers more than 100,000 entries. For more details on ordering a dictionary with this text, contact your Longman sales consultant (Student: ISBN 0-451-18166-2).

Texas Adopters: *The Longman THEA Study Guide* **by Jeannette Harris.**   Created specifically for students in Texas, this study guide includes straightforward explanations and numerous practice exercises to help students prepare for the reading and writing sections of THEA test (Student: ISBN 0-321-20271-6. Value Pack Item Only).

New York Adopters: *Preparing for the CUNY-ACT Reading and Writing Test* **edited by Patricia Licklider.**   This booklet, prepared by reading and writing faculty from across the CUNY system, is designed to help students prepare for the CUNY-ACT exit test. It includes test-taking tips, reading passages, typical exam questions, and sample writing prompts to help students become familiar with each portion of the test. (Student: ISBN 0-321-19608-2. $20 stand alone. Sample through Socrates).

Acknowledgments

I want to thank several people who helped in the making of this book. First, I am indebted to my students and colleagues at Diablo Valley College. They gave me valuable insights about what students need in order to read with greater comprehension and enjoyment. Second, the editorial staff of Longman Publishers made important contributions to this book. Senior editor Steve Rigolosi helped me develop the initial project and supported me through most of the writing process with great enthusiasm and inventiveness. I am also grateful to acquistions editor Susan Kunchandy, who stepped in and helped me finish the project. My developmental editor, Ann Hofstra Grogg, deserves special thanks. Her grasp of everything, from the overall goals to the small details of this book, helped me structure and clarify my ideas. Finally, I thank all my family—Chris, Rachel, Dylan, Carla, Lerryn, Tim, Devon, and Miranda—for their continued patience, love, and support. My deepest gratitude goes to my husband, Robert, for his research contributions, his editorial suggestions, and his consistent good humor and wisdom.

Several reading teachers reviewed earlier drafts, and I am grateful for their suggestions and ideas:

Kristen Gregory, J Sageant Reynolds Community College
Juliet Emanuel, Borough of Manhattan Community College/CUNY
Tammy Frankland, Casper College
Carolyn Conners, Wor-Wic Community College
Bonnie Glaig, Rochester Community and Technical College

Deborah Silvey
Berkeley, California

TO THE STUDENT

WELCOME TO
THE READER'S VOICE

This book was written to help you get more out of your college reading. Reading is more meaningful when you can relate what you read to your own life. So readings in the book are grouped around specific themes—general subjects that are explored from several different perspectives. These themes encourage you to connect the ideas of various writers and to think about how your own experiences relate to them. Each theme is a part, and the book has four parts, each with two or three chapters:

Part I: Learning for Yourself

Part II: Popular Culture

Part III: Men and Women, Boys and Girls

Part IV: Working in America

The Reader's Voice introduces all of its reading instruction through these thematically linked readings. Each chapter uses one of these readings to introduce a new *reading strategy*—a clear plan or method for approaching a reading assignment. You'll practice using strategies like "finding main ideas" and "looking for patterns of thought" with the kinds of readings assigned in your college courses, such as textbooks and journal articles, along with some stories and poems. You'll also find a feature after each chapter called "Time Out for You." Your instructor may assign these "Time Outs," but you can also use them on your own to improve your reading skills and your chances for success in college.

Finally, this book invites you to discover the value of sharing ideas with other readers. The book gives you many opportunities to work in cooperation with other students to increase your understanding of what you read.

As you progress through this book, you will practice ways of reading that increase your ability:

- to discover more about yourself

- to understand college reading assignments

- to work effectively with other students

- to *enjoy* reading!

THE READER'S VOICE

PART I

DISCOVERING THE READER'S VOICE

WITH READINGS ON LEARNING FOR YOURSELF

When is reading really *reading?*

Everyone knows what it's like to go through the motions of reading. You spend time looking at the words on each page, so it seems as if you're reading. But your mind is somewhere else—not on the ideas contained on those pages. After you're through you wonder, "Now, what did I just read?"

You've had another experience of reading, too. Real reading. That happens when you can focus on what the writer is saying. In this kind of reading, you're sometimes aware of the writer "talking" to you. You "hear" the writer's voice as you read his or her words.

But as the reader you also have a voice—the voice in your mind that responds. You respond when you agree or disagree. You respond when you ask a question or become frustrated over a confusing point. You respond when you think about how the ideas relate—or don't relate—to your own life.

This way of reading is called *active reading.* In active reading, you have a kind of conversation with the writer as you "listen" to the writer's voice and respond with the voice in your own mind. Active reading is especially important in college where you're exploring brand new areas of study. For college reading assignments, you need to become fully involved in what you read, so you don't become lost or discouraged.

The Reader's Voice will make you a more involved, active reader. Throughout the book, readings are grouped around themes—general subjects—that invite you to think about your own experiences as you consider each writer's ideas. By voicing your understanding or agreement with those ideas, you help

3

yourself to stay involved. At the same time, voicing your confusion or disagreement also keeps you involved. Active reading puts you in control. It keeps you aware of what you've learned and tells you what new information you might need to look for.

To help you become an active reader, the book also teaches you *reading strategies*—clear plans or methods for approaching a reading assignment. You're first introduced to each strategy as a way to follow the ideas in a specific reading on one of the book's themes. Then you practice the strategy with other readings on that theme.

In Part I, you'll look at the theme of "learning for yourself." You'll read about people facing life's challenges in ways that help them learn who they are and what they can do. As you read each writer's ideas, listen to his or her voice. But also find your own voice, as you "talk back" to the writer. The reading strategy in Chapter 1, **Check In,** shows you how to find your own voice and become involved in a reading. The strategy in Chapter 2, **Respond,** helps you stay involved and "listen" to what you think about the reading.

CHAPTER 1

LISTEN TO YOURSELF FIRST

CHECK IN

Written words have meaning only when they come to life in your mind. That's why *active reading* is like a conversation. The writer's words "speak" to you, the reader; you "listen," and you "talk back." But how do you become involved when you read, so you feel as if you're really having a conversation?

Introduction to the New Strategy: Check In

Strategy 1—**Check In**—gets you involved in a reading from the very beginning. Before starting to read, you get a brief idea of what the reading is about. You do this by looking at the title or other clues about the subject. Next, you **check in** with yourself. What do you have to say about the subject? Listen to yourself first. Recognize your *reader's voice*—the voice in your mind that responds. That way, you're ready with questions and ideas that you'll look for the writer to answer and expand on.

STRATEGY 1: CHECK IN

1 Get a quick first impression of the subject.

2 Relate your experience and feelings to the subject.

Use this strategy to **check in** before reading "Poppa and the Spruce Tree: A Lesson from My Father," by Mario Cuomo, former governor of New York. The reading is on page 7.

The Subject and the Title

1 *Get a quick first impression of the subject.*

Look first at the title of a reading. The title often gives you the *subject*. The subject is what the reading is about; it's the focus for all the ideas. The title of Reading 1 shows that the subject is a lesson the writer learned from his father. The title also shows that the lesson has something to do with a spruce tree.

Your Experience and Feelings

2 *Relate your experience and feelings to the subject.*

Take a moment to see how your experience relates to the subject. You don't need to understand every part of the subject. Use what you do understand to think of ideas and questions you have for the writer. For example, you don't have to know what a spruce tree is or how it is connected to the father's lesson. Instead, focus on what you've learned from your own father, so you have a starting point for your conversation with the writer.

Here are some ways a reader might relate to the subject and begin a conversation with the author, Mario Cuomo.

- Question: "What did I learn from my dad? I guess the best thing was how to get by with very little money. Governor Cuomo, what did you learn from your father? What did a tree have to do with the lesson?"

- Remember: "My father surprised me once by leaving work early to watch me play in an important basketball game. That felt like a lesson—I learned how much he cared. Maybe you learned the same kind of lesson from your father."

- Predict: "It could be that your father showed you how to plant and take care of a tree. I know my father showed me how to do things—not planting, but how to fix my bike, build a desk, program the VCR."

Consider your feelings as well as your ideas about a subject. If you're aware of negative feelings, try to put them aside once you start reading. Otherwise, they can distract you and cause you to miss what the writer is saying. For this reading, your feelings about your father—

positive or negative—will have some influence on your ideas about a father's lessons.

Here's one way a reader might deal with negative feelings before beginning to read:

- Comment: "Most of the lessons I learned from my father were how <u>not</u> to be with your kids. He was not a positive influence. So, Governor Cuomo, I'll just have to see what your father had to teach you. I hope to be a better father than mine was, so maybe I can learn something."

Think of your own ideas and questions to help you get a head start on the conversation with the author. Then, as you read, you'll already be involved in what Mario Cuomo will say back to you.

READING 1   POPPA AND THE SPRUCE TREE: A LESSON FROM MY FATHER
MARIO CUOMO

Mario Cuomo was governor of New York from 1982 to 1994. This reading comes from Diaries of Mario M. Cuomo, *a series of essays Cuomo wrote about the first time he ran for governor.*

Poppa taught me a lot about life, especially its hard times. I remem-   1
bered one of his lessons one night when I was ready to quit a political campaign I was losing, and wrote about it in my diary:

Tired, feeling the many months of struggle, I went up to the den to   2
make some notes. I was looking for a pencil, rummaging° through papers
in the back of my desk drawer, where things accumulate for years, when I
turned up one of Poppa's old business cards, the ones we made up for him,
that he was so proud of: *Andrea Cuomo, Italian-American Groceries—Fine
Imported Products.* Poppa never had occasion to give anyone a calling
card, but he loved having them.

rummaging: looking through

I couldn't help wondering what Poppa would have said if I told him I   3
was tired or—God forbid—discouraged. Then I thought about how he dealt
with hard circumstances. A thousand pictures flashed through my mind,
but one scene came sharply into view.

We had just moved to Holliswood, New York, from our apartment   4
behind the store. We had our own house for the first time; it had some land
around it, even trees. One, in particular, was a great blue spruce° that must
have been 40 feet tall.

spruce: cone-shaped evergreen

Less than a week after we moved in, there was a terrible storm. We   5
came home from the store that night to find the spruce pulled almost
totally from the ground and flung forward, its mighty nose bent in the

scale: climb

asphalt of the street. My brother Frankie and I could climb poles all day; we were great at fire escapes; we could scale° fences with barbed wire—but we knew nothing about trees. When we saw our spruce, defeated, its cheek on the canvas, our hearts sank. But not Poppa's.

Maybe he was five feet six if his heels were not worn. Maybe he weighed 155 pounds if he had a good meal. Maybe he could see a block away if his glasses were clean. But he was stronger than Frankie and me and Marie and Mamma all together.   6

We stood in the street looking down at the tree. The rain was falling. Then he announced, "O.K., we gonna push 'im up!" "What are you talking about, Poppa? The roots are out of the ground!" "Shut up, we gonna push 'im up, he's gonna grow again." We didn't know what to say to him. You couldn't say no to him. So we followed him into the house and we got what rope there was and we tied the rope around the tip of the tree that lay in the asphalt, and he stood up by the house, with me pulling on the rope and Frankie in the street in the rain, helping to push up the great blue spruce. In no time at all, we had it standing up straight again!   7

With the rain still falling, Poppa dug away at the place where the roots were, making a muddy hole wider and wider as the tree sank lower and lower toward security. Then we shoveled mud over the roots and moved boulders to the base to keep the tree in place. Poppa drove stakes in the ground, tied rope from the trunk to the stakes, and maybe two hours later looked at the spruce, the crippled spruce made straight by ropes, and said, "Don't worry, he's gonna grow again. . . ."   8

I looked at the card and wanted to cry. If you were to drive past that house today, you would see the great, straight blue spruce, maybe 65 feet tall, pointing straight up to the heavens, pretending it never had its nose in the asphalt.   9

vengeance: great force

I put Poppa's card back in the drawer, closed it with a vengeance.° I couldn't wait to get back into the campaign.   10

Follow-Up Activities   After you've finished reading, use these questions to respond to "Poppa and the Spruce Tree: A Lesson from My Father." You may write your answers or prepare them in your mind to discuss in class.

1. What did Cuomo's father do to save the spruce tree? Why do you think he went to such trouble to save it?

2. What lesson did Cuomo learn from the way his father dealt with the tree?

3. How did remembering the lesson affect the way Cuomo felt about his political campaign?

4. What is an important lesson you've learned from a parent or other significant adult in your life? How similar or how different was your lesson from the one Cuomo describes?

5. Choose a part of the reading you particularly liked or didn't like. Explain your choice.   ■

Apply the New Strategy: Check In

Now that you understand Strategy 1, put it into practice with Reading 2, "A Role Model of Resiliency: Bouncing Back from Disaster."

1 *Get a quick first impression of the subject.*

Before beginning Reading 2, get as much as you can about the subject from the title. You may not know the word "resiliency," but you can figure it out from the words that follow, "bouncing back from disaster." The title also tells you that someone is a role model of this kind of bouncing back. If the title doesn't tell you enough about the subject, look at the first paragraph or two for more clues. In this reading, the first paragraph and beginning of the second paragraph tell you what that disaster was. You can now see that the subject of the reading is a role model who bounced back from the disaster of an attempted suicide.

2 *Relate your experience and feelings to the subject.*

How can you relate to this subject? Remember: the subject is not suicide, but successfully starting over after a terrible event. Even though most of us have never reached that level of hopelessness, we all know how it feels to go through hard times. What has helped you to bounce back from trouble? Notice your feelings as you relate your own experience to this subject. Don't let negative feelings get in the way of the story Tom Wanamaker has to tell you.

READING 2   A ROLE MODEL OF RESILIENCY:
BOUNCING BACK FROM DISASTER

TOM WANAMAKER

Tom Wanamaker, a staff reporter for the newspaper Indian Country Today, *wrote this article for the March 20, 2002, edition of the paper.*

SALT LAKE CITY—Like many young men, he seemed to have the world at his feet. One of Nevada's top high school athletes, he excelled at both basketball and football and dreamed of playing collegiate and professional sports. But in a split second, Arnold W. Thomas completely transformed his life and his future.   1

despondent: hopeless
wracked: messed up

Despondent° over his father's suicide two years earlier, and wracked°   2
by alcoholism and drug-abuse, Thomas put a rifle under his chin at age 18
and tried to kill himself. He failed, but seriously damaged his face, leaving
himself blind and, for two years, unable to speak. Yet Thomas, a member of
the Shoshone-Paiute Tribes of the Duck Valley Indian Reservation of Idaho

perseverance: determination

and Nevada, has bounced back to become a living lesson in perseverance.°

Arnold Thomas had to start over from scratch.   3

"On top of losing my sight, I couldn't talk—I had to learn to speak   4
again," he told ICT [*Indian Country Times*] recently. "I went to Salt Lake
City to go to a school for the blind and, at 19 years old, I had to learn a new
way of life, [with] independent skills—basic things, like walking down the
street, crossing streets, riding public transportation."

Now, at age 31, Thomas travels throughout the United States and   5
Canada, speaking to school and community groups, both Indian and non-

resiliency: ability to bounce
back from hard times
adversity: hard times

Indian, about suicide and substance abuse. His theme is resiliency,° the
ability to bounce back from adversity°; he compares his personal experiences and struggles to those of Indian country as a whole. He spoke at the
Dancing the Path Wellness Conference . . . at the Turning Stone Casino in
Verona, N.Y.

intuitive: natural

"Resiliency is intuitive° and, to me, spiritual," Thomas explained.   6
"Native people for thousands of years have used the four basic elements to
maintain balance and harmony. . . . By connecting with these elements
through prayer, Native people have always been able to find inner peace
no matter what type of trauma, tragedy or positive experience they go
through. They've been able to take those experiences and find a silver lin-
ing and adapt to and find the beauty in whatever type of situation they are
in and make the best of it."

Seeking strength and balance, Thomas looks to the traditional ways of   7
the Shoshone-Paiute people. . . .

"They're very old, hundreds and thousands of years old," Thomas   8
said. "The songs and language incorporated in the ceremonies tie me and
connect me to the past and help me to maintain that balance in my life. So,
the ceremonies are there to help me maintain balance within my mind
and among my emotions as well as in my physical body. I got away from it
[traditional ceremonies] when I was in high school, but came back when I
got older."

Music has served Thomas as another means for spiritual release. He   9
recorded a selection of songs entitled "Dosa Weehee, Sounds of the Great
Basin." The CD features Thomas singing traditional and original songs in
the Shoshone-Paiute language, accompanied by hand drums, rattles, flutes
and guitars. "Dosa weehee" is Shoshone for "white knife." . . .

In 1999, Thomas graduated from the University of Utah with a master's   10
degree in social work. He views his specialty, clinical therapy, as a way to
help and inspire younger students; if he can overcome the considerable
adversity he's faced, then they can beat the obstacles in their paths as well.

"A lot of the young people I speak to come from broken homes,   11
blended families, interracial families, or have parents who are abusive
in every way we can imagine," said Thomas. "I just let them know
that . . . that they've got the ability to overcome and make a better life for
themselves, but they've got to want to [do] it. I got my degree in clinical
therapy because I feel like a lot of Native people have that [same] ability;
[I just try to] help them to find the positive qualities that are there."

viable: workable

belies: disproves

Despite his blindness, athletic competition remains a key emotional   12
outlet for Thomas as well as a viable° means to a college education for
younger athletes. Once a star basketball player (he competed in a national
foul-shooting contest in junior high and was pursued by collegiate
recruiters in high school) Thomas belies° the idea that a blind man cannot
coach sports. With some help from a sighted assistant, he has coached
youth basketball, stressing commitment and fundamentals from his players. He teaches defense, shooting and dribbling through a combination of
demonstration and explanation.

"In basketball, playing defense, there's a certain defensive stance I'm   13
looking for," Thomas explained. "I actually get out there and show them
how to shuffle and how to have one hand higher than the other. I just kind
of walk them through it, the spring in your feet, the technique, the follow
through, dribbling with the right and left hands and passing. I help them to
visualize" what they're doing.

"I break it down and tell them that, like anything in life, you've got to   14
have the basic fundamentals and then from there build on them," he continued. "I guess the big thing I tell young people is that athletics are 90 percent mental and ten percent physical. The game's won before you get out
on the court."

Although not currently coaching, Thomas carries the message over   15
into his inspirational presentations, asking his listeners to visualize things
with their eyes shut. "When I work with young people I have them close
their eyes throughout my presentation and make reference to various situations in my life," he said. "I run them through some visual images; if you
can visualize things, there are a lot of things that can occur in a positive
way. . . .

"The biggest thing in resiliency that I encourage in people is to have a   16
dream, a vision, a long-term goal," Thomas said. "A lot of people don't
have dreams. Sometimes when they get older, they think they're too old

Resiliency gives us ways to bounce back from hard times.

and they don't need to have a dream. And with young people, I ask them what their dream was when they were younger and the second part of that question is where are you in accomplishing that dream. Have a dream, have a long-term goal, have a vision. We all need it."

Follow-Up Activities   After you've finished reading, use these questions to respond to "A Role Model of Resiliency: Bouncing Back from Disaster." You may write your answers or prepare them in your mind to discuss in class.

1. What did Thomas have to do to "start over from scratch"?

2. What are some ways Thomas finds spiritual strength?

3. How is Thomas able to coach basketball? What lessons does he teach young basketball players? Describe as many lessons as you can.

4. The author of this reading called Thomas "a role model of resiliency." How similar or how different are your ways of being resilient (bouncing back from hard times) from Thomas's ways?

5. Now that you've thought more about the reading, what is your opinion about it? How did your response change from your first impression?   ■

Chapter 1 Summary

How does Strategy 1 help you *use your reader's voice to be an active reader?*

Active reading is like a conversation between you and the writer. You follow what the writer says, but you also have your reader's voice responding in your mind. You "talk back" as you question and as you agree or disagree. You think about how the writer's ideas relate to your own experience. **Checking in** reminds you to see what you have to say about a subject first. You listen to your own voice before reading, so you're ready for the "conversation" as you begin to read.

How does the *checking in* strategy work?

To **check in** you use the title and other clues to identify the subject of the reading. Then you ask yourself what experience and feelings you have in connection with the subject.

STRATEGY 1: CHECK IN

1 Get a quick first impression of the subject.

2 Relate your experience and feelings to the subject.

Are you familiar with the meaning of these terms?

active reading: reading that keeps you involved, as you respond with your own questions and ideas to what the writer says

reading strategies: clear plans for approaching a reading assignment

reader's voice: the voice in your mind that responds as you read what the writer is saying

subject: what the reading is about; the focus for all the ideas

How is the strategy working for you so far?

Explain which parts of **checking in** you've found most helpful in the readings you've practiced with. Which parts have been least helpful?

TIME OUT FOR YOU

How Can Resiliency
Help You in College?

Resiliency is the ability to bounce back from hard times. Psychologists are now studying resiliency to see how it helps people get through life's troubles. Reading 2, "A Role Model of Resiliency: Bouncing Back from Disaster," gives an example of overcoming a major disaster—an attempted suicide. But researchers on resiliency look at how this capacity to bounce back helps us overcome everyday difficulties as well as real tragedies. "When dealing with life's small hassles," says one of the researchers, Nan Henderson, "such as getting stuck in a traffic jam, or diffusing an argument with a co-worker . . . , we draw upon this internal capacity for resiliency. . . . When a major life crisis hits, people draw upon this capacity in a much bigger way."

Why Is Resiliency Important for College Students?

College presents many new challenges. You have a great deal of new material to learn. In addition, you're expected to balance your studying with some kind of social life and usually with a work schedule as well. Nobody faces these challenges without experiencing some setbacks. That's why tapping into your resiliency is so important for your success at college.

Resilient students know how to bounce back from such setbacks as a failed test or a low grade on a paper. "You learn from your mistakes" is not just an empty expression to them. They know how to use their strengths to figure out how to do better the next time.

Becoming a More Resilient Student

Researchers such as Henderson and Deborah Blum agree on two important findings about resiliency:

- People can learn to be more resilient, even as adults.

- People can develop resiliency by identifying the specific qualities that have allowed them to bounce back from trouble in the past.

So, becoming more aware of strengths you've used in the past helps you use them more effectively—when, for example, you run into a problem in college.

Look at the list of qualities that promote resiliency below. Which of these qualities do you think you have? Check the ones that apply to you. If you can think of additional qualities that can help you be resilient, add them on the blank lines provided.

Qualities That Promote Resiliency

[adapted from Henderson]

____ 1. Ability to get support—reaching out to family, friends, a partner, a teacher

____ 2. Faith in future possibilities—may be connected with faith in a higher power

____ 3. Sense of humor—using laughter to deal with life's problems

____ 4. Flexibility—finding ways of coping with change or difficult situations

____ 5. Sense of competence—knowing that you're "good at something"

____ 6. Far-sightedness—looking beyond a present difficulty to see a "bigger picture"

____ 7. Compassion—understanding others, being able to put yourself in others' shoes

____ 8. Creativity—expressing yourself through artistic work of some kind

____ 9. Independence—making your own decisions and taking responsibility for yourself

____ 10. Determination—not giving up, continuing on step-by-step

Other personal qualities, methods, or supports:

_____

_____

_____

_____

Now, take a moment to remember the qualities you used to get through a past difficulty. You may want to write down what you did or share what you did with a classmate.

_____

_____

_____

_____

Handling Typical Setbacks Faced by College Students

Here are three examples of setbacks college students often experience. After each example, think what you would do. Which of the qualities you checked from the list could you use to overcome the setback?

1. You fail your first test. You went to most of the classes, and you thought you'd studied enough for the test. Yet more than half your answers were incorrect.

As a resilient student, you would figure out what went wrong. You'd get help from the professor, fellow students, or perhaps a tutor. You'd find out how to get more out of time spent in class as well as through studying outside of class. In addition, you'd use other resiliency qualities to help see this single setback as part of the bigger picture of college work. Which qualities could you use to help this situation?

_____

_____

_____

_____

2. Your boss changes your work schedule. You started out with a tight schedule for classes and work. Then your boss insisted that you had to work one week during the time your history class meets. You had to miss two classes in a row. In the second class there was a pop quiz that you can't make up.

As a resilient student, you would figure out what to do next. You could explain to the professor what had happened and see if you could do an extra credit assignment. You could talk to your boss to try to prevent future scheduling problems. However, you might need to use other resiliency qualities to get yourself into a better work situation. Which qualities could you use to help this situation?

_____

_____

_____

_____

3. *The material in a course seems too difficult.* Since the beginning of the term you've tried to understand the course material. Now, a few weeks later, you're still not understanding the professor's lectures or the textbook.

As a resilient student, you would decide how to cope with this difficulty. You'd talk with the professor to see if he or she had suggestions. You could also get ideas from other students or join a study group. It might help to talk with a counselor to see if dropping the course would be the best option. In any case, you'd keep your eye on your long-term goal of succeeding in college. Which qualities could you use to help this situation?

_____

_____

_____

_____

Sources

Blum, Deborah. "Finding Strength: How to Overcome Anything." *Psychology Today,* May–June 1998: 32–45.

Henderson, Nan. "The Resiliency Route to Authentic Self-Esteem and Life Success." 2002. http://www.resiliency.com.

CHAPTER 2

STAY INVOLVED IN THE READING

RESPOND

Active reading begins as soon as you **check in.** Your own questions and ideas about the subject get you involved, so you're ready to begin the conversation between you and the writer. To stay involved, you need to continue the conversation as you read. Writers speak to you through their words, and you talk back. You agree or disagree; you notice things you like or dislike. You ask a question and look for an answer. You stay involved because you **respond.**

Try the New Strategy: Respond

Strategy 1, **Check In,** gets you involved in a reading from the start. Strategy 2, **Respond,** keeps you involved, as you consider what you think.

STRATEGY 2: RESPOND

1 Respond while you're reading and after you've finished reading.

2 Make a place or space to respond.

3 Ask questions and say what you think of the writer's ideas.

Notice how you **respond** as you read "The Struggle to Be an All-American Girl," by Elizabeth Wong. To give you practice, space is provided for you to **respond** at various points in the reading. At these points, pause briefly. Think about things you like or dislike; notice how Wong's ideas relate (or do not relate) to your own experiences; see what new questions and possible answers you now have. When you've finished the reading, be ready to **respond** by sharing your ideas and questions with others in the class.

| READING 3 | THE STRUGGLE TO BE AN ALL-AMERICAN GIRL |

ELIZABETH WONG

CHECK IN
- What does being an "all-American" girl or boy mean to you?
- Did you have any sort of struggle to be that kind of person? Or, did someone you know well go through such a struggle?
- Did you ever decide <u>not</u> to be "all-American"? If so, why?

stoically: showing no emotion

defiant: rebellious

maniacal: crazy

Elizabeth Wong first wrote this account of her growing up in San Francisco's Chinatown for the Los Angeles Times.

It's still there, the Chinese school on Yale Street where my brother and   1
I used to go. Despite the new coat of paint and the high wire fence, the school I knew ten years ago remains remarkably, stoically° the same.

Every day at 5 P.M., instead of playing with our fourth- and fifth-grade   2
friends or sneaking out to the empty lot to hunt ghosts and animal bones, my brother and I had to go to Chinese school. No amount of kicking, screaming, or pleading could dissuade my mother, who was solidly determined to have us learn the language of our heritage.

Forcibly, she walked us the seven long, hilly blocks from our home to   3
school, depositing our defiant° tearful faces before the stern principal. My only memory of him is that he swayed on his heels like a palm tree, and he always clasped his impatient twitching hands behind his back. I recognized him as a repressed maniacal° child killer, and knew that if we ever saw his hands we'd be in big trouble.

Jot down your questions and comments:

_____

_____

_____

We all sat in little chairs in an empty auditorium. The room smelled like   4
Chinese medicine, an imported faraway mustiness. Like ancient mothballs or dirty closets. I hated that smell. I favored crisp new scents. Like the soft French perfume that my American teacher wore in public school.

There was a stage far to the right, flanked by an American flag and the   5
flag of the Nationalist Republic of China, which was also red, white and
blue but not as pretty.

Although the emphasis at the school was mainly language—speaking,   6
reading, writing—the lessons always began with an exercise in politeness.
With the entrance of the teacher, the best student would tap a bell and

kowtow: bow deeply

everyone would get up, kowtow° and chant, "Sing san ho," the phonetic
for "How are you, teacher?"

Jot down your questions and comments:

_____

_____

_____

ideographs: picture symbols
representing a thing or idea

Being ten years old, I had better things to learn than ideographs° copied   7
painstakingly in lines that ran right to left from the tip of a *moc but,* a real
ink pen that had to be held in an awkward way if blotches were to be
avoided. After all, I could do the multiplication tables, name the satellites of
Mars, and write reports on *Little Women* and *Black Beauty.* Nancy Drew, my
favorite book heroine, never spoke Chinese.

The language was a source of embarrassment. More times than not, I   8
had tried to disassociate myself from the nagging loud voice that followed
me wherever I wandered in the nearby American supermarket outside
Chinatown. The voice belonged to my grandmother, a fragile woman in her
seventies who could outshout the best of the street vendors. Her humor

raunchy: slang expression
meaning "crude"

was raunchy° her Chinese rhythmless, patternless. It was quick, it was
loud, it was unbeautiful. It was not like the quiet, lilting romance of French
or the gentle refinement of the American South. Chinese sounded pedes-
trian. Public.

Jot down your questions and comments:

_____

_____

_____

In Chinatown, the comings and goings of hundreds of Chinese on their   9
daily tasks sounded chaotic and frenzied. I did not want to be thought of as

gibberish: confused,
nonsensical speech

mad, as talking gibberish° When I spoke English, people nodded at me,
smiled sweetly, said encouraging words. Even the people in my culture
would cluck and say that I'd do well in life. "My, doesn't she move her lips

fast," they would say, meaning that I'd be able to keep up with the world outside Chinatown.

My brother was even more fanatical than I about speaking English. He 10
was especially hard on my mother, criticizing her, often cruelly, for her

**pidgin:** simplified speech combining two or more languages

pidgin° speech—smatterings of Chinese scattered like chop suey in her conversation. "It's not 'What it is,' Mom," he'd say in exasperation. "It's 'What *is* it, what *is* it, what *is* it!'" Sometimes Mom might leave out an occasional "the" or "a," or perhaps a verb of being. He would stop her in mid-sentence: "Say it again, Mom. Say it right." When he tripped over his own tongue, he'd blame it on her: "See, Mom, it's all your fault. You set a bad example."

Jot down your questions and comments:

_____

_____

_____

What infuriated my mother most was when my brother cornered her 11
on her consonants, especially "r." My father had played a cruel joke on Mom by assigning her an American name that her tongue wouldn't allow her to say. No matter how hard she tried, "Ruth" always ended up "Luth" or "Roof."

After two years of writing with a *moc but* and reciting words with mul- 12
tiples of meanings, I finally was granted a cultural divorce. I was permitted to stop Chinese school.

I thought of myself as multicultural. I preferred tacos to egg rolls; I 13
enjoyed Cinco de Mayo° more than Chinese New Year.

**Cinco de Mayo:** May fifth, celebration by Mexican-Americans of 1862 defeat of French in Mexico

Jot down your questions and comments:

_____

_____

_____

At last, I was one of you; I wasn't one of them. 14
Sadly, I still am. 15

What question or comment do you have for Wong about her last sentence?

_____

_____

_____

Get a Close-Up of the New Strategy: Respond

You already know that just going through the motions of reading is a waste of time. Your mind has to be involved as you read. When you **respond,** you keep your mind on the writer's ideas. You think about what these ideas mean to you.

Time for Responding

1 *Respond while you're reading and after you've finished reading.*

When you read, pause here and there to think about what the writer said, just as you did now while reading "The Struggle to Be an All-American Girl." Ask the writer questions; agree or disagree; notice things you like or dislike. You'll stop to **respond** more or less often depending on the reading. For example, when reading in a subject you already know a lot about, you may not need to stop at all. But readings about unfamiliar subjects may require several stops. In fact, when reading a difficult part of a college textbook, you may need to pause every two or three sentences so you can see how to connect the new information with what else you have learned.

Responding to a reading doesn't stop when you've read the last word. Instead, the conversation goes on in your mind as you continue to talk back to the writer with your own ideas and questions. Even after you've put your book aside, your mind will return to a reading at odd times—when taking a shower, walking to class, or talking with a friend.

College instructors will often ask you to **respond** to a reading by answering questions or writing a paper. But even if there is no specific assignment, you'll learn material more quickly by putting your thoughts down on paper as soon as you've finished reading.

Space for Responding

2 *Make a place or space to respond.*

It's helpful to set aside places for your responses during and after reading. Here are some possibilities.

Your own mind. First, make space in your own mind to **respond.** Listen to your reader's voice—the voice in your own mind—as you think about what the writer has said.

Margin notes. Read with a pencil in your hand. That way, you can respond in the margin of the reading. There are many ways to make useful *margin notes.* Put a pencil mark next to a sentence you really liked. Or put a frown next to one you disagree with, or a question mark next to a confusing spot. You'll learn other ways of marking ideas later in this book.

Journal or reading log. You can use a *journal* or *reading log* for writing down your ideas. It can be a separate notebook or simply a few sheets of paper. Jot down responses as you read and after you've finished reading. Your instructor may give you guidelines for using a journal or reading log.

Reading partner. Reading with someone else can sometimes be helpful, especially for difficult readings. You both read the same text silently. After each paragraph you pause for each of you to respond aloud. This technique allows you to share your responses and find answers to questions.

Questions and Comments

3 *Ask questions and say what you think of the writer's ideas.*

Questions. Ask questions as if the writer were there to answer you. In a way, the writer is there, because often the answer can be found when you read a little further. If not, you may find the answer when you reread a passage or get help from a fellow student or your instructor.

Agreements and disagreements. What do you think of the writer's ideas? Do you agree or disagree with an idea? Voice your opinion as you read. Remember, you can change your mind when you get more information. For example, you might disagree with Wong's mother, who made her children attend Chinese school, or with Wong's brother, who was always correcting his mother's speech.

Likes and dislikes. What parts do you like in a reading? What parts do you dislike? In this reading, you might like Wong's strong spirit as a child. She knew what she wanted: escape from the daily Chinese school and association with the Chinese language. And she finally got her wish. But you might dislike other parts of the reading. Perhaps you didn't like the fact that, as a child, Wong rejected her own culture. Or perhaps you were put off by some of the scenes at the school. Maybe they reminded you of unpleasant schoolrooms you've known. What were your likes and dislikes in this reading?

Connections. See how you can compare what you find in a reading with what you've experienced in your own life or with what you've learned from other sources—reading, TV, a movie. How does your own experience compare with Wong's? How do other books or movies you've read or seen compare with her story?

Talking with others. Share your questions and comments with others once you've finished reading. Discussion can often clear up questions. Then, too, others' comments help make the writer's ideas come to life, even if you don't always agree with what someone else has said.

Follow-Up Activities Throughout This Book

The Reader's Voice gives you many ways to **respond** when you've finished reading. The "Time Out for You" on learning styles at the end of this chapter may help you think about the kind of responding that works best for you. In this book there is a section of follow-up activities after each reading. Beginning with this chapter, the following types of questions will always be included:

- *Grab your first impressions.* What do you feel and think right after you've finished reading?

- *Ask and answer questions.* Try to answer the questions that are provided. Then, try to ask and answer your own questions.

- *Form your final thoughts.* After you're sure you've understood the writer, decide what you think about the reading.

These questions may be answered in a variety of ways, depending on your instructor's guidelines. You may:

- Prepare them in your mind to discuss in a small group or with the class.

- Work with classmates to prepare your answers. Questions with the icon 🧍 are especially good for discussion with fellow classmates.

- Write out your answers either in a journal (or reading log) or as a separate written assignment. When writing answers, be sure to use your own words (don't just copy from the reading).

Follow-Up Activities for Reading 3   After you've finished reading, use these activities to respond to "The Struggle to Be an All-American Girl." You may write your answers or prepare them in your mind to discuss in class.

Grab your first impressions.

1. What about the reading did you like? What didn't you like? Explain your choices.

2. What surprised you most about this reading? Why?

Ask and answer questions.

1. How did Wong's desires about how she wanted to spend her time as a young child differ from her mother's plans for her?

2. What were some of the things Wong disliked about going to Chinese school?

3. How did both Wong and her brother feel about the Chinese language?

4. When she was able to stop going to Chinese school, Wong says, "At last, I was one of you; I wasn't one of them." What group did she feel she had joined? What group had she left behind?

5. Wong's very last sentence is, "Sadly, I still am." What is Wong sad about now, as she looks back on her childhood?

 Ask and answer your own question.

Write a question of your own. Share your question with others, and work together on an answer.

Form your final thoughts.

1. Wong and her mother had a conflict over the way to grow up in America. What kinds of conflicts did you and your parents experience? How did you resolve these conflicts?

 2. Imagine that your class or small group were able to talk with Elizabeth Wong. What more would you like to know about her childhood or her present life? ■

Apply the New Strategy: Respond

Now that you understand Strategy 2, put it into practice with Reading 4, "Self-Esteem." This time, pause from time to time and **respond** in the margins, as suggested on page 22. Reminder boxes in the margins will suggest places to respond, but feel free to mark any ideas you want to question or comment on.

READING 4   SELF-ESTEEM

JOSEPH A. DEVITO

This reading comes from the chapter called "The Self in Communication" in the textbook Human Communication, *by Joseph A. DeVito, a professor of communication at Hunter College of the City University of New York.*

CHECK IN
- The first sentence defines "self-esteem." Using that definition, what would you say about your own self-esteem?
- Be aware of positive or negative feelings you might have about this subject.

Textbooks and academic writers give credit for material borrowed or quoted from others. Parentheses point you to a full credit at the end of a reading, called "Works Cited" or "References."

Personal self-esteem refers to the way you feel about yourself—how much you like yourself, how valuable a person you think you are, how competent you think you are. These feelings reflect the value you place on yourself; they're a measure of your self-esteem.   1

There's also group self-esteem, or your evaluation of yourself as a member of a particular cultural group (Porter & Washington, 1993). Personal self-esteem is influenced by your group self-esteem. If you view your racial or ethnic group membership negatively, then it's especially difficult to develop high positive self-esteem. Conversely, if you view your membership positively, then you're more likely to develop high positive self-esteem. Pride in one's group (racial, ethnic, religious, or gender, for example) and a supportive community contribute to group self-esteem and consequently to personal self-esteem.   2

There are also significant cultural differences in the way we're taught to view ourselves (Gudykunst & Ting-Toomey,1988). For example, in the United States, Australia, and western Europe, people are encouraged to be independent. Members of these cultures are taught to get ahead, to compete, to win, to achieve their goals, to realize their unique potential, to stand out from the crowd. In many Asian and African cultures, on the other hand, people are taught to value an *inter*dependent self. Members of these cultures are taught to get along, to help others, and not to disagree, stand out, or be conspicuous. Although self-esteem depends largely on achieving your goals, your culture seems to select the specific goals.   3

RESPOND:
Questions? Comments?

ATTACK YOUR SELF-DESTRUCTIVE BELIEFS

RESPOND:

Self-destructive beliefs are those beliefs that damage your self-esteem and prevent you from building meaningful and productive relationships. They may be about yourself ("I'm not creative," "I'm boring"), your world ("The world is an unhappy place," "People are out to get me"), and/or your relationships ("All the good people are already in relationships," "If I ever fall in love, I know I'll be hurt"). Identifying these beliefs will help you examine them critically and see that they're both illogical and self-defeating. A useful way to view self-destructive beliefs is given in the Building Communication Skills box entitled "How Can You Attack Self-Defeating Drivers?"   4

drivers (box): beliefs that may motivate—or drive—you to act in certain ways, in this case ways that are self-defeating

BUILDING COMMUNICATION SKILLS

HOW CAN YOU ATTACK SELF-DEFEATING DRIVERS?

Another approach to unrealistic beliefs is to focus on what Pamela Butler (1981) calls "drivers"°— beliefs that may motivate you to act in ways that are self-defeating. Because these drivers embody unrealistically high standards, they make it impossible for you to accomplish the very things you feel are essential for gaining approval from others and from yourself. Recognizing that you may have internalized such drivers is the first step to eliminating them. The second step involves recognizing that these drivers are in fact unrealistic and self-defeating. The third step is to substitute realistic and self-affirming beliefs for these self-defeating drivers. How would you restate each of these five drivers as realistic and productive beliefs?

■ The drive *to be perfect* impels you to try to perform at unrealistically high levels at work, school, and home; anything short of perfection is unacceptable.

■ The drive *to be strong* tells you that weakness and any of the more vulnerable emotions (like sadness, compassion, or loneliness) are wrong.

■ The drive *to please others* leads you to seek approval from others; you assume that if you gain the approval of others, then you're a worthy and deserving person—and that if others disapprove of you, then you're worthless and undeserving.

■ The drive *to hurry up* compels you to do things quickly, to try to do more than can reasonably be expected in any given amount of time.

■ The drive *to try hard* makes you take on more responsibilities than any one person can be expected to handle.

ENGAGE IN SELF-AFFIRMATION

RESPOND:

Remind yourself of your successes from time to time. To enhance self-affirmation focus on your good deeds, strengths, and positive qualities. Also, look carefully at the good relationships you have with friends and relatives. Concentrate on your potential, not your limitations (Brody, 1991):

■ I'm a good team worker.

■ I keep confidences.

5

- I respect other people.

- I'm goal directed.

- I'm open to new ideas.

- I nurture others and allow others to nurture me.

- I'm creative.

- I'm willing to share what I have and what I know.

- I like myself.

- I deserve to have good things in my life.

SEEK OUT NURTURING PEOPLE

RESPOND:

Seek out positive, optimistic people who make you feel good about   6
yourself. Avoid those who find fault with just about everything. Seek to
build a network of supportive others (Brody, 1991). At the same time, however, realize that you do not have to be loved by everyone. Many people
believe that everyone should love them. This belief traps you into thinking
you must always please others so they will like you.

Television talk show hosts, especially Oprah Winfrey, often emphasize the importance of self-
esteem. Here she seems to be comforting basketball star Dennis Rodman. Do you feel self-
esteem is important to your own personal and professional success?

WORK ON PROJECTS THAT WILL RESULT IN SUCCESS

Try to select projects you can complete successfully. Success builds   7
self-esteem. Each success makes achieving the next one a little easier.
Remember, too, that the failure of a project is not the failure of you as a
person; failure is something that happens, not something inside you.
Everyone faces defeat somewhere along the line. Successful people are
those who know how to deal with setbacks. Further, one defeat does not
mean you'll fail the next time. Put failure in perspective, and don't make it
an excuse for not trying again.

Another activity that has been shown to contribute to self-esteem is   8
exercise. In a study of adults between the ages of 60 and 75, those who
exercised—and it didn't matter what exercise it was—increased their self-
esteem. The exercise seems to have made the individuals feel better physically; this gave them a feeling of increased physical strength and hence
control over their environment (McAuley, Blissmer, Katula, Duncan, &
Mihalko, 2000).

References

Brody, J. E. (1991, April 28). How to foster self-esteem. *New York Times Magazine,* pp. 26–27.

Butler P. E. (1981). *Talking to yourself: Learning the language of self-sup-port.* New York: Harper & Row.

Gudykunst, W. B., & Ting-Tooney, S., with Chua, E. (1988). *Culture and interpersonal communication.* Thousand Oaks, CA: Sage.

McAuley, E., Blissmer, B., Katula, J., Duncan, T. E., & Mihalko, S. L. (2000). Physical activity, self-esteem, and self-efficacy relationships in older adults: A randomized controlled trial. *Annals of Behavioral Medicine, 22* (Spring), 131–139.

Porter, J. R., & Washington, R. E. (1993). Minority identity and self-esteem. *Annual Review of Sociology, 19,* 139–161.

Follow-Up Activities   After you've finished reading, use these activities to
respond to "Self-Esteem." You may write your answers or prepare them in your
mind to discuss in class.

Grab your first impressions.

1. As you checked in, you thought about your own self-esteem. What more
   have you learned about your self-esteem now that you've finished the
   reading?

2. Did this reading convince you that self-esteem is important to your own
   success? Explain your answer.

Ask and answer questions.

1. How can group self-esteem affect one's personal self-esteem? How do you think group self-esteem affected Elizabeth Wong in Reading 3, "The Struggle to Be an All-American Girl"?

2. What is the definition of "self-defeating drivers" provided in the Building Communication Skills box? What are the steps given for eliminating these "drivers"?

3. What is the value of engaging in "self-affirmation"?

4. Why does exercise contribute to self-esteem?

5. In Paragraph 7, DeVito explains the value of selecting projects you can complete successfully. He says, "Each success [in completing a project] makes achieving the next one a little easier." Give an example of a project you could complete successfully. How would that success help you with the next project?

 Ask and answer your own question.

Write a question of your own. Share your question with others, and work together on an answer.

Form your final thoughts.

1. What parts of the reading did you find most useful in thinking about your own self-esteem? What step or steps might you take to increase your self-esteem?

 2. Share your ideas about this reading with someone else or with a group. What similarities or differences do you find in your responses?   ■

Chapter 2 Summary

How does Strategy 2 help you use your reader's voice *to be an active reader?*

In active reading, you carry on a kind of conversation with the writer. **Checking in** prepares you for that conversation, as you discover what you have to say about the subject before beginning to read.

Responding during and after reading keeps this conversation going. You use your reader's voice to ask questions and make comments about what the writer says, just as you would if you were speaking with him or her.

How does the *respond* strategy work?

To **respond** you give yourself the time and space during and after reading to talk back to the writer. Here are the three reminders for Strategy 2.

STRATEGY 2: RESPOND

1 Respond while you're reading and after you've finished reading.

2 Make a place or space to respond.

3 Ask questions and say what you think of the writer's ideas.

Are you familiar with the meaning of these terms?

journal or *reading log:* a place for writing down your ideas about a reading

margin notes: words, phrases, or symbols written in the margin next to a sentence or sentences you want to respond to in some way

How is the strategy working for you so far?

Explain which parts of **responding** you've found most helpful in the readings you've practiced with. Which parts have been least helpful?

TIME OUT FOR YOU

WHAT IS YOUR LEARNING STYLE?

Each of you has certain preferences about the way you learn something new. These preferences add up to your *learning style*. Here are some questions that can help you decide on your personal style.

- *Learning environment.* In what environment is your mind most alert? For example, what time do you learn best: early in the morning or late at night? Consider, too, the place that you learn best. Is it in your room, in the library, or with other students in the cafeteria?

- *Social situation.* What social situation works best for your learning? For example, do you prefer learning in small groups, in pairs, or on your own?

- *Sensory information.* Which senses do you tend to rely on when taking in new information? Do you prefer to see visual images? Hear explanations? Try things out with your hands and body?

Another way of thinking about your learning preferences is based on the theory of *multiple intelligences,* developed by Dr. Howard Gardner of Harvard University. In 1983, Gardner put forward that we have seven intelligences—five more than the traditional verbal and logical/mathematical intelligences tested by IQ tests. While everyone has all seven, each of us has some intelligences that are especially well developed. Read the following summaries, and think about how these intelligences apply to you. After each description, you'll find suggestions for making use of that specific intelligence in your college studying.

- *Verbal intelligence*—understands and expresses itself through words and language. Verbal activities include writing, reading, poetry, stories, discussion, and debate.
  Study suggestions: Use note taking, reading, talking things over with others, and writing to understand and remember. Try audio tapes for another way to take in verbal information.

- *Logical/Mathematical intelligence*—emphasizes logic and mathematical reasoning. This intelligence stands out in experimentation and organized, step-by-step approaches to solving problems.

  Study suggestions: Disorganization can be frustrating to you, so identify the structure of an assignment before starting. Use reasoning to work through the steps of writing or study assignments.

- *Visual/Spatial intelligence*—gives the ability to think in pictures and create strong mental images. Visual/spatial thinkers have a good sense of direction and of how things relate to one another in space. They may have a talent for art or design.

  Study suggestions: Draw, chart, or diagram information. Relate pictures, photos, and other visuals to written information. Use different colors and symbols to show different ideas or parts.

- *Musical intelligence*—gives the ability to respond to and create music, through a sensitivity to rhythm, pitch, and melody.

  Study suggestions: Find music that can help you focus on studying, not distract you. Take occasional "musical breaks" with a favorite piece. Use rhythm to help you remember words and phrases.

- *Physical intelligence*—covers the mental abilities that coordinate bodily movements. It includes a good sense of balance, good eye-hand coordination, and skill in handling objects.

  Study suggestions: Role play or act out scenes in subjects like English, history, or sociology. Walk through your house as you test yourself on new information; connect ideas to different spots in the house. Take "exercise breaks" to get a better mind-body connection.

- *Interpersonal intelligence*—"reads" feelings, behaviors, and motives of others. It allows a person to see things from another's point of view and to communicate well both verbally and nonverbally.

  Study suggestions: Study with other people; discuss ideas and test one another. Find a study partner or organize your own study group. Telephoning or even e-mailing study partners can substitute for actual meetings if scheduling is a problem.

- *Intrapersonal intelligence*—emphasizes self-awareness, an understanding of one's own feelings and motivations. It gives a person a strong sense of moral beliefs and an ability to work alone and independently.

Study suggestions: You need to believe in what you're doing—to have a strong purpose for doing it. For some course work, your instructor might allow you to do an independent project to fulfill an assignment in your own way.

Remember: your learning style covers many different areas of your personality as well as your intelligences. A useful learning styles inventory can be found at the Web site for Diablo Valley College, where the author of this book teaches. Go to the college Web site: www.DVC.edu/, find the search box there, and type "learning styles survey" into the box. For a multiple intelligences inventory, you can try www.surfaquarium.com/MIinvent.htm.

PART I

ADDITIONAL READINGS ON
LEARNING FOR YOURSELF

The readings that follow will give you further practice in using the first two strategies—**Check In** and **Respond**—with a variety of readings on the theme of "learning for yourself."

READING I-A   LEARNING TO WRITE

RUSSELL BAKER

CHECK IN
- What was your experience learning to write papers in high school English classes?
- What do you like about writing? What do you dislike?
- What careers did you start thinking about in high school? Why?

Belleville: a town in New Jersey

lackluster: dull

chloroform: chemical used widely in the past for making surgery patients unconscious or for putting animals to sleep

RESPOND while you're reading and when you've finished reading.

notorious: famous for doing something wrong

prim: stuffy, neat, overly proper and formal

Macbeth: play by Shakespeare

ferocity: vicious cruelty

Russell Baker wrote a regular column for the New York Times *from 1954 to 1998. This reading comes from* Growing Up, *Baker's story of growing up in America during the Great Depression of the 1930s.*

The notion of becoming a writer had flickered off and on in my head   1
since the Belleville° days, but it wasn't until my third year in high school that the possibility took hold. Until then I'd been bored by everything associated with English courses. I found English grammar dull and baffling. I hated the assignments to turn out "compositions," and went at them like heavy labor, turning out leaden, lackluster° paragraphs that were agonies for teachers to read and for me to write. The classics thrust on me to read seemed as deadening as chloroform°.

When our class was assigned to Mr. Fleagle for third-year English I   2
anticipated another grim year in that dreariest of subjects. Mr. Fleagle was notorious° among City students for dullness and inability to inspire. He was said to be stuffy, dull, and hopelessly out of date. To me he looked to be sixty or seventy and prim° to a fault. He wore primly severe eyeglasses, his wavy hair was primly cut and primly combed. He wore prim vested suits with neckties blocked primly against the collar buttons of his primly starched white shirts. He had a primly pointed jaw, a primly straight nose, and a prim manner of speaking that was so correct, so gentlemanly, that he seemed a comic antique.

I anticipated a listless, unfruitful year with Mr. Fleagle and for a long   3
time was not disappointed. We read *Macbeth*° Mr. Fleagle loved *Macbeth* and wanted us to love it too, but he lacked the gift of infecting others with his own passion. He tried to convey the murderous ferocity° of Lady Macbeth one day by reading aloud the passage that concludes

. . . I have given suck, and know

How tender 'tis to love the babe that milks me.

I would, while it was smiling in my face,

Have plucked my nipple from his boneless gums. . . .

The idea of prim Mr. Fleagle plucking his nipple from boneless gums   4
was too much for the class. We burst into gasps of irrepressible° snicker-
ing. Mr. Fleagle stopped.

irrepressible: unmanageable

"There is nothing funny, boys, about giving suck to a babe. It is the—   5
the very essence° of motherhood, don't you see."

essence: core, real meaning

RESPOND
Questions? Comments?

He constantly sprinkled his sentences with "don't you see." It wasn't a   6
question but an exclamation of mild surprise at our ignorance. "Your pro-
noun needs an antecedent, don't you see," he would say, very primly. "The
purpose of the Porter's scene°, boys, is to provide comic relief from the hor-
ror, don't you see."

Porter's scene: scene in
Macbeth when the porter
or gatekeeper makes jokes

Late in the year we tackled the informal essay°. "The essay, don't you   7
see, is the . . ." My mind went numb. Of all forms of writing, none seemed
so boring as the essay. Naturally we would have to write informal essays.
Mr. Fleagle distributed a homework sheet offering us a choice of topics.
None was quite so simpleminded as "What I Did on My Summer Vacation,"
but most seemed to be almost as dull. I took the list home and dawdled°
until the night before the essay was due. Sprawled on the sofa, I finally
faced up to the grim task, took the list out of my notebook, and scanned it.
The topic on which my eye stopped was "The Art of Eating Spaghetti."

essay: composition, paper

dawdled: hung around,
wasted time

This title produced an extraordinary sequence of mental images.   8
Surging° up out of the depths of memory came a vivid recollection of a
night in Belleville when all of us were seated around the supper table—
Uncle Allen, my mother, Uncle Charlie, Doris, Uncle Hal—and Aunt Pat
served spaghetti for supper. Spaghetti was an exotic treat in those days.
Neither Doris nor I had ever eaten spaghetti, and none of the adults had
enough experience to be good at it. All the good humor of Uncle Allen's
house reawoke in my mind as I recalled the laughing arguments we had
that night about the socially respectable method for moving spaghetti from
plate to mouth.

surging: rising, moving up
in waves

RESPOND

Suddenly I wanted to write about that, about the warmth and good   9
feeling of it, but I wanted to put it down simply for my own joy, not for Mr.
Fleagle. It was a moment I wanted to recapture and hold for myself. I
wanted to relive the pleasure of an evening at New Street. To write it as I
wanted, however, would violate all the rules of formal composition I'd
learned in school, and Mr. Fleagle would surely give it a failing grade.
Never mind. I would write something else for Mr. Fleagle after I had written
this thing for myself.

When I finished it the night was half gone and there was no time left to   10
compose a proper, respectable essay for Mr. Fleagle. There was no choice

reminiscence: memories

next morning but to turn in my private reminiscence° of Belleville. Two days passed before Mr. Fleagle returned the graded papers, and he returned everyone's but mine. I was bracing myself for a command to report to Mr. Fleagle immediately after school for discipline when I saw him lift my paper from his desk and rap for the class's attention.

"Now, boys," he said, "I want to read you an essay. This is titled "The 11 Art of Eating Spaghetti.'"

And he started to read. My words! He was reading my words out loud 12 to the entire class. What's more, the entire class was listening. Listening attentively. Then somebody laughed, then the entire class was laughing, and not in contempt and ridicule, but with openhearted enjoyment. Even

repress: hold back

Mr. Fleagle stopped two or three times to repress° a small prim smile.

I did my best to avoid showing pleasure, but what I was feeling was 13 pure ecstasy at this startling demonstration that my words had the power to make people laugh. In the eleventh grade, at the eleventh hour as it were, I had discovered a calling. It was the happiest moment of my entire school career. When Mr. Fleagle finished he put the final seal on my happiness by saying, "Now that, boys, is an essay, don't you see. It's—don't you see—it's of the very essence of the essay, don't you see. Congratulations, Mr. Baker."

Follow-Up Activities   After you've finished reading, use these activities to respond to "Learning to Write." You may write your answers or prepare them in your mind to discuss in class.

Grab your first impressions.

1. What surprised you most about this reading? Why?

2. Baker uses descriptive details throughout this reading. Choose a paragraph you like that describes his teacher, his family, or his writing process. What details help give you an especially clear picture?

Ask and answer questions.

1. Baker was bored by his English teacher, Mr. Fleagle. What else did he hate about his English courses?

2. In Paragraph 2, Baker uses the word "prim" over and over to describe Mr. Fleagle. He repeats "prim" for every detail about the teacher's appearance to show us just how "stuffy, neat, proper, and formal" the teacher looked. What words did Mr. Fleagle often use that showed his prim speech?

3. What made Mr. Fleagle's reading of the passage from *Macbeth* seem so ridiculous?

4. How did Baker come to realize that he wanted to write for himself—"for his own joy"—not for Mr. Fleagle?

5. What did Baker learn from the experience of hearing his essay being read aloud? What did he learn about Mr. Fleagle?

 Ask and answer your own question.

Write a question of your own. Share your question with others, and work together on an answer.

Form your final thoughts.

1. Baker discovered that he loved writing through doing an assignment he had dreaded. What example can you think of from your own experience where you've learned something positive from an assignment you hadn't wanted to do?

 2. Russell Baker has had a long career doing something he loves to do: write. If you could talk with him, what would you like to ask him about his life and his career?   ■

READING I-B ## PANDORA'S BOX: HOPE AND THE POWER OF POSITIVE THINKING

DANIEL GOLEMAN

CHECK IN
• What role does hope play in your life?
• When do you find it hard to be hopeful?
• Do you believe in the power of positive thinking? Explain your answer.

hypothetical: possible, but imaginary

bolster: increase

A superscript number indicates that credit for material borrowed or quoted from others will be given under that number in the "Notes" at the end of a reading.

Daniel Goleman is a professor of psychology at Harvard University. This reading comes from his book Emotional Intelligence: Why It Can Matter More Than IQ. *IQ is short for "intelligence quotient" (a number that comes from an intelligence test). According to Goleman, emotional intelligence means our ability to respond emotionally in appropriate and helpful ways to life's challenges.*

College students were posed the following hypothetical° situation: 1

Although you set your goal of getting a B, when your first exam score, worth 30% of your final grade is returned, you have received a D. It is now one week after you have learned about the D grade. What do you do?[1]

Hope made all the difference. The response by students with high levels of hope was to work harder and think of a range of things they might try that could bolster° their final grade. Students with moderate levels of hope thought of several ways they might up their grade, but had far less deter-   2

demoralized: discouraged, depressed

theoretical: academic

correlated: connected

aptitudes: abilities

equivalent: equal

afflictions: burdens, miseries

malaise: depression

antidote: cure

solace: comfort

potent: powerful

onerous: difficult, tiring

mination to pursue them. And, understandably, students with low levels of hope gave up on both counts, demoralized°.

The question is not just theoretical°, however. When C. R. Snyder, the University of Kansas psychologist who did this study, compared the actual academic achievement of freshman students high and low on hope, he discovered that hope was a better predictor of their first-semester grades than were their scores on the SAT, a test supposedly able to predict how students will fare in college (and highly correlated° with IQ). Again, given roughly the same range of intellectual abilities, emotional aptitudes° make the critical difference.   3

Snyder's explanation: "Students with high hope set themselves higher goals and know how to work hard to attain them. When you compare students of equivalent° intellectual aptitude on their academic achievements, what sets them apart is hope."[2]   4

As the familiar legend has it, Pandora, a princess of ancient Greece, was given a gift, a mysterious box, by gods jealous of her beauty. She was   5

told she must never open the gift. But one day, overcome by curiosity and temptation, Pandora lifted the lid to peek in, letting loose in the world the grand afflictions°—disease, malaise°, madness. But a compassionate god let her close the box just in time to capture the one antidote° that makes life's misery bearable: hope.

Hope, modern researchers are finding,   6
does more than offer a bit of solace° amid affliction; it plays a surprisingly potent° role in life, offering an advantage in realms as diverse as school achievement and bearing up in onerous° jobs. Hope, in a technical sense, is more than the sunny view that everything will turn out all right. Snyder defines it with more specificity as "believing you have both the will and the way to accomplish your goals, whatever they may be."

People tend to differ in the general   7
degree to which they have hope in this sense. Some typically think of themselves as able to get out of a jam or find ways to solve problems, while others simply do not see themselves as having the energy, ability, or means to accomplish their goals. People with high

Pandora opens the box. (By the illustrator Walter Crane)

RESPOND
Questions? Comments?

formidable: tough

defeatist: negative, accepting
defeat

maneuver: guide oneself

levels of hope, Snyder finds, share certain traits, among them being able to motivate themselves, feeling resourceful enough to find ways to accomplish their objectives, reassuring themselves when in a tight spot that things will get better, being flexible enough to find different ways to get to their goals or to switch goals if one becomes impossible, and having the sense to break down a formidable° task into smaller, manageable pieces.

From the perspective of emotional intelligence, having hope means   8
that one will not give in to overwhelming anxiety, a defeatist° attitude, or depression in the face of difficult challenges or setbacks. Indeed, people who are hopeful evidence less depression than others as they maneuver° through life in pursuit of their goals, are less anxious in general, and have fewer emotional distresses.

Notes

[1] C. R. Snyder et al., "The Will and the Ways: Development and Validation of an Individual-Differences Measure of Hope," *Journal of Personality and Social Psychology* 60, 4 (1991), p. 579.

[2] I interviewed C. R. Snyder in the *New York Times* (Dec. 24, 1991).

Follow-Up Activities   After you've finished reading, use these activities to respond to "Pandora's Box: Hope and the Power of Positive Thinking." You may write your answers or prepare them in your mind to discuss in class.

Grab your first impressions.

1. Has reading "Pandora's Box" given you a new way to think about the role of hope in your own life? Why or why not?

2. What ideas in this reading do you agree with? What ideas do you disagree with? Explain your reasons.

Ask and answer questions.

1. In the study discussed in Paragraphs 1 and 2, what did the students with high levels of hope say they would do if they got a D? How would the students with low levels of hope respond?

2. How does the psychologist C. R. Snyder explain why hope is a better predictor of first semester grades than scores on the SAT?

3. Paragraph 6 gives Snyder's definition of hope as "believing you have both the will and the way to accomplish your goals, whatever they may be." How would you state his definition in your own words?

4. What are the essential traits, or qualities, Snyder finds that people with high levels of hope all have in common?

5. What does the legend of Pandora's box show about the role hope plays in our lives?

 Ask and answer your own question.

Write a question of your own. Share your question with others, and work together on an answer.

Form your final thoughts.

1. C. R. Snyder's study showed three levels of hope: high, moderate, and low. What level of hope do you think you generally have? Do you think you could become more hopeful if you wanted to?

 2. What is your definition of hope? Compare your definition with that of other students, and discuss the importance of hope in your lives. ■

READING I-C   **I MAY, I MIGHT, I MUST**

MARIANNE MOORE

Poets—even more than other writers—expect that you'll connect your own experience to the words you read. Words in a poem may make you think of a similar idea, a past event, or a familiar picture. In this short poem, the poet Marianne Moore (1887–1972) asks you to bring your own thoughts and feelings to what she suggests with her words.

*To **check in** for this poem, give yourself a chance to see what you get from the title alone. Then read the poem at least twice. It's best to read this poem aloud, line by line. That way you can hear the rhythm and the places where the rhyme emphasizes certain words.*

I May, I Might, I Must

If you will tell me why the fen°
appears impassable°, I then
will tell you why I think that I
can get across it if I try.

Follow-Up Activities   After you've finished reading, use these activities to respond to "I May, I Might, I Must." You may write your answers or prepare them in your mind to discuss in class.

Grab your first impressions.

1. What about the poem did you like? What didn't you like? Explain your choices.

2. Think now about how you could relate this poem to your own life. You'll come back to this question after you've had a chance to think more about it and discuss it with others.

Ask and answer questions.

1. What would make a fen seem "impassable"—impossible to get through?

2. How does the poet say she would respond if someone told her it's impossible to get through the fen?

3. Now that you've read the poem, give your understanding of the words in the title. Why does the poet end the title with "I must"?

4. "Fen" and "then" are two words in the poem that rhyme. The other rhyming words all have the same vowel sound as "why." What are all the words that rhyme with "why"? Why do you think these words are especially important in the poem?

5. Try to put the poem's message in your own words.

Ask and answer your own question.

Write a question of your own. Share your question with others, and work together on an answer.

Form your final thoughts.

1. Now that you've thought about more about the poem, how can you relate it to your own life?

2. Choose another reading from Part I to compare with Moore's poem. What similarities do you see between the message in the poem and the ideas in the other reading? ■

PART I REVIEW
DISCOVERING THE READER'S VOICE

You've completed Part I. Now take some time to look back at both the theme and the strategies introduced in this part.

Theme: Learning for Yourself

The theme of Part I is "learning for yourself"—learning that gives you insight about who you are and how you can meet life's challenges. Write down or discuss with others in class the ideas you found most helpful on this theme. Which were your favorite readings? Why?

_____

_____

_____

_____

_____

Strategies: Check In and Respond

Part I showed you how the first two strategies help you become an involved, active reader throughout the reading process. Like any process, reading has a beginning, middle, and end. In the beginning stage, you *get started*. You **check in** and voice your thoughts about the title (or other clues). In the next stage, you *read*. As you do, you **respond** to what the writer says. At the end, you *follow up* by **responding**. Even after you've read the last word, your mind is still involved in the reading, thinking over what you've read.

Look at the chart on the next page to remind yourself when each of the first two strategies is used.

Using Strategies Throughout the Reading Process

GET STARTED   Begin with strategies that help you think about the subject and find out about what the writer will say.

■ **Check in**

READ   Use strategies that help you read with greater understanding, interpret the language, and respond with your own questions and ideas.

■ **Respond**

FOLLOW UP   End with strategies that help you look more closely at the language and ideas in the reading, assess your understanding, and respond in a thoughtful way.

■ **Respond**

How Are the Strategies Working for You?

Answer the following questions to help you evaluate what you have learned. Then compare your answers with other students, and ask your instructor for ideas on how to get more out of the strategies.

1. How much time are these strategies taking? (Remember that all strategies take more time while you're learning them, but because they will help you understand more easily, they will save you time later.)

_____

_____

_____

2. Overall, how helpful have the strategies been in increasing your concentration and your understanding and/or enjoyment of what you read?

_____

_____

_____

3. What can you do to make the strategies work better for you?

_____

_____

_____

PART II

PREDICTING AND QUESTIONING

WITH READINGS ON POPULAR CULTURE

Popular culture is something you know a lot about. It's what you see and hear all around you at home, in the car, and at the mall or supermarket. It is the culture of everyday life. From popular music to advertising, movies to sports—all of us share in some aspects of this culture. Each reading in Part II deals with one of these aspects. Because you already know about the popular culture of our day, your knowledge and experience will help you relate to what each writer has to say on this theme.

To think more about the theme, look over this list of everyday activities. Check the entries that are regular parts of your life or that you consider important. Think about aspects of popular culture so you can discuss them with others in class.

- Going to the movies
- Watching a video or DVD
- Watching TV programs
- Listening to music
- Talking on the phone
- Using slang expressions
- Surfing the Net
- Communicating by e-mail
- Other?

In Part I you discovered your reader's voice as you became involved in a conversation with the writer. The new strategies in Part II, "Predicting and Questioning," develop your reader's voice and keep you involved with the writer's ideas. Strategies 3 and 4 (**Use Context Clues** and **Find the Right Definition**) help you predict the definition of new words and clarify their meaning, so unfamiliar words don't keep you from **responding** to a reading. With Strategy 5, **Ask Questions,** you learn to question the writer so you can better understand his or her ideas. You get started on a reading by asking questions that help you think ahead about what the writer will say. Then you read to answer your own questions and see how accurate your predictions were.

CHAPTER 3

WORK WITH
NEW WORDS

USE CONTEXT CLUES

You're reading along, **responding** to what the writer is saying. But then unfamiliar words get in your way. College reading often presents this challenge: difficult vocabulary becomes a barrier to your understanding. Strategy 3 will help you figure out the meaning of new words as you read, so you can stay involved in your conversation with the writer.

Introduction to the New Strategy: Use Context Clues

Strategy 3, **Use Context Clues,** helps you remove barriers posed by new vocabulary. The word *context* refers to the surroundings. Often, the surrounding words and ideas give you clues about the meaning of a word. These clues—called *context clues*—allow you to predict, or make an educated guess, about a word's definition. That way you don't need to stop your reading to turn to the dictionary.

STRATEGY 3: USE CONTEXT CLUES

1 Use the "sense of the sentence," or logic clues.

2 Let examples act as clues.

3 Watch for contrast clues.

4 Notice actual definitions.

Logic Clues

1 *Use the "sense of the sentence," or logic clues.*

Logic clues are the most common type of context clues. You may not realize that you sometimes use these clues already. When you guess the meaning of a new word in order to go on reading, you use "the sense of the sentence"—that is, the logic of the rest of the sentence and perhaps the sentences around it. However, with practice you can use logic clues more effectively to predict the meaning of new words. Read the following paragraph about cell phones. You'll find a few underlined words that are probably unfamiliar to you. See if you can use your understanding of the rest of the paragraph to figure out the meaning of these words.

> Until a few years ago, it was somewhat shocking to see someone walking down the street talking loudly to the air. If you carried on a conversation when no one else was around, people assumed you were <u>demented</u>, or at least a little unbalanced mentally. Nowadays, talking loudly to an invisible listener may annoy or even <u>infuriate</u> the people around you. But no one is shocked, as long as you're holding a cell phone to your ear. In fact, half the people around you may also be <u>prattling</u> on. Like you, they're speaking to someone far away, a "cell mate" at the other end of the cell phone connection.

Look, for example, at the word "demented" in the second sentence of the paragraph on cell phones. The sentence gives you a good clue in the phrase "or at least a little unbalanced mentally." The phrase shows that being "mentally unbalanced" is a possible meaning for "demented."

You can use the same kind of logic clues to predict the meaning of two more words from the paragraph, "infuriate" and "prattling." "Infuriate" must mean something that's even stronger than "annoy." So, "infuriate" means "to make angry." What logic clues tell you that "prattling" is another word for "talking"?

Example Clues

2 *Let examples act as clues.*

An example shows one case or instance of a general idea. *Example clues* use examples to suggest the meaning of a word. What do the examples in this next passage tell you about the meaning of "defiance"?

> Bart Simpson, of TV's *The Simpsons,* is known for his expressions of <u>defiance</u>; for example, three of his favorite sayings are, "Outta my way, man," "Eat my shorts," and "No way, man."

SIGNALS FOR
EXAMPLES
  for example
  for instance
  such as
  included are
  like or like the following

The phrase, "for example," signals the three specific examples of Bart's expressions. His words show the meaning of "defiance": "noncooperation," or "rebelliousness." Look in the margin for some phrases used to signal an example clue.

Contrast Clues

3 Watch for contrast clues.

Sometimes two words in a sentence are clearly the opposite of each other—they contrast with each other. If you know the meaning of one of those words, you can predict that the new word must have the opposite meaning. For example, see how you can use *contrast clues* to figure out the meaning of "diligent."

Bart Simpson has a reputation at school for being a lazy student, but his sister Lisa is known to be <u>diligent</u> about her studies.

SIGNALS FOR
CONTRAST
  but
  however
  on the other hand
  on the contrary
  instead
  although or even though

The sentence makes a contrast between Bart and Lisa. The "but" shows you that "diligent" must be the opposite of "lazy"—"hardworking." More signal words for contrast are given in the margin.

Definition Clues

4 Notice actual definitions.

Don't forget that writers often give you a definition of a word that might be unfamiliar. The writer may say exactly what the word means. In the next paragraph, for example, the first sentence is a complete definition of the underlined word.

An <u>emoticon</u> is a combination of keyboard characters, typically representing a facial expression or emotion, used especially in e-mail. The most common emoticon, the smiley face, is in the space below. You can see it by tilting your head a bit to the left.

:-)

Often, however, the definition is given through a *synonym*, a word or phrase that means the same thing as the new word. The synonym is usually set off by parentheses, commas, or dashes. Note how the dashes signal the synonym in this next sentence.

Some people are <u>diffident</u>—shy and withdrawn—in face-to-face communication. But even they like using emoticons in their e-mail communication.

SIGNALS FOR DEFINITION

Punctuation clues: dashes, commas, and parentheses

Words or phrases:
  or
  that is
  in other words

Either punctuation or words can signal *definition clues*. Signals for definition are given in the margin.

Practice Exercises

To more clearly understand Strategy 3, do these practice exercises for **using context clues**. Write out your answers. Work with classmates to prepare your answers if your instructor tells you to do so. Don't use the dictionary!

Exercise 1: Using context clues. For each of the following sentences, use the context clue provided to help you predict the meaning of the underlined word.

Example: I remember her kitchen being filled with <u>pungent</u> odors like garlic, onion, vinegar, and ginger. clue: examples

strong , sharp, stimulating, especially to the sense of smell

1. A trumpet solo began the <u>coda</u>—the concluding section of the musical piece.

   _____ clue: definition

2. The doctor had an <u>amiable</u> manner that made people want to get to know him as a friend.

   _____ clue: logic

3. A trained collie can quickly round up a flock of sheep. On the other hand, an untrained dog of a different breed will just as quickly <u>disperse</u> the entire flock.

   _____ clue: contrast

4. He was afraid that hiking in the mountains might involve <u>perils</u> like the following: getting hit by a falling rock, being bitten by a snake, or sliding off a narrow ledge.

   _____ clue: examples

5. She was so distracted that she wheeled the wrong shopping cart to her car and didn't realize her <u>blunder</u> until she got home with two bags of someone else's groceries.

   _____ clue: logic

Exercise 2: Using context clues. For each of the following sentences, look for the context clues that can help you predict the meaning of the underlined word. Then state what kind of context clue you used: logic, example, contrast, or definition.

Example: Some students seemed <u>hostile</u> to the new teacher's methods, but others were welcoming and open to her ideas.

*opposed or resistant*_____ clue: *contrast*

1. Although the first medication was too weak to have any effect on the infection, the second medication was very <u>potent</u>.

_____ clue: _____

2. The mountain bike was designed to <u>maneuver</u> easily through the twists and turns of a hilly, wooded pathway.

_____ clue: _____

3. Guards stood at the ancient castle's <u>portal</u> (a grand door or entrance) to warn of enemy approaches.

_____ clue: _____

4. A childhood <u>trauma</u>, such as losing a parent, suffering a severe illness, or experiencing physical cruelty, may scar a child for life.

_____ clue: _____

5. The typewriter has fallen out of use and become <u>obsolete</u>; almost everyone types on a computer nowadays.

_____ clue: _____

6. Cave paintings from the <u>Paleolithic</u>, or Old Stone Age, show that creativity existed in the earliest human beings.

_____ clue: _____

7. Last year's basketball team was practically unbeatable. However, this year's team seems quite <u>vulnerable</u>.

_____ clue: _____

8. Included in the <u>strenuous</u> activities offered at the gym are: dancing, jogging, cycling, swimming, and playing tennis.

_____ clue: _____

9. People used to believe that complete bed rest <u>facilitates</u> a patient's recovery from surgery. On the contrary, too much bed rest holds back recovery.

_____ clue: _____

10. Praising children when they've successfully met a challenge helps bolster their confidence and increases their ability to meet the next challenge.

_____ clue: _____

Apply the New Strategy: Use Context Clues

Now that you understand Strategy 3, put it into practice with Reading 5, "Sounds of Home: An 8,690-Mile Echo." Some unfamiliar words in the reading are defined for you in the margin. Other unfamiliar words are underlined. In the space provided in the margin, write down the meaning you can predict for each of these words by using context clues. You'll find that logic clues are the most common.

For the first eight paragraphs, you will find margin notes next to each underlined word. These notes tell you what type of context clues to use and indicate specific words and phrases from the sentences that help you define each word. From Paragraph 9 to the end, continue to use the context clues given for each underlined word to predict its definition. At the end of this reading, you can check to see how close your definitions are to the dictionary's.

READING 5   **SOUNDS OF HOME: AN 8,690-MILE ECHO**

SARA RIMER

This reading, adapted from a New York Times *article, is about a new musical group made up of young Cambodian-Americans. This group, pictured on page 46, performs a blend of hip-hop and traditional Cambodian music. Cambodia, a small Southeast Asian country, has been known in America mainly for its terrible history during 1975 to 1979. At that time the Khmer Rouge°, led by the military dictator Pol Pot, had taken over the country. They killed at least one million Cambodians.*

Now, these young people are bringing a positive side of Cambodian culture into a popular musical form. Journalist Sara Rimer describes a festival on the Merrimack River in Lowell, Massachusetts.

Khmer Rouge: "Cambodian" is the English term for "Khmer"; "rouge" means red.

CHECK IN
- What music is part of your cultural tradition?
- What types of popular music do you like?
- What do you think of blending a traditional culture with current pop culture?

hovering: moving back and forth near a place (in this case the temperature)

Southeast Asian Water Festival: definition clues—"a celebration . . . hundreds of years"

emulate: logic clues—the women are performing songs by famous singers, "doing their best to . . ."

Seasia: the name of the band

regime: government in power

emigrating: logic clues—"family fled," "living in . . . refugee camp," "before . . . to Chicago"

ghetto: logic clues—"poor neighborhood . . . called . . . Khmer ghetto"

With the temperature hovering° around 95, the river provided the only hint of a cooling breeze as an estimated 50,000 people converged on Lowell for the annual <u>Southeast Asian Water Festival</u>, a celebration of regional culture modeled on the water festivals that have been held in Cambodia for hundreds of years. Started in 1996, . . . the festival serves as the summer highlight for thousands of Southeast Asian immigrants from around the United States.

The day began with Cambodian monks blessing the river and the launching of eight colorful dragon boats. Then the action moved to the main stage—performances of traditional music and dance alternating with young Cambodian women doing their best to <u>emulate</u> Whitney Houston ("I Will Always Love You") and Celine Dion ("My Heart Will Go On"). . . .

At about 5 P.M. a group of three men in their 20's, dressed in baggy jeans, football jerseys and sneakers, took over the stage. "Lowell city, how ya doing?" the leader of the band, Tony Ayeth Roun, 24, called out, waving the microphone with one hand, a bottle of water with the other; his cornrows tight against his head as he strutted around the stage. "Are you feeling this, Lowell? Everyone got Khmer pride, Asian pride?" The crowd roared its response.

Seasia° had arrived. Finally. The band, a highlight of the festival, had been delayed, partly because two members had been stuck in traffic and then had to walk a half mile because they didn't want to shell out $5 for the parking lot fee. (Popular they may be. Rich they are not.). . . As about 20 young Cambodian men and women climbed up on stage to join it, Seasia (pronounced see-AH-sha) went into a new song. . . .

It's been a long journey to this place for Tony Roun and his band mates, Sambath Hy, 25, and Felix Sros Khut, 24. Mr. Roun's family fled the Khmer Rouge regime° shortly after he was born, living for the next five years in a Cambodian refugee camp on the Thailand border before <u>emigrating</u> to Chicago, and then to Lowell when he was 10. The two other Seasia members also spent their early years in refugee camps. . . .

The first Cambodian immigrants came to Lowell in the mid-1980's as part of a federal refugee resettlement program, and then thousands followed, drawn by the manufacturing jobs that required little English and few technical skills. . . .

But the journey for these three young men has been more than just the physical distance of the 8,690 miles from Cambodia to Lowell. They spent their early years in Lowell in a poor neighborhood—"We called it the Khmer <u>ghetto</u>," Mr. Khut said—and sharing the streets with local gang members. The three friends resisted joining the gangs, not, however, without something of a struggle to find their own identity.

1

2

3

4

5

6

7

killing fields: the Khmer
Rouge killed people mainly
in the countryside

"When I was young, I didn't care about being Khmer or Cambodian,"   8
Mr. Khut said on the Friday night before the festival performance. . . . "My
parents didn't want to talk about the killing fields?" he said. "They didn't
want to know about Cambodia. They just wanted to start a new life here.
Then Arn came along. He said you've got to be proud of who you are. He
showed us the light."

captors: use logic clues
_____

mission: use example clues
_____

Arn is Arn Chorn-Pond, a 37-year-old Cambodian-American flute player.   9
He is determined to bring back the traditional music that was outlawed
when Pol Pot's Khmer Rouge military regime took over the country from
1975 to 1979, and began its campaign to wipe out the educated classes,
including musicians. . . . Mr. Roun formed Seasia in 1995 and met Mr.
Chorn-Pond three years later when he heard him perform at a local community college. After the performance, Mr. Chorn-Pond, who had been forced
to play for his captors at a death camp, talked about his mission: to rediscover the handful of forgotten Cambodian masters who had survived Pol
Pot, and to enlist them in teaching their music to a new generation. . . .

RESPOND
Pause from time to time;
relate what you've read
to your own experience.

Ms. [Carolyn] Langevin, [the band's unpaid manager] . . . helped raise   10
the money to send [the band members] to Cambodia with Mr. Chorn-Pond
last year. They performed with the masters. They appeared on Cambodian
television. They visited the killing fields, and that night Mr. [Sambeth] Hy
wrote a rap about it: "As I reflect in the glass, in the back of skull frac-
tures . . . who could give me answers to all this killing?"

It was a far cry from their early exposure to the music business. Com-   11
ing of age in Lowell, and wanting to be a singer, Tony Roun says he had no
role models. "There were no Cambodian entertainers," he said. "I thought
I'm going to be the first group that breaks the barrier." He broke the first
one when he joined the show choir back at Lowell High School. "I was the
only Cambodian, the only Asian," he said. "We were singing stuff like 'Give
my regards to Broadway.'"

widespread: use contrast
clues
_____

At the time, traditional Cambodian music was [not widespread but]   12
something he heard only once in awhile at weddings, or when his father
played it at home. . . . [But] one night, they heard a Latin group perform at a
club. "That changed everything," Mr. Roun said. "We thought, 'We can do
it, too, man.' I said, 'Guys, we got to put a group together.'"

Seasia was born, with Mr. [Felix] Khut, another friend from high   13
school, later joining them. At first their friends discouraged them. "They
said 'You're short, you're Cambodian,'" said Mr. Rhoun, who is 5-foot, 2-
inches. "'You're never going to make it.'"

Mr. Hy said: "There were no cool Cambodians."   14

It's the Sunday after the festival, and the band members have dropped   15
in on their music teacher, Bin Phan, 72, who is in his garage in shorts and
bare feet, making a traditional Cambodian wooden drum. The heat is

oppressive: hard to bear; burdensome

sarong: cloth worn as a skirt by men and women in parts of Southeast Asia and the Pacific islands

revere: use logic clues
_____

oppressors: use logic clues
_____

jam: take part in a spur-of-the-moment musical session

trou sou: Use logic clues
_____

virtue: use logic clues
_____

oppressive°, and Mr. Phan has an electric fan turning at the foot of his workbench.

His lined face lights up when Mr. Roun, wearing a green sarong°, a 16
white tank top and a cellphone on his hip, walks into the garage with the other two band members. "I saw you on TV," Mr. Phan says in Khmer, with Mr. Roun translating, explaining that the heat had kept him home from the show. "It was good."

Mr. Roun and the other band members smile shyly. They <u>revere</u> Mr. 17
Phan as a Cambodian master, one of a small group of musicians who survived Pol Pot, and he has been a central influence as the band created their distinctive sound: a blend of traditional Cambodian music and hip hop. Under the Khmer Rouge, Mr. Phan was forced to spend his days working as a blacksmith, and his nights playing revolutionary music for his <u>oppressors</u>. Most of the other musicians were killed. He does not like to talk about that time. Right now he would rather jam° with his young friends.

He picks up his two-stringed <u>trou sou</u>, which he had made using the 18
wood of a New England maple instead of bamboo from Cambodia, and a piece of a Coca-Cola can, and draws his bow across it. The haunting notes of "Hero in My Eyes," a song Mr. Roun's group had written in honor of the masters, floats through the garage. Tapping out the beat with their flip-flops and slicing the air with their hands, Mr. Roun and Mr. Hy begin rapping over the old man's traditional Cambodian sound:

> Once, in my life, I was lost, now I'm found 19
> I've been, searching for, my roots in the ground
> All the types of sounds and sights that I've seen
> Couldn't explain my purpose or my reason being
> Now if I was to let go—like a wounded angel—foot off the pedal, I'll be buried in the meadows
> Just when I was about to give up, you charged my life, and changed my luck, huh!
> In my eyes you're a hero, a man beyond <u>virtue</u>. . . .

Definitions of Unfamiliar Words in Reading 5 Note that "Southeast Asian Water Festival" (Paragraph 1), "Seasia" (Paragraph 4), and "trou sou" (Paragraph 18) are special names. You wouldn't find them in a dictionary. "Southeast Asian Water Festival" is defined in the same sentence in which it is found. Seasia is the name of the band. "Trou sou" is a Cambodian stringed musical instrument, played with a bow, like a violin.

1. emulate: imitate

2. emigrating: leaving a country to live elsewhere

3. ghetto: a part of a city where members of a minority group live, especially because of social, legal, or economic pressure

4. captors: people who take others by force, or capture them

5. mission: task taken on with a sense of purpose

6. widespread: common, well known

7. revere: to see as worthy of great honor

8. oppressors: people who force heavy burdens on someone

9. virtue: goodness, righteousness

Follow-Up Activities   After you've finished reading, use these activities to respond to "Sounds of Home: An 8,690-Mile Echo." You may write your answers or prepare them in your mind to discuss in class.

Grab your first impressions.

1. Which people in this reading would you be most interested in meeting? Why? What more would you like to know about them?

2. The group found a way to blend its traditional music with a hip-hop style. What do you think are the similarities between its music and the music you like? What are the differences?

Ask and answer questions.

1. The band in the reading, Seasia, was "a highlight" of the Southeast Asian Water Festival. Describe what happened at the festival before the band arrived.

2. What brought the three band members from their own country to Lowell, Massachusetts? What was life like for them as they grew up there?

3. What made Arn Chorn-Pond want to work with the band members? How did he help them rediscover their Cambodian roots?

4. Why was it especially hard for Tony Roun and the others to get started as musicians? At what moment did they decide they could put a group together?

5. At the end of the reading the different generations play the song, "Hero in My Eyes." Why is their playing that song together important? How does it help to sum up the whole reading?

Ask and answer your own question.

Write a question of your own. Share your question with others, and work together on an answer.

Form your final thoughts.

 1. This reading shows how music can be a way for generations to work together. What ways have you seen music, art, sports, or other activities bring people of different backgrounds together?

 2. What experiences did the two older musicians share? What experiences did the young musicians share? How important are shared experiences for members of each generation?

3. What music would you like to share with others in the class? What parts of the music do you think your classmates would respond to most—the words, melody, rhyme, or rhythm? Bring in some samples of your music if your instructor agrees. ■

Chapter 3 Summary

How does Strategy 3 help you *use your reader's voice to be an active reader?*

As an active reader, you **respond** in your reader's voice to what the writer has to say. But sometimes unfamiliar words become a barrier between you and the writer's ideas. Strategy 3, **Use Context Clues,** helps you predict the meaning of these new words so you can continue responding as you read.

How does the *use context clues* strategy work?

To **use context clues,** you look for clues in the surrounding words and sentences that suggest the meaning of a new word. Here are the four reminders for Strategy 3 (see page 60).

STRATEGY 3: USE CONTEXT CLUES

1 Use the "sense of the sentence," or logic clues.

2 Let examples act as clues.

3 Watch for contrast clues.

4 Notice actual definitions.

Are you familiar with the meaning of these terms?

context: the surroundings in which you find a word

context clues: clues from surrounding words and ideas that suggest the meaning of a new word

contrast clues: clues that suggest that the meaning of a new word is the opposite of a word you already know

definition clues: words or punctuation marks that show you a new word is being defined for you

example clues: clues that use examples or instances to suggest the meaning of a new word

logic clues: clues about the meaning of a word that come from the logic of the rest of the sentence

synonyms: two words or phrases that have the same meaning

How is the strategy working for you so far?

Explain which parts of **using context clues** you've found most helpful in the readings you've practiced with. Which parts have been least helpful?

TIME OUT FOR YOU

WHAT HELPS YOU PLAN AHEAD?

As a college student, you have a lot going on in your life. Your week is filled with going to class, studying, and outside responsibilities, such as work or family. On top of all that, you need time for friends and fun. Planning ahead—for the day, the week, and beyond—can help you keep track of all these demands on your time. Try these suggestions for good planning. See which ones work best for you.

Use a Weekly Schedule

Make a photocopy of the schedule on page 62. Write in the class meeting times for each of your courses. Then write down additional hours for work or other regularly scheduled activities, such as picking up your sister at school or playing a weekly game of soccer (see the sample schedule on page 63). You can make several copies of your schedule with the times for classes, work, and scheduled activities filled in. Then, for each week, fill in the empty spaces with what you need to do that week.

Use a Calendar

Start with the syllabus (course description and schedule) for each course. On a calendar, write down the due dates for tests, papers, and other major assignments listed on the syllabus. In addition, write down time-consuming events outside of school, such as a friend's wedding. Try one or more of these calendars:

- A small pocket calendar you can carry along with you

- An easy-to-see wall calendar

- A desk calendar

Weekly Schedule

Hour	Sun.	Mon.	Tues.	Wed.	Thurs.	Fri.	Sat.
7:00							
8:00							
9:00							
10:00							
11:00							
12:00							
1:00							
2:00							
3:00							
4:00							
5:00							
6:00							
7:00							
8:00							
9:00							
10:00							
11:00							
12:00							

Sample of a Student's Weekly Schedule

Hour	Sun.	Mon.	Tues.	Wed.	Thurs.	Fri.	Sat.
7:00							
8:00							work
9:00	free		P.E.		P.E.		work
10:00	free	History		History		History	work
11:00	free	Math	Math	Math	Math	Math	work
12:00	free						
1:00	study	work	Reading	work	Reading	work	soccer game
2:00	study	work	Reading	work	Reading	work	soccer game
3:00	study	pick up sister	work	work	pick up sister	work	soccer game
4:00			work	errands	work		meet friends
5:00		study group	work	errands	work		
6:00		soccer practice				soccer practice	
7:00		soccer practice	study	study	study	soccer practice	
8:00	study		study	study	study	meet friends	
9:00	study						
10:00							
11:00	sleep	sleep	sleep	sleep	sleep		
12:00						sleep	sleep

Make "To Do" Lists

Try writing a list of specific tasks you need to get done for the day or week. Write the list in a small notebook or on an index card to carry with you. Some students find special satisfaction in checking off the completed tasks.

Make Visual Reminders

For many students, the more visual the information, the better. Clear, colorful information is easier to notice and remember. Here are some tools for making visual reminders.

- An oversized schedule or wall calendar—helps you see the important things coming up. These are inexpensive and can be found in office supply stores.

- Colored pens, highlighters, or sticky notes—can call attention to special events or tasks. Write down the most important assignments for the term on the calendar, circled in a bright color. Your most important social events—such as an out-of-state trip—can be circled in a different color.

- Sticky notes—provide flexible ways to call attention to the things you need to do. Small notes of different colors are great for putting on the calendar. They remind you of things that don't have a definite date. For example, you can add a sticky note reminding yourself to start writing a paper a week before it is due. If something else comes up that day, you can move the sticky note to the next day. Larger sticky notes can be used all around your room to remind you of things you have to do.

CHAPTER 4

WORK WITH NEW WORDS

FIND THE RIGHT DEFINITION

Strategy 3, **Use Context Clues,** helps you predict the meaning of new words. But sometimes the context doesn't give you enough clues. You need Strategy 4, **Find the Right Definition,** to help you define and learn new words.

Introduction to the New Strategy: Find the Right Definition

Finding the right definition helps you investigate new words. This strategy gives you ways to use word parts and the dictionary to help you figure out the meaning of words and expand your vocabulary. To make these new words part of your vocabulary, learn the system presented in the "Time Out for You" at the end of this chapter.

STRATEGY 4: FIND THE RIGHT DEFINITION

1 Use word parts.

2 Make the dictionary work for you.

Word Parts

1 *Use word parts.*

Read the following paragraph about pay phones. As you read, see what you notice about the underlined words.

> When I was young [pay phones] were just there, a given, often as stubborn . . . as the <u>curbstone</u> <u>underfoot</u>. They were instruments of torture sometimes. You had to feed them <u>fistfuls</u> of change . . . and the operator was a real person who stood maddeningly between you and whomever you were trying to call.
>
> —Ian Frazier, "Dearly Disconnected"

You probably noticed that a couple of these words were made up of two smaller words. It's easy to see the two little words in "curbstone"("curb" and "stone") and "underfoot" ("under" and "foot").

Sometimes words contain only one little word that can stand by itself. For example, "fistfuls" begins with the word "fist"; "fuls" isn't a word by itself. But it is a *word part*—an element of a word that has a constant meaning. In this case, you probably recognize "ful" as a word part meaning "full."

When you come across a new word, it helps to watch for a familiar word within it. But English words don't always contain little words that can stand alone. More frequently, they are made up of other word parts known as *prefixes, roots,* and *suffixes.* If you learn the most common of these word parts, you can often predict the meaning of new words, and you'll multiply the number of words you can add to your vocabulary.

Prefixes. Prefixes come at the beginning of a word. They add meaning to the word. You may already know that "pre-" in "prefix" means "before." If so, it's easy to understand and remember it as the word part that comes before the rest of a word. "Pre" added to "view" makes "preview," which means to "view before." "Pre" added to "pay" makes "prepay," which means to "pay before." Here are three more common prefixes you probably already know:

"re-" (back; again): return, review

"un-" (not): unhappy, unlucky

"bi-" (two): bicycle, bimonthly

Learn additional common prefixes to get a head start in figuring out the meaning of hundreds more words.

Roots. Roots may come at the beginning, middle, or end of a word. A root gives the word its core meaning. The root "dict," for example, means "say" or "word." The word "pre*dict*" combines the prefix "pre" with the root "dict," meaning "say," so the whole word means "say before." The word "*dict*ate" means "say to someone"; the word "*dict*ionary" means "a book about words." "Port" is another common root, meaning "carry." See how it is used first as a word by itself and then as a root combined with other word parts:

> *port* = place where ships carry things in and out
>
> *port*able = able to be carried
>
> ex*port* = carry out
>
> im*port* = carry in

Suffixes. Suffixes come at the end of a word. They tell you what form or part of speech the word is, that is, how the word is used in a sentence. The main forms are: noun (names a person, place, or thing), verb (shows action or state of being), adjective (describes a noun), or adverb (describes a verb or an adjective). Here are some common suffixes:

> "-ist" (noun suffix) indicates a person who does something: artist, violinist
>
> "-ize" (verb suffix) shows action: criticize, sanitize, baptize
>
> "-ful" (usually adjective suffix) describes being "full of": colorful, helpful, playful
>
> "-ly" (adverb suffix) shows how something is done: quickly, sweetly, cruelly

The following charts give lists of common prefixes, roots, and suffixes.

Common Prefixes

Prefix	Sample words
a (or *ab*): without or not	*a*moral (without morals); *ab*normal (not normal)
anti: against	*anti*freeze (against freezing)

auto: self	*auto*biography (writing about yourself—your life)
bi: two; *tri:* three	*bi*cycle (two wheels); *tri*cycle (three wheels)
circ (or *circum*): round or around	*circ*le (round shape); *circum*ference (boundary around)
co (or *con*): together or with	*co*operate (work together); *con*join (join together)
counter: opposing or opposite to	*counter*argument (opposing argument); *counter*clockwise (opposite from clockwise direction)
de: down or showing a reversal	*de*grade (downgrade); *de*activate (make inactive)
dis: not	*dis*agree (not agree)
ex (or *e*): out or out of	*ex*port (take out of the country); *e*ject (throw out)
hyper: over	*hyper*active (overactive)
in (or *il, im, ir*): in OR not	*in*spect (look into); *il*legal (not legal); *im*moderate (not moderate); *ir*regular (not regular)
inter: between OR among	*inter*mediate (placed in between); *inter*national (among nations)
mal: bad	*mal*nutrition (bad nutrition)
mono: one	*mono*tone (one tone)
pre: before	*pre*marital (before marriage)
post: after	*post*date (date after)
pro: forward	*pro*gress (move forward)
re: again or back	*re*do (do again); *re*ject (throw back)
sub: under	*sub*marine (boat for under water)
syn (or *sym*): with or together	*syn*chronize (set the same time); *sym*phony (instruments playing together)
tele: far	*tele*scope (instrument for far sight)
trans: across	*trans*port (carry across)

Common Roots

Roots	Sample words
bio: life	*bio*logy (study of life)
chron: time	*chron*ic (continuing a long time)
-cide: kill (always at end of word)	insecti*cide* (killing insects)
cred: belief	*cred*ible (able to be believed)
dict: word; say	*dict*ionary (book of words); pre*dict* (say beforehand)
fus: pour or blend as if by melting	in*fus*e (pour into); *fus*e (verb meaning blend together)
graph: writing or drawing	bio*graph*y (writing about someone's life); *graph* (drawing that diagrams information)
log; logy: knowledge, record, or study of	cata*log* (record of knowledge); zoo*logy* (study of animals)
mort: death or dying	*mort*ician (one who prepares the dead for burial); im*mort*al (not dying)
path: feeling or suffering	sym*path*y (feeling with someone)
phobia: irrational fear of	claustro*phobia* (fear of enclosed spaces)
port: carry	trans*port* (carry across)
psych (or *psycho*): mind	*psycho*analysis (analysis of the mind)
spec (or *spect*): look or see	in*spect* (look inside)
theo: God or gods	*theo*logy (the study of religion or God)
ven (or *vent*): come	con*vent*ion (coming together)

Common Suffixes

Suffixes for nouns (person)	Sample words
-er, -or	teach*er*, doct*or*
-ist	dent*ist*, real*ist*

Suffixes for nouns (quality or condition)	Sample words
-ance, -ence	assist*ance*, refer*ence*
-ation	imagin*ation*, realiz*ation*
-ion	act*ion*, tens*ion*
-ism	pessim*ism*, real*ism*
-ity	activ*ity*, human*ity*
-ness	good*ness*
Suffixes for verbs	**Sample words**
-ate	initi*ate*, gener*ate*
-ify	just*ify*, simpl*ify*
-ize	apolog*ize*, symbol*ize*
Suffixes for adjectives	**Sample words**
-able, -ible	stretch*able*, sens*ible*
-ful	sorrow*ful*, beauti*ful*
-ive	act*ive*, destruct*ive*

The Dictionary

2 Make the dictionary work for you.

You can often predict the meaning of a word from the context or by analyzing word parts. However, you also need the dictionary to confirm that your prediction was correct and to give you a more precise definition.

When to look up a word. Does an unfamiliar word keep you from following what you're reading? If so, you may need to look it up right away. But usually, you don't need to interrupt your reading. As you read, underline unknown words, or make a list. After reading, look them up.

Try this method in reading the following paragraph written by the author about smoking. Underline any new words. See how well you can follow the ideas without stopping to use the dictionary.

In recent decades, the dangers of smoking have become much clearer, and cigarettes have lost much of their appeal. Yet tobacco leaders remain sanguine about future earnings from cigarettes. It is true that regulations against smoking are in force everywhere today, from restaurants to airplanes, college campuses to office buildings. In fact, smokers often have to huddle together outside in the cold, just to find a place to smoke. But if the tobacco industry is losing customers here, it's gaining them overseas. In developing countries, more people than ever are taking up the habit, and many of them will have a hard time kicking it.

You probably got the overall message: Americans smoke less, but the tobacco industry sees continuing profits from overseas sales. But for a better understanding, you need more information about an unusual word in the second sentence—"sanguine." Now is the time to look it up. You'll find a complete definition in the sample dictionary entry below.

Dictionary entries. A dictionary entry gives many different ways of looking at a word. Dictionaries vary, but their entries help you answer the same basic questions. The sample entry (below) comes from the *American Heritage Dictionary* that is on the Internet. Many dictionaries

sanguine

a.	SYLLABICATION:	san·guine
b.	PRONUNCIATION:	AUDIO: săng'gwĭn KEY
c.	ADJECTIVE:	**1a.** Of the color of blood; red. **b.** Of a healthy reddish color; ruddy: *a sanguine complexion.* **2.** *Archaic* **a.** Having blood as the dominant humor in terms of medieval physiology. **b.** Having the temperament and ruddy complexion formerly thought to be characteristic of a person dominated by this humor; passionate. **3.** Cheerfully confident; Optimistic.

multiple meanings (See "Choosing the definition that fits", p. 72)

d.	ETYMOLOGY:	Middle English, from Old French *sanguin,* from Latin *sanguineus,* from *sanguis, sanguin-,* blood.
e.	OTHER FORMS:	**san'guine·ly**—ADVERB **san'guine·ness, san·guin'i·ty**—NOUN

from *American Heritage On-Line Dictionary*
Sample Dictionary Entry

now have a version on the Internet. These are called *on-line diction-aries*. On-line dictionaries and dictionaries on CD-ROM have an audio portion that gives the correct pronunciation of a word.

a. Syllabication—how is the word broken into syllables?

b. Pronunciation—how is the word pronounced? To use the pronun-ciation symbols, use the key—usually at the bottom of the page. In this on-line version you'd click on "AUDIO" to hear the correct pro-nunciation, and "KEY" to get to the pronunciation key.

c. Form of the word—what form (or part of speech) is the word? In this case it is an adjective.

d. Etymology—what are the origin and history of the word? The *etymology* gives more information about one or more of the word parts that make up the word.

e. Other forms—what are the different forms made by changing the word's suffix (ending) or adding a new one? In this case, adding "-ly" makes it an adverb; "-ness" or "-ity" makes the word a noun.

Choosing the definition that fits. Many words have more than one meaning. Think of how the word is used in the context—the surround-ing words and ideas—before choosing a definition. Then you can be sure to pick the definition that fits. The sample entry gives three main definitions for "sanguine," with specific variations for the first two. Which definition seems the right one for the context?

1a. Of the color of blood; red. b. Of a healthy reddish color; ruddy: *a sanguine complexion?* Nothing in the context suggests that the leaders look red or have a reddish complexion.

2. Archaic. Seeing "Archaic" (or the abbreviation, "Arch.") before a definition tells you that this meaning is "old"; it was once in regular use but is now out-of-date. It does give you more history of the word that may be helpful in understanding its current meaning. For example, this definition helps you see the relationship between "red" and "blood" and definition 3.

3. This one makes sense. Tobacco leaders are "cheerfully confident; optimistic" about future earnings because of overseas sales of ciga-rettes.

Choosing the right dictionary. It's best to have two dictionaries. A pocket dictionary is helpful for finding a brief definition when you're away from home. A desk or collegiate dictionary is better for getting a clear understanding of a word's meaning. *Merriam-Webster's Collegiate Dictionary, The American Heritage Dictionary,* and *The Random House Dictionary* are three widely used collegiate dictionaries. You can also use the on-line versions of those dictionaries.

Practice Exercises

To gain a clearer understanding of Strategy 4, do these practice exercises for **finding the right definition.** Write out your answers. Work with classmates to prepare your answers if your instructor tells you to do so.

Exercise 1: Using word parts in real words. Each of the following ten words contains at least one prefix, root, or suffix found in the charts on the previous pages. Follow these steps to figure out their meanings:

- Give the meaning of each prefix, root, or suffix found in the charts.

- Say what the whole word means.

    Example: predict = "before" and "say"; the word means "to say before."

1. subfloor _____

2. malfunction _____

3. counterattack _____

4. autograph _____

5. exporter _____

6. apathy _____

7. hypersensitive _____

8. inspector _____

9. biocide _____

10. convene _____

 Exercise 2: Using word parts in "made-up words." A. The following words are not real words, but they are made up of commonly used

prefixes and roots that do have real meanings. Part of the word is given for you. You give the meaning of the word part in italics:

Example: pre*spect* = to _____ before

Answer: "to see before."

1. mal*port*: to _____ badly

2. *cred*ology: the study of _____

3. *inter*spect: to see _____

4. *dict*phobia: an irrational fear of _____

5. circum*fuse*: to _____ around

B. Now, use prefixes and roots from the charts on pages 67–69 to put together five "made up" words. Say what each part means and then what your new word would mean.

1. _____

2. _____

3. _____

4. _____

5. _____

Exercise 3: Making the dictionary work for you. Read this paragraph about marketing clothes to teenagers. Then, for each word, follow the directions for using the dictionary. The first word is done for you.

> To be successful, retailers marketing to teenagers must first find the hippest fashion—"clean grunge" is big now—then set the prices. Pollsters say teenagers want to spend no more than $200 on a season like back-to-school and expect to get four or five items. At such low prices, it is tough to find both fit and fashion. What usually suffers is quality. But teenagers' style is so evanescent that long before the clothes fall apart, they will have been shoved to the back of the closet.
>
> —Tracie Rozhon, "The Race to Think Like a Teenager"

Example: retailer You probably won't find the word "retailer" in the dictionary. How can you find the meaning?

The list of suffixes on pages 69–70 tells you the suffix "-er" means "some-one who," that is, a person. Take off that ending, and look up "retail."

"Retailer" means "someone who retails," that is, "someone who sells in small quantities directly to consumers."

1. <u>hippest</u> Take off the suffix "-est" (meaning "the most"). Then see how many definitions for "hip" you find in the dictionary entry. What are at least two ways you can tell which definition fits this context?

   _____

2. <u>grunge</u> This is a slang word that was first used in its adjective form, "grungy," meaning dirty. Here is the second definition of "grunge" in the Merriam-Webster on-line dictionary:
   (2) Rock music incorporating elements of punk rock and heavy metal; also: the untidy working-class fashions typical of fans of grunge

   From this definition and the ideas in the paragraph, what guess can you make about what "clean grunge" means? How can "grunge" be "clean?"

   _____

3. <u>pollster</u> This word is defined as "one who conducts a poll." Which is the best definition of "poll" for this context?
   (1) the number of votes cast or recorded
   (2) a survey of the public or of a sample of public opinion to acquire information

   _____

4. <u>evanescent</u> Look up this word in your dictionary. In your own words, what does the writer mean by saying that teenage style is "so evanescent"?

   _____

5. In this same article, teenage customers are referred to as "mercurial customers." Which of the following four definitions for "mercurial" best fits the context of this article?
   (1) pertaining to the Greek god Mercury or the planet Mercury
   (2) having the characteristics of eloquence, shrewdness, swiftness, and thievishness attributed to the god Mercury
   (3) containing or caused by the action of the element mercury
   (4) being quick and changeable in character

   _____

CHECK IN
- What are some slang expressions you use often?
- When do you feel comfortable using slang? How do you feel about others using slang?
- Do you ever find it frustrating when you can't understand a slang expression? Why or why not?

Apply the New Strategy: Find the Right Definition

Now that you understand Strategy 4, put it into practice with Reading 6, "Flappers 2 Rappers: American Youth Slang." Some unfamiliar words in the reading are defined for you in the margin. Others are underlined. Follow the suggestions in the margin next to each underlined word for using Strategy 3, **Use Context Clues,** or Strategy 4, **Find the Right Definition** of the new word. At the end of this reading, you can check to see if you have chosen the right meanings.

READING 6   FLAPPERS 2 RAPPERS: AMERICAN YOUTH SLANG

TOM DALZELL

"Slang" is an informal and playful language made up of surprising new uses of words and made-up words. Words like "cool" (having style) or "goof" (silly mistake) are two common slang words. In this reading, Tom Dalzell talks about why and how slang has been used by young Americans since the beginning of the twentieth century. The reading is adapted from the introduction to his book Flappers° 2 Rappers°: American Youth Slang. *At the end of the reading, you can see how many of the slang words (in bold) you know. They're defined for you right after the reading. But also note the underlined words. They are the ones you'll work with in the follow-up activities.*

Flapper: young woman of the 1920s, known for breaking social rules of behavior and dress

Rapper: performer of rap (rhyming and rhythmic chanting to music)

vernacular: use logic clues

counterculture: break up the word; the prefix "counter" means "opposed to"

Harlem: section of New York with large African-American community

advocates: use logic clues and the contrast clues, "I believe otherwise"

As I worked my way through the century, I came to several broad conclusions about youth slang from that of the Flapper to that of the Rapper. First, one cannot help but be struck by the powerful influence of African-American <u>vernacular</u> on the slang of all 20th-century American youth. Jazz musicians of the 1930s and rappers of the 1980s and 1990s defined the popular youth slang of the late 1930s, the 1940s, the <u>counterculture</u> 1950s, the 1960s, and the 1990s. There were other influences, to be sure, on the slang of America's young, but none as powerful as that of the streets of Harlem° and Chicago.

As a second observation, it is my distinct belief that the young do not use slang to conceal the meaning of their speech from their parents and other authority figures. This theory has its <u>advocates</u>, most notably Robert Chapman, author of the *New Dictionary of American Slang....* Still, I believe otherwise. My sense is that most young people do not even use slang in front of adults. If slang is not used in front of adults, it cannot be said that it is used to cloak the meaning of what is said.

1

2

RESPOND
Remember to make a comment or question the writer from time to time.

station: use the sentence that follows for logic clues. Be sure your meaning fits the context.

status: use logic clues

defying: context clues may not work here, but finish the reading before using the dictionary

reemerged: you know the prefix "re-"; use logic clues to help with "emerge"

vengeance: use logic clues

reincarnation: you know the prefix "re-"; use logic clues to help with the "incarnation"

Instead, the primary purposes of youth slang, it seems to me, are threefold. First, slang serves to change the level of conversation towards the informal. Slang serves the important function of identifying other young people as members of a group; because you use certain words or expressions, I know that we are from the same tribe and that I can speak freely and informally with you. Second, slang establishes <u>station</u> ... [and] ... the speaker's <u>status</u> .... Beginning (hello) and ending (good-bye) conversations smoothly is a learned social skill, and the risk of embarrassing oneself and losing face is great. Youth slang confronts this problem by providing established ... greetings and farewells. The third function of youth slang is to satisfy youth's drive for <u>defying</u> authority.   3

My next observation on the slang of 20th-century American youth is that there is very little that is new. Certain words are cyclical; **groovy, mellow,** and **solid** all come to mind as examples of words that were popular with the youth of the 1940s, fell into disfavor in the 1950s, and then <u>reemerged</u> with a <u>vengeance</u> in the 1960s.   4

How does this happen? How is it that **groovy** was so thoroughly forgotten as a big word of the 1940s and sounded so new when it leapt into the spotlight in 1965 or so?   5

Robert Chapman believes that there is no single cause for the <u>reincarnation</u> of slang. ...   6

Other words, such as **dope, drag, freak, rap,** or **trip** assumed different meanings in different decades. ... Of course, there is the incomparably adaptable *hip,* which has survived in one form or another (**hip, hep, hipster, hepster, hep-cat, hippy, hippie,** and **hip-hop**) for the entire [twentieth] century.   7

Definitions of Slang Words in Reading 6 These definitions come from *The American Heritage On-Line Dictionary.*

1. groovy: wonderful, excellent; hip

2. mellow: pleasant, having a relaxed style

3. solid: excellent

4. dope: illegal drug or information (as in "the inside dope")

5. drag: someone or something that's very tiresome

6. freak: passionate fan (as in "computer game freak")

7. rap: form of music using rhythmic speaking in rhyme, or sentence to serve time in prison

8. trip: getting high on a mind-altering drug, or an all-absorbing interest (as in a "health-food trip")

9. virtue: goodness, righteousness

Follow-Up Activities   After you've finished reading, use these activities to respond to "Flappers 2 Rappers: American Youth Slang." You may write your answers or prepare them in your mind to discuss in class.

Grab your first impressions.

1. How important is slang as a way to express yourself? Explain your answer.

2. As Dalzell reminds us, there are many slang expressions for saying "Hello" or "Good-bye." What is a slang expression you or others around you use for those purposes? Slang words are also commonly used to say "That's great" or "That's terrible." What are some slang words that express these or other emotions? You can refer to the list on page 77 if you need to.

Work with new words.

Several of the unfamiliar words from the reading have multiple meanings. Choose the definition that best fits the context. The first item is done for you.

1. vernacular: 1. The standard native language of a country or locality. 2. The idiom of a particular trade or profession. __1__

2. advocate: 1. One that argues for a cause or an idea. 2. A lawyer. _____

3. station: 1. The place, building, or establishment from which a service is provided or operations are directed. 2. Social position or rank. _____

4. status: 1. Position relative to that of others; standing. 2. High standing; prestige. _____

5. defy: 1. To oppose or resist with boldness and assurance. 2. To challenge or dare (someone) to do something. _____

6. emerge: [note: the word in the reading is "reemerge"; choose the best definition for "emerge," and recognize that the prefix "re-" adds the meaning "again."] 1. To rise from or as if from immersion: Sea mammals must emerge periodically to breathe. 2. To come forth from obscurity: new leaders who may emerge. _____

7. "<u>with a vengeance</u>": 1. With great violence or force. 2. To an extreme degree. _____

8. <u>reincarnation</u>: 1. Rebirth of the soul in another body. 2. A reappearance or revitalization in another form; a new embodiment. _____

Ask and answer questions.

1. What are the two types of African-American musicians who have had a powerful influence on slang?

2. Dalzell disagrees with the theory that says young people use slang to hide the meaning of what they say from people in authority. Why does he disagree?

3. Dalzell says that the third function of youth slang is "to satisfy youth's drive for defying authority." What does "defy" mean? Why is using slang a way of defying authority?

4. What are examples of slang words that came back into use after disappearing from the language? What are examples of slang words that came back into use, but with new meanings?

5. According to Dalzell, the first function of youth slang is to give young people a particular, informal way of talking to one another that lets other young people know the speaker is one of their group. He says the second function is to establish "station" and "the speaker's status." What does he mean by adding that having "established . . . greetings and farewells" helps someone avoid the "risk of embarrassing oneself and losing face" (or status)?

Ask and answer your own question.

Write a question of your own. Share your question with others, and work together on an answer.

Form your final thoughts.

1. In a group, share some of your favorite slang expressions. Which expressions do you have in common? Which are different? How would you explain these similarities and differences?

2. Did your attitude and ideas about slang change because of learning more about the subject? Refer to specific details in the reading that help explain why or why not. ■

Chapter 4 Summary

*How does Strategy 4 help you use your reader's voice
to be an active reader?*

Using context clues helps you handle unfamiliar words. But sometimes you need more help with those words. Strategy 4, **Find the Right Definition,** gives you ways to find out a more exact meaning of new vocabulary words, so you can keep **responding** to the writer's ideas.

How does the find the right definition strategy work?

Find the Right Definition shows how word parts and the dictionary can improve your ability to understand and learn new words. Here are the two reminders for Strategy 4.

STRATEGY 4: FIND THE RIGHT DEFINITION

1 Use word parts.

2 Make the dictionary work for you.

Are you familiar with the meaning of these terms?

etymology: origin and history of a word

on-line dictionary: dictionary on the Internet

prefix: a word part that comes at the beginning of a word; it indicates such information as direction (in, out, under) and number

root: a word part that gives a word its core meaning; it may come at the beginning, middle, or end of a word

suffix: a word part that comes at the end of a word; it shows how the word is used in the sentence (noun, verb, adjective, or adverb)

word part: element of a word that has a constant meaning

How is the strategy working for you so far?

Explain which parts of **finding the right definition** you've found most helpful in the readings you've practiced with. Which parts have been least helpful?

TIME OUT FOR YOU

HOW CAN YOU IMPROVE
YOUR VOCABULARY?

Do you want to improve your vocabulary? Most college students say they do. But how? A good dictionary and a knowledge of common word parts give you a good start. Still, words only become part of your vocabulary when you make them your own. Here's a system for doing that.

Deciding What Words to Learn

Look for words you want to become part of your vocabulary. In addition to any words your instructor assigns, choose your own words to learn:

- words you've run into several times

- words you can imagine using in writing or conversation

- words that relate to subjects that interest you

Learning Words with Vocabulary Cards

Make your own vocabulary cards for self-study. Here's how:

1. On the front of a 3 x 5 index card, write the word in context (plus pronunciation symbols if needed). On the back, write the definition, along with other helpful information or drawings to help you remember a word. See the sample cards on page 83.

2. To study the word, look at the front side only. See if you can say the definition. Then turn the card over to see if you remembered the correct definition.

3. Carry the cards with you so you can test yourself whenever you have a few extra minutes—for instance, when you're stuck waiting in line.

4. Mix up the cards so you don't have to depend on learning words in a set order.

5. Put aside the cards of words you've learned, so you concentrate on the words you don't know yet.

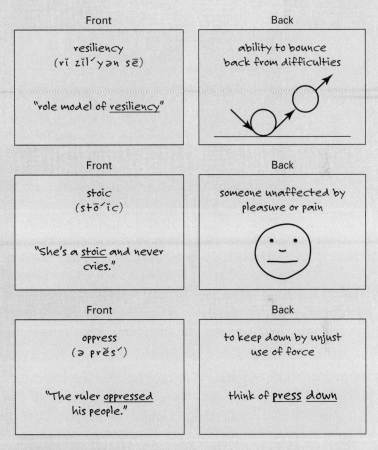

Sample Vocabulary Cards

CHAPTER 5

ASK
QUESTIONS

As an active reader you involve yourself in a conversation with the writer. In addition to "listening" and "talking back," you ask the writer questions. Strategy 5, **Ask Questions,** helps you make your questions more effective. You continue asking about what catches your interest, as you've been doing when **checking in** and **responding.** But there are also questions to ask before getting started that can help you predict what the reading will be about. Then you know what to look for as you read. Other questions you ask during and after reading can help you identify the writer's most important ideas.

Introduction to the New Strategy: Ask Questions

A questioning mind keeps you interested and helps you think clearly about a reading. Strategy 5, **Ask Questions,** gives you three ways to use questions to improve your understanding before, during, and after reading.

STRATEGY 5: ASK QUESTIONS

1 Ask questions about what catches your interest.

2 Before reading, ask questions to get an overview.

3 During and after reading, ask and answer questions.

Use this strategy as you prepare to read "Movie Censorship: A Brief History," on pages 90–93. **Asking questions** keeps you connected to the reading. Questions also help you find the reading's most important ideas.

Questions for Connecting with the Reading

You've learned to **check in** before reading to make a connection with the subject. Don't forget that asking questions helps you make that first connection. You can ask such questions as, "What experience have I had with the subject?" or "How can this subject relate to me?" or "How do I feel about this subject?" For example, think about the next reading, "Movie Censorship: A Brief History."

What would your check-in questions be? Here are some examples: "How would I feel if I were told I couldn't see a certain movie?" "What kinds of movies do I object to?" "I didn't know that movie censorship had a history; were there movies my parents or grandparents couldn't see?" These personal questions get you involved from the beginning. But remember that asking questions is also part of **responding** and staying involved. As you read, **ask questions** about any ideas that interest you. Continue reading to find answers.

Questions for Getting an Overview

Your **check-in** reminds you of your own ideas on the subject of a reading. But what about the writer's ideas? An *overview* shows you what the writer will say on the subject. So, before reading, stop a little longer to get an *overview.*

An overview is the big picture. It's the kind of view you get of a city when you take off or land in an airplane. From up high, you don't see each small building or even each neighborhood. Instead, you see the entire city and are able to pick out major locations. Getting an overview means looking at the big picture so you have a sense of the entire reading and don't get lost in the details. Asking questions as you get an overview helps you *predict,* that is, use information to see what to expect about the important ideas in a reading.

Title as key to the subject. To get an overview before reading, start with the title. Use it as a key for finding out more about the subject. For example, think about the title of Reading 7, "Movie Censorship:

A Brief History." The reading will be about censoring movies in the past and maybe in the present, too.

Turn the title into a question that can guide the rest of your overview. For most titles, use a "what," "why," or "how" question. Here are three ways of asking a question based on the title:

1. "What has been the history of movie censorship?"

2. "Why were movies censored in the past—and what's the current situation?"

3. "How did they censor movies in the past—and maybe in the present?"

Any one of these questions will help you get an overview.

Other important cues. In addition to the title, writers and editors use other parts of a reading to capture your attention. These *cues,* which can lead you to important ideas, are shown in the table on page 89. Now, see how each cue helps you ask questions and make predictions about "Movie Censorship: A Brief History." Remember to relate these cues to the title.

Notes before a Reading   Notes given before a reading, like the ones before magazine articles or textbook readings, give helpful information about the author and the reading. For example, the note before Reading 7 shows that the reading comes from a textbook about current mass media°. Thus, you can expect the "brief history" to include current as well as past movie censorship.

mass media: forms of public communication, such as TV, movies, radio, newspapers

Headings   Headings are words or phrases that act as titles for sections of a reading. The first heading in Reading 7 is about issues (or questions) of morality° in the early years of movies. You might ask, "Was morality the reason why movie censorship got started? If so, how did it happen?" Look at the second and third headings:

morality: ideas about right and wrong; a sense of decency

- Movies and Changing Moral Values

- Current Movie Code

What do these headings add to your questions and predictions about the history of movie censorship?

Introduction   A reading's introduction is found in the first paragraph or paragraphs. The introduction to Reading 7—its first paragraph—

adds to your predictions. It mentions today's movie rating system. Today our rating system simply "alerts" people to movies they might disapprove of. You might ask, "What happened in the past that led to today's rating system?"

Conclusion   The last paragraph or two often sum up an entire reading. This reading doesn't have such a conclusion because it is an excerpt from a longer textbook chapter.

Illustrations   Pictures and other types of visual information make your overview easier. The photograph on page 93 gives you an idea about a current problem some people have with movies.

Captions for Visual Features   Captions found under visual features explain what is portrayed and often add other important information. Don't forget to read them. How does the caption for the photograph on page 93 explain the current problem? How does that problem relate to questions about movie censorship?

Boxed Information   Some information may be set off in a box. Putting the information in a box—usually near the ideas it is related to—shows that it is different from the main part of the reading but gives important added ideas or summaries of ideas.

The overall point and the umbrella question. The *overall point* of a reading is the writer's most important message. Think of it as an "umbrella idea." Like an umbrella, the overall point covers—or includes—all of the other important ideas in the reading (see the diagram on page 88). The overall point can be summed up in a statement about the whole reading.

How can you use your overview to predict the overall point? Go back to the question you asked based on the title. That will become your *umbrella question*—the question that is answered by the overall point. Because your overview gives you more cues, you may need to change your question slightly. Here are the questions about "Movie Censorship: A Brief History" from page 86. Notice that the second and third questions have been modified slightly to cover all the cues. That way any of the three could become your umbrella question.

1. "What has been the history of movie censorship?" [This question works as is, because it covers the present as well as the past.]

2. "Why were movies censored?" [This question covers all cues as long as you add "and what's the current situation?"]

3. "How did they censor movies in the past?" [This question would cover all cues as long as you added something like "and what are they doing about censorship nowadays?"]

Ask your umbrella question. Then use all the cues from your overview to answer the question, giving you the predicted overall point. Here's an example:

- Umbrella question: "What has been the history of movie censorship?"

- Answer (predicted overall point): "Questions of morality came up early on in movie history, so probably movie censorship started then. But over the years, there were changes in moral values, and now we have a code that just 'alerts' people to movies they might object to."

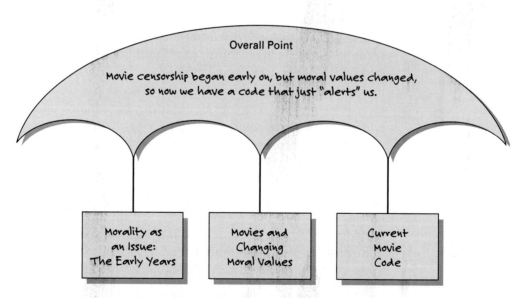

This umbrella diagram shows how the overall point for Reading 7 acts as an umbrella that covers all the other important ideas.

Answers and New Questions

3 *During and after reading, ask and answer questions.*

As you read, see how the writer answers the questions you thought of during your overview. Continue to ask and answer new questions.

- Mark in the margins. Put check marks by the sentences where you find answers to your questions.

- Ask new questions as you read. Put a question mark in the margin if you're unable to find an answer.

- Use headings, the introduction, the conclusion, and illustrations. Let these reading cues help you answer questions as you read.

After reading, look over what you've read. See if the reading answered your questions. Plan to ask other students or the instructor for help with any questions you still can't answer. Continue thinking and talking about the reading.

- Use the questions in the follow-up activities. Answer these questions, and ask and answer similar types of questions of your own.

- Exchange questions and answers with your classmates. Work together to deepen your understanding of the reading.

What to Look For in an Overview

What	Where	Why
Title	Just before the reading	Tells (or suggests) subject of entire reading
Notes before a reading	Before the reading (mainly in magazines or collections of readings by many authors)	Gives information about the author and the reading
Headings	Spaced throughout a reading	Tells the subject of a specific section of the reading
Introduction	The first paragraph (or first few paragraphs)	1) Captures your interest and/or 2) Lets you know the overall point

Conclusion	The last paragraph (or last few paragraphs)	1) Gives a final example or comment and/or 2) Sums up the information
Illustrations (photos, charts, tables, maps, and other visual features)	Usually near a relevant piece of information	Shows examples to help you picture ideas; adds interest
Captions for visual features	Under or beside the feature	Explains visual feature; often adds important information
Boxed information	Usually near a relevant piece of information	Gives added ideas or summaries of ideas

Try the New Strategy: Ask Questions

Your questions and predictions have already prepared you to follow the ideas in "Movie Censorship: A Brief History." Take a moment now to **check in** and make a personal connection with the reading. As you read, ask and answer new questions.

Words that may be unfamiliar are underlined. Strategy 3, **Use Context Clues,** and Strategy 4, **Find the Right Definition,** will help you understand them.

READING 7   MOVIE CENSORSHIP: A BRIEF HISTORY

JOHN VIVIAN

CHECK IN
- Were you kept from seeing a movie as a teenager? Explain your answer.
- What kinds of movies do you object to, if any?
- Do you pay any attention to the movie rating system now?

This reading comes from the textbook The Media of Mass Communication, *by John Vivian. The textbook is used in courses that examine how all forms of current media—from movies to TV, newspapers to the Internet—communicate with a mass audience.*

The movie industry has <u>devised</u> a five-step rating system that alerts   1
people to movies they might find <u>objectionable</u>. Despite problems . . . in any rating scheme, the NC-17, R, PG-13, P and G system has been more successful than earlier self-regulation attempts to quiet critics.

MORALITY AS AN ISSUE: THE EARLY YEARS

RESPOND
Pause from time to time to compare your ideas and experience with the writer's information.

Victorian: time of Queen Victoria, known for strict moral standards

elder: officer or leader in a church

Depression: economic collapse of 1929 that lasted through the 1930s

"moral bankruptcy": complete breakdown of morals

It was no wonder in Victorian° 1896 that a movie called *Dolorita in the*   2
Passion Dance caused an uproar. There were demands that it be banned—
the first but hardly last such call against a movie. In 1907 Chicago passed a
law restricting objectionable motion pictures. State legislators across the
land were insisting that something be done. Worried movie-makers created the Motion Picture Producers and Distributors of America in 1922 to
clean up movies. Will Hays, a <u>prominent</u> Republican who was an elder° in
his Presbyterian church, was put in charge. Despite his efforts, movies with
<u>titillating</u> titles continued to be produced. A lot of people shuddered at
titles such as *Sinners in Silk* and *Red Hot Romance.* Hollywood scandals
were no help. Actor William Reid died from drugs. Fatty Arbuckle [famous
star of early movies] was tried for the drunken slaying of a young actress.
When the Depression° struck, many people linked the nation's economic
failure with "moral bankruptcy°." Movies were a target.

Under pressure, the movie industry adopted the Motion Picture Pro-   3
duction Code in 1930, which <u>codified</u> the kind of thing that Will Hays had
been doing. There was to be no naughty language, nothing sexually suggestive, and no bad guys going unpunished.

Ask your questions: _____

_____

_____

Church people led intensified efforts to clean up movies. The 1930   4
code was largely the product of Father Daniel Lord, a Roman Catholic
priest, and Martin Quigley, a Catholic <u>layperson</u>. In 1934 . . . U.S. [Catholic]
bishops organized the Legion of Decency, which worked closely with the
movie industry's code administrators.

The legion, which was <u>endorsed</u> by religious leaders of many faiths,   5
moved on several fronts. Chapters sprouted in major cities. Some chapters
<u>boycotted</u> theaters for six weeks if they showed condemned films. Mem-
bers slapped stickers marked "We Demand Clean Movies" on car bumpers.
Many theater owners responded, vowing to show only approved movies.
Meanwhile, the industry itself added teeth to its own code. Any members
of the Motion Picture Producers and Distributors of America who released
movies without approval were fined $25,000.

Ask your questions: _____

_____

_____

MOVIES AND CHANGING MORAL VALUES

exhibition: system for showing movies

First Amendment: part of U.S. Constitution that guarantees free expression

mores: moral values or customs

racy: indecent, sexually suggestive

In the late 1940s the influence of the policing agencies began to <u>wane</u>. The 1948 Paramount court decision was one factor. It took major studios out of the exhibition° business. As a result, many movie houses could rent films from independent producers, many of which never subscribed to the code. A second factor was the movie *The Miracle,* which became a First Amendment° issue in 1952. The movie was about a simple woman who was sure Saint Joseph had seduced her. Her baby, she believed, was Christ. Critics wanted the movie banned as <u>sacrilege</u>, but in the *Miracle* case, the Supreme Court sided with exhibitors on grounds of free expression. Film-makers became a bit more <u>venturesome</u>.   6

At the same time, with <u>mores</u> changing in the wake of World War II, the influence of the Legion of Decency was slipping. In 1953 the legion condemned *The Moon Is Blue,* which had failed to receive code approval for being a bit racy°. Despite the legion's condemnation, the movie was a box-office smash. The legion contributed to its own undoing with a series of <u>incomprehensible</u> recommendations. It condemned significant movies such as Ingmar Bergman's *The Silence* and Michelangelo Antonioni's *Blowup* in 1966 while endorsing the likes of *Godzilla vs. the Thing.*   7

Ask your questions: _____

_____

_____

CURRENT MOVIE CODE

Movie-makers sensed the change in public attitudes in the 1950s but realized that audiences still wanted guidance they could trust on movies. Also, there remained some moralist critics. In 1968 several industry organizations established a new rating system. No movies were banned. Fines were out. Instead, a board representing movie producers, distributors, importers and exhibitors, the Classification and Rating Administration Board, placed movies in categories to help parents determine what movies their children should see. Here are the categories, as modified through the years: 8

- G: Suitable for general audiences and all ages.

- PG: Parental guidance suggested because some content may be considered unsuitable for preteens.

- PG–13: Parental guidance especially suggested for children younger than 13 because of partial nudity, swearing or violence.

Violence and Kids. Movie executives apologized for a "lapse in judgment" after the Federal Trade Commission reported in 2000 that studios were marketing violent fare to children. Sony acknowledged that its marketing planners had included kids as young as 9 in focus groups for R-rated movies. In Congressional hearings, movie companies were told to clean up their act or face government regulation. They said they would.

- R: Restricted for anyone younger than 17 unless accompanied by an adult.

- NC-17: No children under age 17 should be admitted.

Whether the rating system is widely used by parents is questionable.   9
One survey found that two out of three parents couldn't name a movie their teenagers had seen in recent weeks.

Follow-Up Activities   After you've finished reading, use these activities to respond to "Movie Censorship: A Brief History." You may write your answers or prepare them in your mind to discuss in class.

Grab your first impressions.

1. What did you find most surprising about the way movies have been regulated from the early days until now?

2. Why did people from the late 1920s to the late 1940s want a strict movie code? What do you think would be positive about such a code? What would be negative?

Work with new words.

Some words in this reading may be unfamiliar to you. Use the methods of Strategies 3 and 4 to explain what the listed words mean.

1. Use context clues.

   a. devised (Paragraph 1) (use logic clues)

   _____

   b. titillating (Paragraph 2) (note that movie titles act as example clues)

   _____

   c. endorsed (Paragraph 5) (use logic clues)

   _____

   d. wane (Paragraph 6) (use logic clues)

   _____

   e. sacrilege (Paragraph 6) (use logic clues)

   _____

   f. mores (Paragraph 7)

   _____

2. Use word parts.

   a. objectionable (Paragraph 1) (two suffixes have been added to the verb "object")

   _____

   b. codified (Paragraph 3) (note that the verb suffix "-ify" was added to "code"; the "y" was changed to "i" and "-ed" was added for the past tense)

   _____

   c. venturesome (Paragraph 6) (note the root "venture," as in the word "adventure"; use logic clues to help)

   _____

   d. incomprehensible (Paragraph 7) ("comprehend" means "understand"; how do the prefix "in-" and the suffix "-ible" change that meaning?)

   _____

3. Use the dictionary.

Choose the correct definition of these words as they are used in the context of this reading.

a. prominent (Paragraph 2) (note how the prefix "pro-" helps you understand this word)

_____

b. layperson (Paragraph 4)

_____

c. boycotted (Paragraph 5) (note the special history of this word)

_____

Ask and answer questions.

1. What specific things did the Motion Picture Production Code of 1930 prevent people from seeing in movies? How did that code calm fears the public had about movies' influence on people's morality?

2. What was the Legion of Decency of the 1930s? How did this organization prevent certain movies from being shown?

3. What made moviemakers decide to establish a new rating system?

4. What is the difference between a rating of PG and a rating of PG-13? What is the difference between a rating of R and a rating of NC-17?

5. Why were *The Miracle* and *The Moon Is Blue* important movies in the history of movie censorship? Explain what happened in each case.

 Ask and answer your own question.

Write a question of your own. Share your question with others, and work together on an answer.

 Answer the umbrella question to state the overall point.

You've answered important questions about the reading. Now, make a statement that answers your umbrella question, "What has been the history of movie censorship?" How close is your current answer to the predicted overall point on page 88?

Form your final thoughts.

1. What are some examples of movies, television programs, or song lyrics you wouldn't want young children to see or hear? What about teenagers? Explain why you feel as you do.

2. Do you think our present movie code works better than the stricter regulations of the past? Why or why not? ■

Apply the New Strategy: Ask Questions

Now that you understand Strategy 5, put it into practice with Reading 8, "The Day Athletics Won Out Over Politics." Before reading, **check in.** Then get an overview. **Ask questions** and make predictions based on the title and other cues in this reading. For example, look at the information given in these cues:

■ Note before the reading: the reading tells about the 1936 Olympics in Berlin, Germany, under the rule of Hitler and the Nazis.

■ Headings: "Help for a Fellow Athlete," "A Defeat for Hitler," "Lasting Friendship"

Put together the information you gather from these and other cues. Then write your umbrella question, and answer the question with your predictions about the overall point.

Umbrella question:_____

_____

_____

_____

Answer (predictions about the overall point): _____

_____

_____

_____

Continue asking questions as you read. Jot down a question in each **"Ask Questions"** margin box or in the margin at other points where you have a question. Read to find answers.

Words that may be unfamiliar are underlined. Strategy 3, **Use Context Clues,** and Strategy 4, **Find the Right Definition,** will help you understand them.

READING 8   THE DAY ATHLETICS WON OUT OVER POLITICS

RON FIMRITE

This reading comes from a 1996 issue of Sports Illustrated. *However, it tells about events that took place in 1936, shortly before World War II. In that year, the Olympics were held in Berlin, Germany, then under the rule of Hitler and the Nazis.*

Jesse Owens of the U.S. had already won the 100 meters and had run two Olympic-record-breaking heats° in the 200 at the Berlin Games when, inexplicably, he had trouble qualifying in what may have been his best event—the long jump. Owens was the world-record holder at 26' 8¼", a standard that would last more than 25 years. But under the baleful gaze of Adolph Hitler, he fouled on his first two jumps. Owens had one chance remaining to qualify for the finals. The qualifying distance, 23' 5½", was no problem for him; hitting the takeoff board° legally was.

1

HELP FOR A FELLOW ATHLETE

Owens was silently berating himself alongside the jumping pit when he was approached by another competitor, Germany's Luz Long. Tall, blond and blue-eyed, Long was the personification of the pure Aryan° that Hitler and his henchmen thought of as the Übermensch°. In reality, Long shared none of the Führer's° crackpot racial notions, and in the African-American Owens he saw only a fellow athlete in need of counsel.

2

Not only speaking flawless English but also spicing it with American slang, Long first introduced himself and then asked Owens, "What's eating you? You should be able to qualify with your eyes closed." Long suggested that Owens draw a line a few inches in front of the board and use that mark as his takeoff point. Owens thanked him for the advice and qualified easily on his next jump.

3

In the finals later that day, Owens reached 25' 5½" and 25' 10" on his first two jumps. Long tied him at 25' 10" on his fifth jump, spurred on by his new friend's competitiveness, Owens then cleared 26 feet on his fifth jump and on his final effort reached 26' 5½", the winning leap and an Olympic record. . . . Owens won two more gold medals, with an Olympic record 20.7 in the 200 and running the first leg on the U.S. 4 x 100 relay team, which set a world record (39.8 seconds).

4

Sidebar

CHECK IN
- What role has sports played in your life?
- Did you watch the last Olympic Games on TV? Why or why not?
- How could you help someone who's afraid of failing?

heats: beginning races to see who qualifies for the final competition

takeoff board: place that marks the starting point for the jump

Aryan: Nazi name for Germanic and other Northern European white people

Übermensch: German for "superman" or "super race"

Führer: German for "leader," title taken by Hitler for himself

ASK QUESTIONS:

Long's advice may have cost him the long jump gold medal but won him a friend in Owens.

A DEFEAT FOR HITLER

RESPOND
Remember to pause during your reading for a comment as well as a question.

Owens's <u>feat</u> of winning four gold medals in men's track and field was not equaled until 1984, when another U.S. sprinter-jumper, Carl Lewis, won gold medals in the same four events as Owens had. But Owens's achievements had consequences far beyond the arena, for they effectively <u>debunked</u> the myth of Aryan superiority, right in front of Hitler. In fact, by themselves, the 10 African-Americans on the U.S. track team outscored all other national teams, winning eight gold, three silver and two bronze medals.   5

Though he undoubtedly might have liked to, the Nazi leader did not— as myth has it—snub the great black American athlete. Two days before the long jump competition, in a fit of national pride, Hitler had summoned the Games' first gold medal winner, German shot-putter° Hans Woellke, to his box to offer him personal congratulations. He also congratulated two more gold medallists, a German and a Finn, before he left Olympic Stadium while the competition was still going on. Hitler was not present when another African-American, Cornelius Johnson, won the high jump at 6' 8". So if anyone was snubbed, it was Johnson, not Owens.   6

shot-putter: participant in shot put, a field event where a heavy metal ball (shot) is thrown as far as possible

That evening Hitler was advised by International Olympic Committee president Count Henri de Baillet Latour that it was not the Führer's function as <u>patron</u> of the Games to congratulate any of the winners, and that if he chose to honor one he must honor all. Hitler elected henceforth to congratulate no one, at least publicly. "Anyway," Owens said, "I didn't come to Berlin to shake his hand."   7

ASK QUESTIONS:

LASTING FRIENDSHIP

After the long jump competition, in which Long held on to win the   8
silver, Owens and Long walked arm-in-arm away from the landing pit. They
did not see each other after the Berlin Games, but they continued to correspond. After Long was killed in Italy during World War II, Owens dutifully
kept in touch with his family.

Before he died of lung cancer at 66 in 1980, Owens wrote: "You can   9
melt down all the medals and cups I have and they wouldn't be plating on
the 24-carat friendship I felt for Luz Long." It was one memorable occasion
when the Olympic spirit triumphed over <u>tawdry</u> international politics.

Follow-Up Activities   After you've finished reading, use these activities to
respond to "The Day Athletics Won Out Over Politics." You may write your
answers or prepare them in your mind to discuss in class.

Grab your first impressions.

1. What sentence or sentences did you find personally meaningful in this
   reading? Explain your choice.

2. Imagine that you were Jesse Owens during the 1936 Berlin Olympics.
   What sorts of thoughts and feelings would you have had during those
   games? What sorts of thoughts and feelings would Luz Long have had?

Work with new words.

Some words in this reading may be unfamiliar to you. Use the methods
of Strategies 3 and 4 to explain what the listed words mean.

1. Use context clues.

   a. baleful (Paragraph 1) (use logic clues)

   _____

   b. feat (Paragraph 5) (use logic clues)

   _____

   c. debunked (Paragraph 5) (use logic clues; also note that the prefix "de-"
      means "away")

   _____

   d. patron (Paragraph 7) (use logic clues)

   _____

2. Use word parts.

  a. crackpot (Paragraph 2) (find the two words, and use logic clues)

  _____

  b. counsel (Paragraph 2) (a "counselor" is someone who gives "counsel")

  _____

3. Use the dictionary.

  Choose the correct definition of these words as they are used in the context of this reading.

  a. inexplicably (Paragraph 1) (the prefix "in-" means "not' in this word)

  _____

  b. berating (Paragraph 2)

  _____

  c. henchmen (Paragraph 2)

  _____

  d. tawdry (Paragraph 9)

  _____

Ask and answer questions.

1. What had Jesse Owens accomplished before he started having trouble qualifying for the long jump?

2. What was Long's advice to Owens? What made his friendly gesture so important to Owens?

3. Why do you think Hitler was so troubled by the success of Owens and the other African-Americans on the U.S. track team? What prevented him from snubbing Owens?

4. Right after the long jump competition, Owens and Long showed their friendly feelings toward each other by walking away "arm-in-arm." What evidence does the reading give of their "lasting friendship" in the years following the Olympics?

5. Owens was quoted as saying, "You can melt down all the medals and cups I have and they wouldn't be plating on the 24-carat friendship I felt for Luz Long." What did he mean by that? Why was their friendship so important in the history of the Olympic Games?

Ask and answer your own question.

Write a question of your own. Share your question with others, and work together on an answer.

Answer your umbrella question to state the overall point.

You've answered important questions about the reading. Now, make a statement that answers your umbrella question. Here is an example of an effective question: "How did athletics—the experience athletes share—win out over politics?" How close is your current answer to your predicted overall point on page 96?

Form your final thoughts.

1. The Olympic competition brought Long and Owens together in spite of their national and ethnic differences. Have sports or some other group activity helped you get to know someone from a different ethnic or national background? Explain your answer.

2. This story about Owens and Long took place more than 60 years ago. What meaning does it have for us today?   ■

Chapter 5 Summary

How does Strategy 5 help you *use your reader's voice to be an active reader?*

Asking questions develops your reader's voice. You question, then read to find the writer's answers. Then you **respond,** with your own ideas and perhaps more questions. Your questions help you stay interested. They also help you look for the important ideas in a reading.

How does the *ask questions* strategy work?

With Strategy 5, **Ask Questions,** you maintain a questioning mind-set, so you stay involved with the reading. Before reading, you get an overview by asking questions that help you predict important ideas. You also use questions during and after reading to develop your understanding of the writer's ideas. Here are the three steps for Strategy 5.

STRATEGY 5: ASK QUESTIONS

1 Ask questions about what catches your interest.

2 Before reading, ask questions to get an overview.

3 During and after reading, ask and answer questions.

Are you familiar with the meaning of these terms?

cues: parts of a reading that lead you to important ideas

headings: words or phrases that act as titles for each section of a reading

notes before a reading: notes about the author and the reading

overall point: the writer's most important message that covers—or includes—all of the other ideas in a reading

overview: an overall sense of the entire subject, indicating what is important in a reading

predict: use all the cues in a reading to see what to expect

umbrella question: question based on the title and other cues from your overview

How is the strategy working for you so far?

Explain which parts of **ask questions** you've found most helpful in the readings you've practiced with. Which parts have been least helpful?

TIME OUT FOR YOU

How Can You Take Notes in Class?

Taking notes in class helps you focus and stay alert to important information. Good notes also give you a record to come back to later. You don't have to produce "picture-perfect" notes. Here are some guidelines.

Prepare

Come to class with your notebook and pen. Do the assigned reading, so you know what the class will be about. If you run out of time to do the assignment, you can prepare by getting an overview of the reading.

Notice Cues

Instructors use various cues to call attention to important information. Write down that information. Don't try to get down every word—just necessary words and phrases. Here are three main types of cues:

- *Announcing.* Notice phrases such as these: "This is important. . . ." "Here are three different possibilities. . . ." and "Finally, we should remember that. . . ." The instructor may even say, "This is likely to be on the test." If so, put a star by that note.

- *Repeating.* Repetition shows the instructor thinks the information is important.

- *Writing on the board or using an overhead projector.* Instructors usually expect you to write down some or all of what they write in class.

Leave Space on the Page

Leave enough room so your words aren't too crowded and you can add something later—a definition, example, or other information.

Use Signals

Use graphic signals such as arrows, equal signs, question marks, or stars. These will make your notes more useful for review.

Save Time with Abbreviations

Use standard abbreviations and your own personal ones. (See the abbreviations list on page 152.)

Practice with Your Own Learning Style

Review what you learned about your learning style (see page 32). Regardless of your learning style, some writing is necessary for taking notes, but you can make some modifications. You might combine tape recording (with the instructor's permission) with note taking. You could make more visual or graphic notes, adding color, charts, or diagrams. You might write only a few key words you'll use for a quick review with a study partner after class.

Try to jot down some notes for each class. Take a moment after class to look over your notes. That way you can straighten out any confusions while you still remember what the instructor said. With practice, your notes can help you succeed in all your courses.

PART II

ADDITIONAL READINGS ON
POPULAR CULTURE

The readings that follow will give you further practice in using the strategies from Part I and Part II with a variety of readings on the theme of popular culture, the culture of our everyday lives.

BUT WEIGHT!

ROBERT A. WALLACE

This reading comes from the biology textbook, Biology: The World of Life, *by Robert A. Wallace. Wallace gives a biologist's view of a subject discussed daily on television, in magazines, and other media: how to lose weight.*

Before reading, **check in.** *Then,* **ask questions** *about the title and other cues. Note especially the headings and the introduction (first paragraph). Put these cues together. Try writing the following:*

Umbrella question: _____

_____

_____

_____

Answer (predictions about the overall point): _____

_____

_____

_____

Continue asking questions as you read. Jot down a question in the margin at points where you want more information. Read to find answers.

Words that may be unfamiliar are underlined. Strategy 3, **Use Context Clues,** *and Strategy 4,* **Find the Right Definition,** *will help you understand them.*

About 51 million Americans are regarded as overweight and many, if not most, of them have tried to slim down. Only the most determined, it seems, are able to meet their weight goals and 90 percent of them will have regained that lost weight within the year. Why is it so difficult to lose weight and keep it off?   1

PROBLEMS IN LOSING WEIGHT AND KEEPING IT OFF

Actually, there are a lot of reasons. First, though, let's establish that we're not talking about a few pounds. That's usually no problem. Since   2 obesity is regarded as being 25 percent heavier than "ideal" (a figure that varies widely among health professionals), we're talking about significant weight loss. And what happens is that after those first few pounds disappear, the body seems to resist losing any more. In fact, the body seems to interpret weight loss as starvation and immediately makes certain

metabolic: chemical processes in the body, necessary for life

metabolic° changes to retain the rest of the fat. It begins to burn fat more slowly and to increase the internal stimuli that signal "hunger." (We are descended from a long line of "survivors," and many of our ancestors survived adversity because their bodies were able to make those metabolic changes. Little did they know the problems that would cause for us!) Many people dig in and diet harder even as the body fights back, so there can be a roller coaster ride on the scales (which can cause heart problems).

It seems that genetics is also powerfully involved with weight control, 3 and that each individual is born with a "fat-ostat,"° a kind of sensory mechanism that tells the body how much fat to carry. Some people believe that

"fat-ostat": a "made-up" word, with the same root as "thermostat" (automatic device for regulating temperature)

mechanism can be altered by smoking, pills, or whatever, but scientific evidence is hard to come by.

Others believe that weight can be reduced through exercise, and 4 they're partly right. They are often surprised to learn, however, that to lose a pound of fat requires burning about 3500 calories of energy. Jogging burns about 560 calories an hour for the average person, so that person would have to jog about 6.25 hours to lose 1 pound! So this means that losing a pound through jogging would mean hitting the road for about an hour a day, every day for a week. Exercise may have an unexpected benefit, however, in altering the metabolic rate, at least temporarily, and causing more calories to be burned per unit time, so there may be a carry-over effect.

Most nutritionists agree that long-term weight loss involves a combi- 5 nation of moderate dieting (say, eating 200 to 500 fewer calories a day than your body requires) and moderate exercise, both of which usually involve

behavior modification: systematic substitution of desirable behaviors for undesirables ones

some behavior modification°. If the regimen is too difficult, most people simply just won't stay with it.

DANGEROUS WEIGHT LOSS

Although Wallis Warfield Simpson once said, "You can never be too 6 thin or too rich," she may have been half wrong. Some people *are* too thin not by circumstance, but by choice. The two main disorders leading to extreme weight loss on purpose are called *anorexia nervosa*° and *bulimia*°.

anorexia nervosa and bulimia: note how these serious eating disorders are defined for you in paragraphs 7–8

Anorexia nervosa is most commonly found in women in their teens 7 and early twenties, a time that psychologists tell us is often marked by self-doubt and feelings of insecurity. These women may see themselves as fat even as they waste away. Their greatest fear may be of being fat and hungry, and so they diet, and often exercise, <u>obsessively</u>. Young girls may behave this way as a means of avoiding the natural development that signals growing up. Others are anorexic because they are, in a sense, highly driven to achieve and to be "in control," and weight loss is something they can accomplish on their own. In extreme cases anorexia can be fatal, as any of several body systems simply gives out from lack of nourishment.

Bulimia refers to "eating like an ox," which is what some people do, 8 sometimes taking in twenty times the calories of a normal diet. Then the person vomits, or takes a laxative, to rid themselves of the food, both of which can be damaging. The constant vomiting puts intense pressure on the gut and <u>diaphragm</u>, and the acid contents of the stomach can dissolve the enamel of the teeth. Repeated use of laxatives can damage the intestinal wall and cause chronic diarrhea. Bulimics often maintain normal weight, but bulimia has been known to kill by <u>rupturing</u> the stomach, or causing kidney or heart failure. Like anorexics, bulimics are often hard-driving (and sometimes frustrated) perfectionists seeking to gain control of some aspect of their lives. Both bulimia and anorexia can be difficult to treat, and long-term <u>psychotherapy</u> may be required.

OTHER APPROACHES TO WEIGHT

A discovery in 1995 is being regarded as a "breakthrough" in weight 9 loss: a hormone°, called leptin, that makes animals—even thin ones—lose body fat. It operates by causing the brain to modify its control over metabolic pathways. Of course, several years of human testing will be necessary before it is available.

hormone: chemical messenger that regulates bodily functions

Many people are beginning to argue that weight adjustment should 10 not be done at all, that their weight is a personal thing and that, unless health is an issue, society should learn to accept a range of body types.

Follow-Up Activities   After you've finished reading, use these activities to respond to "But Weight!" You may write your answers or prepare them in your mind to discuss in class.

Grab your first impressions.

1. What new information about weight problems did you learn in this reading?

2. How does your experience (or the experience of someone you know well) relate to this reading? Choose a specific part to show the relationship.

Work with new words.

Some words in this reading may be unfamiliar to you. Use the methods of Strategies 3 and 4 to explain what the listed words mean.

1. Use context clues.

a. obesity (Paragraph 2) (use logic clues)

_____

b. adversity (Paragraph 2) (use logic clues)

_____

c. altered (Paragraph 3) (use logic clues)

_____

d. regimen (Paragraph 5) (use logic clues)

_____

2. Use word parts.

a. stimuli (Paragraph 2) (plural for "stimulus"; has the same root as "stimulate")

_____

b. sensory (Paragraph 3) (has the same root as "sense")

_____

c. insecurity (Paragraph 7) (what does the prefix mean here?)

_____

d. psychotherapy (Paragraph 8)

_____

3. Use the dictionary.

Choose the correct definition of these words as they are used in the context of this reading.

a. genetics (Paragraph 3)

_____

b. obsessively (Paragraph 7)

_____

c. diaphragm (Paragraph 8)

_____

d. rupturing (Paragraph 8)

_____

4. List below additional words you're unsure of from the reading. Use one of
these methods to discover their meaning.

_____   _____

_____   _____

_____   _____

Ask and answer questions.

1. How does the body react after a person loses the first few pounds in a
weight-loss program?

2. Burning off calories through exercise can take a lot of time and effort.
However, Wallace says that exercise has an "unexpected benefit." What
is that benefit? How does it work?

3. What are two possible causes of anorexia in young women?

4. What serious health problems does bulimia cause?

5. Why does Wallace say that long-term weight loss usually requires behavior modification?

Ask and answer your own question.

Write a question of your own. Share your question with others, and work
together on an answer.

Answer your umbrella question to state the overall point.

You've answered important questions about the reading. Now, make a
statement that answers your umbrella question. Here is an example of an
effective question: "How can you lose weight safely?" How close is your current answer to your predicted overall point on page 105?

Form your final thoughts.

1. What advice would you give to someone who felt he or she had a weight
problem? Use any new information you learned as well as what you
already knew about this subject.

2. Our culture seems obsessed with being thin. At the same time, recent medical research shows an alarming rise in obesity among Americans. Discuss this contradiction with your group. What do you think can be done to develop more healthy attitudes and behaviors?

3. Why do you think Wallace used the title "But Weight!" for his information on weight loss?   ■

READING II-B NEW ADVERTISING HITS CONSUMERS EVERYWHERE

KAREN TALASKI

ambient: present on all sides or everywhere

This reading is adapted from a newspaper article by Karen Talaski, titled "Ambient° Advertising Invades Consumers." It was first published on October 21, 2001, in the Detroit News with the subtitle "Floors, vehicles [are the] latest spots for ads." In her article Talaski reports on the increasing numbers of ads turning up in unexpected places.

Before reading, **check in.** Then, **ask questions** about the title and other cues. Note especially the headings, the boxed information, the illustration, and the introduction (first paragraph). Put these cues together. Try writing the following:

Umbrella question: _____

_____

_____

_____

Answer (predictions about the overall point): _____

_____

_____

_____

CHECK IN
• What ads have annoyed you? Why?
• What ads have you enjoyed? Did you buy the products they advertised? Explain your answer.
• Have you noticed ads appearing in unexpected places? Where?

Continue **asking questions** as you read. Jot down a question in the margin at points where you want more information. Read to find answers.

Words that may be unfamiliar are underlined. Strategy 3, **Use Context Clues,** and Strategy 4, **Find the Right Definition,** will help you understand them.

Note the many short paragraphs in this reading, typical of a newspaper article.

Advertisers, increasingly struggling to grab buyers' attention, are fill- 1
ing every nook and cranny of consumers' lives.

At the gas station, a talking pump announces a sale on wiper fluid. Go 2
to the grocery store, and an ad for laundry soap is glued to the floor. A sign at the mall reminds you to watch the latest television reality show.

It's called ambient advertising and invades consumers' <u>consciousness</u> 3
like elevator music (see box). <u>Advocates</u> like to call it <u>stealth</u> marketing because of its sometimes subtle touch. But critics see it more often as an in-your-face promotion to captive audiences.

AMBIENT ADVERTISING

Ambient advertising is a catchall term for outdoor ads outside of billboards that are meant to grab our attention in unusual ways. Here are some examples:

On the move: trucks, gas pumps, telephones

On the town: drink coasters, bathroom stalls

Pester power: school books, cafeteria trash bins

Retail: floor panels, baby-changing stations

Strange: taxis, bicycles, dry-cleaning bags

Source: *Posterscope*

RESPOND
Bring in your own experience as you read.

Desperate to stand out from the crowd, ad firms are embracing its potential. Finding consumers in this on-the-go society requires more creativity, they say. And hitting people in places where they have idle time has proven an effective way to spread their message. 4

"You can't help but see them," said Munir Kazaleh, a 69-year-old Farmington resident who passes dozens of advertisements during his daily walks around Metro Detroit malls. 5

Both businesses and individuals are exploiting the concept for their own benefit. . . . Drivers willingly wrap their vehicles in ads to bypass car payments. One New York couple even tried to sell naming rights° for their infant son over the Internet. 6

naming rights: offer to advertise a company by giving the child the company's name

"There's new frontiers everywhere," said Jack Neff, a contributing editor at *Advertising Age* magazine. "There's an endless number of new entrepreneurs looking for ways to attach advertising to new ideas." 7

Kroger: a big supermarket chain

Look closely at the bananas at your local Kroger°. Not only do they have a sticker from producer Del Monte, but a second label encourages you to "Try Kellogg's cereal." 8

Even beaches have potential. Beach 'n Billboard, a New Jersey–based company, has a contract with Silver Lake State Park on the state's west side to carve commercials on the sand. 9

Critics who watch advertising's creep say they are wary of its long-term impact. . . . 10

"We are more bombarded than ever," said Susan Douglas, a communication studies professor and director of the University of Michigan's mass communication graduate program in Ann Arbor. "The over-reaching message is that consuming is the solution to all the problems we have." 11

Laurino Scafone II, president of Let's Wrap, will wrap advertisements on vehicles depending on where a person plans to drive.

Unchecked, experts say, advertising will continue to consume more of   12
the environment. Already, its <u>practitioners</u> are busy creating more sophisti-
cated versions and documenting their impact. And as corporations expand
their investment, ambient advertising is sure to secure a permanent place
in ad budgets and in our lives. . . .

FRAGMENTING MARKETS

It used to be easier for advertisers to reach people. They could sponsor   13
a popular radio show, or place an ad on one of television's few channels
and be relatively sure their target audience was watching. Magazines also
were a ripe market—practically everyone read *Life* or *Reader's Digest.*

However, times changed and audiences became fragmented. Radio   14
stations grew more diverse. Cable television added hundreds of channels
for our viewing pleasure. Magazines exploded with hundreds of titles from
Arthritis Today to *Yoga Journal.* And the Internet created another medium
for information and entertainment.

It is estimated that North Americans see an average of 3,000 ads every   15
day. But because advertising is a one-way communication, it is hard to say
how many were hitting their mark, said Alice K. Sylvester, a vice-president
at advertising firm Foote, Cone and Belding in Chicago and co-author of
Advertising and the Mind of the Consumer.

"Consumers aren't just waiting with open eyes and open ears for mes-   16
sages," she said. "We've had to go out in search of the consumer.". . .

COMMERCIAL CULTURE

How much is too much? Critics worry that constant exposure to adver- 17
tising will <u>warp</u> our values. Even worse, they say, it may harm our children,
who face commercial messages at home and school. . . .

[Susan Douglas] believes too much advertising makes people <u>obses-</u> 18
<u>sive</u> about keeping up with their neighbors.

"It urges us to constantly think of ourselves as individuals in a compet- 19
itive relationship with others. Is my car bigger? Are my clothes nicer? Is my
wine cooler?" Douglas said.

Gary Ruskin is one of advertising's most active critics. He is the execu- 20
tive director of Commercial Alert, a Portland, Ore., organization that
"strives to keep the commercial culture within its proper sphere."

Some things should not be for sale, Ruskin said. This includes our 21
schools, where companies are wooing administrators with promises of
extra <u>revenue</u> if they allow ads inside cafeterias, football stadiums and
hallways.

"It sets up an alternative authority structure that parents have no con- 22
trol over," Ruskin said.

It is this lack of control that worries groups like Scenic Michigan, a 23
landscape preservation organization in Petoskey, [Michigan].

"If we're in our households, we can turn off the radio. We can turn off 24
the TV. We can choose whether we pick up a newspaper or magazine. But
(billboards) are in our right of way. We can't turn them off," said Scenic
Michigan President Debbie Rohe.

COMBATING ADVERTISING'S STEADY INCREASE

What can consumers do to combat advertising's creep? Douglas recom- 25
mends people focus on advertising's goal: to spread a commercial message.
For example, product placement in movies is hardly <u>coincidental</u>—corporations pay for consumers to see their product in the hands of a big star.

Douglas believes children learn from experience. She bought her 26
daughter a product she knew could not live up to its advertised <u>allure</u>. Her
daughter quickly saw the difference between what was on television and
reality. It was a $15 lesson that will last a lifetime, Douglas said.

Complaints sometimes work. Poor customer feedback has all but killed 27
talking pumps at Shell's gasoline stations. "They're seen as <u>intrusive</u> when
people are trying to fill up," said Shell spokesman Iain Hildreth.

Kazaleh, a retired electrician, said his daily mall walks have failed to 28
change his mind about most advertising. "It doesn't stay with me, unfortunately for them," Kazaleh said. "When I see it the next day, I'm surprised
it's still here."

Missing the target is a risk all advertisers face, Douglas said.   29

"Not all advertising is bad. Some of it is very important in alerting us   30
to good new products," she said. "On the other hand, the more advertising
people are bombarded by, the less advertising they remember."

Follow-Up Activities   After you've finished reading, use these activities to
respond to "New Advertising Hits Consumers Everywhere." You may write your
answers or prepare them in your mind to discuss in class.

Grab your first impressions.

1. What were the most surprising places for advertisements?

2. What is your opinion about putting ads in these and other unexpected
   places? Explain.

Work with new words.

Some words in this reading may be unfamiliar to you. Use the methods
of Strategies 3 and 4 to explain what the listed words mean.

1. Use context clues.

   a. consciousness (Paragraph 3) (use logic clues)

   _____

   b. entrepreneurs (Paragraph 7) (use logic clues)

   _____

   c. wary (Paragraph 10) (use logic clues)

   _____

   d. warp (Paragraph 17) (use logic clues)

   _____

   e. allure (Paragraph 26) (use logic clues)

   _____

2. Use word parts.

   a. bombarded (Paragraph 11) (find a familiar little word in "bombarded,"
      and use logic context clues)

   _____

    b. practitioners (Paragraph 12) (the first part of the word is the same as "practice")

    _____

    c. obsessive (Paragraph 18) (how does the suffix change the meaning of the verb "obsess?")

    _____

    d. intrusive (Paragraph 27) (use logic clues to see if the prefix means "into" or "not" in this word)

    _____

3. Use the dictionary.

   Choose the correct definition of these words as they are used in the context of this reading.

    a. advocates (Paragraph 3)

    _____

    b. stealth (Paragraph 3)

    _____

    c. potential (Paragraph 4)

    _____

    d. revenue (Paragraph 21)

    _____

    e. coincidental (paragraph 25)

    _____

4. List below additional words you're unsure of from the reading. Use one of these methods to discover their meaning.

    _____   _____

    _____   _____

    _____   _____

    _____   _____

    _____   _____

Ask and answer questions.

1. The box on page 111 lists places where ads grab our attention in unusual ways. What places are mentioned in the reading itself? What types of things are advertised in these places?

2. In the past, it was easier for advertisers to reach their audiences. They could use popular radio shows, a small number of television channels, and popular magazines. How did these audiences become "fragmented" and harder to reach?

3. What are some concerns expressed by critics of this new type of advertising?

4. What can consumers do to fight against the steady increase of ads in our lives?

5. At the end of the reading, Susan Douglas is quoted as saying, "the more advertising people are bombarded by, the less advertising they remember." What does she mean by that statement?

 Ask and answer your own question.

Write a question of your own. Share your question with others, and work together on an answer.

 Answer your umbrella question to state the overall point.

You've answered important questions about the reading. Now, make a statement that answers your umbrella question. Here is an example of an effective question: "How is advertising in so many new places affecting us?" How close is your current answer to your predicted overall point on page 110?

 Form your final thoughts.

1. Where would you draw the line in terms of giving space for advertising? For example, are you bothered by the ads that "pop up" on the Internet? Or are you worried about how ads in schools affect children? Discuss your ideas with others.

2. What changes do you predict for the future of advertising? Will it become more invasive? If so, how will consumers respond? ∎

READING II-C **runnin**

JAMILA Z. WADE

This poem comes from the 2001 anthology of poetry, bum rush the page: a def poetry jam, *edited by Tony Medina and Louis Reyes Rivera. The anthology features the popular new trend of spoken-word poetry. This poetry is often performed for others; it uses the same kind of rhyme and rhythm heard in rap, or hip-hop, lyrics. Be sure to read this poem out loud to get a sense of how the arrangement and sound of the words affect the meaning.*

CHECK IN
- Do you listen to hip-hop music?
- What feelings do you have about poetry? What about hip-hop? If you have negative feelings, can you put them aside?
- What comes to mind when you think about "running from yourself"?

runnin

yesterday
i was runnin
from myself
goin so fast
had dust and   5
fear like death
comin
caught all in
my conscious
going so fast   10
sanity got left
7 miles
back
3 revolutions ago
runnin from myself   15
runnin from my
self
runnin from
my
self   20
was goin
so fast
head tryin ta
catch my tail
tongue tryin ta   25
catch my mind

mind tryin ta
catch my soul
wasn't gonna happen
though   30
not yesterday
not any day
had to slow my
self
down   35
catch hold of
breath and
reason
had to slow my
self   40
down
claw my way
to answers
and truth
had to slow   45
my
self
down
rebuild
strength and   50
dignity yesterday
was runnin
from my self
was goin too
fast   55
this day
findin my
self whole
once more
faith and   60
determination
alive in my palm

RESPOND
Pause to consider your
thoughts and feelings
before rereading the
poem.

Follow-Up Activities   After you've finished reading, use these activities to respond to "runnin." You may write your answers or prepare them in your mind to discuss in class.

Grab your first impressions.

1. What did you like most about the poem? What didn't you like?

2. Throughout the poem, words and phrases are repeated in slightly different ways. Which of these repetitions seemed most effective? Why?

Ask and answer questions.

1. Why do you think the poet didn't capitalize letters and used unconventional spelling, such as "runnin" for "running" and "tryin ta" instead of "trying to?" Was this an effective technique for the poem? Explain your answer.

2. The poem starts with "yesterday" (line 1). What change takes place between "yesterday" and the end of the poem, "this day" (line 56)?

3. What do these phrases from the poem mean to you?

   lines 5–9:

   had dust and
   fear like death
   comin
   caught all in my
   conscious

   lines 21–26:

   was goin
   so fast
   head tryin ta
   catch my tail
   tongue tryin ta
   catch my mind

4. How does the poem give a sense of speed—of running? What are some of the ways the poem changes to a slower pace?

5. What is the meaning of slowing down in this poem? Why is slowing down so important?

Ask and answer your own question.

Write a question of your own. Share your question with others, and work together on an answer.

Form your final thoughts.

1. What ideas in the poem about running from yourself did you find most meaningful? How does this reading relate to another reading you've read in Part I or in Part II?

 2. As a group, practice reading this poem aloud. You might want to have each person say a few lines before "handing off" to the next person. Does speaking the poem with others make it more meaningful? Explain your answer.

PART II REVIEW
PREDICTING AND QUESTIONING

You've completed Part II. Now take some time to look back at both the theme and the strategies introduced in this part.

Theme: Popular Culture

The theme of Part II is popular culture—the culture of our every-day lives. Write down or discuss with others in class the ideas you found most interesting on this theme. Which were your favorite readings? Why?

_____

_____

_____

_____

_____

Strategies: Use Context Clues, Find the Right Meaning, and Ask Questions

Part II showed you how predicting and questioning can help you find the meaning of new words. Predicting and questioning also improve your understanding of a reading. Look at the following chart to remind yourself when you use the three new strategies, **Use Context Clues, Find the Right Meaning,** and **Ask Questions.** The new strategies are in white.

Using Strategies Throughout the Reading Process

GET STARTED   Begin with strategies that help you think about the subject and find out about what the writer will say.

- Check in
- Ask questions

READ   Use strategies that help you read with greater understanding, interpret the language, and respond with your own questions and ideas.

- Use context clues
- Find the right meaning
- Ask questions
- Respond

FOLLOW UP   End with strategies that help you look more closely at the language and ideas in the reading, assess your understanding, and respond in a thoughtful way.

- Find the right meaning
- Ask questions
- Respond

How Are the Strategies Working for You?

Answer the following questions to help you evaluate what you have learned. Then compare your answers with other students, and ask your instructor for ideas on how to get more out of the strategies.

1. How much time are these strategies taking? (Remember that all strategies take more time while you're learning them, but because they will help you understand more easily, they will save you time later.)

_____

_____

_____

2. Overall, how helpful have the strategies been in increasing your ability to figure out the meaning of new words and understand and enjoy what you read?

_____

_____

_____

3. What can you do to make the strategies work better for you?

_____

_____

_____

PART III

UNDERSTANDING MAIN IDEAS

WITH READINGS ON
MEN AND WOMEN, BOYS AND GIRLS

A hundred years ago, men's and women's roles overlapped very little. Today, thanks to the rights women have won over the last century, there are far fewer differences between what a woman and a man can choose to do. But even today, important differences between the sexes remain, and men and women often find it hard to understand each other.

Each reading in Part III looks at a different aspect of what it means to be a man or a woman in today's society. As you read, think of your knowledge and experience of your own sex and the opposite sex. To think about this theme, consider these questions.

- What differences between the two sexes have you observed? How do these differences make it hard to get along?

- When you were a child, which games and toys seemed either for girls only or for boys only? Have your ideas about sex differences in children's play changed since then? Explain your answer.

- Look back at your own family history. How were your great-grandparents' lives affected as women gained legal rights and a wider role in society? How were your grandparents' and parents' lives affected?

- If you're a woman, how do you think your work and family life will differ from your mother's? If you're a man, how will your work and family life differ from your father's?

The new strategies in Part III—Understanding Main Ideas—give you more ways to be an active reader. As you continue practicing the strategies already introduced, you'll learn Strategies 6 and 7, **Find Topics and Main Ideas** and **Find the Support.** These help you find the most important ideas and the details that support or explain them. Strategy 8, **Look for Patterns of Thought,** helps you recognize the way these ideas are presented.

CHAPTER 6

FIND TOPICS
AND
MAIN IDEAS

As you get an overview, Strategy 5, **Ask Questions,** helps you predict what the writer will say. Strategy 6, **Find Topics and Main Ideas,** uses this preparation to help you find the writer's most important ideas. When you understand them, you can respond more fully to what the writer says.

Introduction to the New Strategy: Find Topics and Main Ideas

Before reading, you get an overview—a sense of the big picture—so you'll know what to expect from the writer. By asking questions about the title and other cues, you learn more about the subject, and you try to predict the writer's overall point.

When you begin to read, Strategy 6, **Find Topics and Main Ideas,** reminds you to keep this big picture in mind even as you shift your focus to specific parts of a reading. You recognize a *topic*—what one part of the reading is about—by seeing how that part relates to the subject as a whole. You then read to find out what the writer says *about* the topic. In other words, you read to find the *main idea*—a general, or overall idea about a topic. As you read, you see how the main ideas work together to support or explain the writer's overall point. You can make these topics and main ideas stand out by marking them with a pencil or pen.

STRATEGY 6: FIND TOPICS AND MAIN IDEAS

1 Use your umbrella question to help find main topics.

2 Find the main idea about each topic.

3 See how the main ideas relate to the overall point.

4 Read with a pencil or pen.

Umbrella Question and Main Topics

> **1** Use your umbrella question to help find main topics.

Before you read, your overview shows you what to look for in the reading. During and after reading, keep your questions and predictions in mind.

Umbrella question. Your umbrella question from your overview is especially useful. It reminds you to consider how each topic in a reading relates to the writer's message as a whole. For example, an overview of Reading 9 (page 129) might produce this effective umbrella question: "How *do* money fights ruin a marriage?" This question helps you look for the ways money fights damage marriages.

Main topics. A *topic* is what one part or section of the reading is about. As you read, look for topics that relate to your umbrella question. Each reading deals with a small number of topics—usually between three and five. Like the subject of the reading as a whole, a topic can be stated in a word or phrase.

Headings and main topics. If a reading has headings, the words in the heading usually indicate the topic of the group of paragraphs under that heading. Sometimes, however, you need your umbrella question to help clarify the topic. For example, in Reading 9, the first heading is "What Am I Worth If I Lose My Job?" But the topic is not just about losing a job. The umbrella question—"How do money fights ruin a marriage?"—reminds you to add "money fights" to this heading. The complete topic is: "money fights when one member of the couple loses a job."

In Reading 9 there are four headings, indicating four separate topics—four different types of money fights:

- "What Am I Worth If I Lose My Job?" (fighting when one member of the couple loses a job)

- "Whose Money Is It Anyway?" (fighting about what's his, hers, and theirs)

- "Why Should I Have to Beg for Money?" (new parents fighting when her income stops)

- "Why Can't We Get Out of Debt?" (fighting over credit card debt)

Readings without headings. In a reading without headings your umbrella question is even more important for finding main topics. You'll practice finding topics in a reading without headings later in the chapter, in Reading 10.

Main Topics and Main Ideas

2 Find the main idea about each topic.

When you find a main topic, look for what the writer says *about* that topic. A *main idea* is a general, or overall, idea about that topic. Sometimes it is stated directly in a sentence, and sometimes you find it by adding up all the information, or details, the writer provides.

Main Ideas and the Overall Point

3 See how the main ideas relate to the overall point.

Each main idea fills in part of the answer to your umbrella question. A reading's overall point is thus a summary statement of all the main ideas. It gives a complete answer to your umbrella question. A reading's introduction often states the overall point. So, along with your umbrella question, the overall point can help guide you to the main ideas during and after your reading.

Try the New Strategy: Find Topics and Main Ideas

Before reading "Money Fights Can Ruin a Marriage," **check in.** Then, complete your overview, begun as part of the introduction to Strategy 6. **Ask questions** about the following cues: the introduction, the conclusion, and the boxed information at the end of the reading. Put these cues together, and write your umbrella question. Then answer the question with your predictions about the overall point.

Umbrella question: *"How do money fights ruin a marriage?"*

Topics (note the four headings): _____

_____

Answer (predictions about the overall point): _____

_____

_____

As you read, try using a pencil or pen to mark topics and main ideas as well as the overall point (details about marking follow the reading).

Words that may be unfamiliar are underlined. Strategy 3, **Use Context Clues,** and Strategy 4, **Find the Right Definition,** will help you understand them.

READING 9   MONEY FIGHTS CAN RUIN A MARRIAGE

DIANNE HALES

CHECK IN
You've practiced answering questions to **check in.** Now try this on your own. The subject is money fights in a marriage. How can you relate your experience and feelings to this subject?

Dianne Hales, the author of this reading, has written many articles and books for helping people understand themselves and their relationships. In this reading, excerpted from a Woman's Day *article, she deals with typical money conflicts men and women face in marriage.*

Whether couples are rich, poor or somewhere in between, whether they have two steady incomes or one that's <u>erratic</u>, most fight about money. And as money gets tight—which is increasingly common these days—battles over the budget increase.   1

"When couples are forced to set priorities, someone has to give up something—and that's when the fights begin," explains Victoria Felton-Collins, author of *Couples and Money: Why Money Interferes with Love and What to Do About It.* Once money spats flare up, they can turn ugly. "Money is a magnet that draws in all the frustrations in our lives," she observes.   2

It doesn't have to be this way, but you do have to <u>delve</u> beyond the dollars-and-cents dilemmas before you can stop the fights. Says Felton-Collins: "Money is a <u>metaphor</u> for power, freedom, self-esteem and love. You must understand how you and your spouse view and use money if you're going to stop fighting about it."   3

Consider how some real couples—who asked that their names be   4
changed—handled these typical situations.

"WHAT AM I WORTH IF I LOSE MY JOB?"

Despite 15 years' seniority, Ned was fired when his company was sold.   5
At first, he and his wife were thankful they had Pam's salary. But after
months of fruitless job hunting, Ned started making <u>snide</u> remarks. "I can't
spend a dime without getting her highness's approval," he complained.
And Pam grew resentful. "I'm working extra hours just to pay our mortgage, utility and food bills," she said.

"When I get home at night, I'd like to feel appreciated."   6

Losing a job is a blow to ego as well as to income—especially for men,   7
who define manhood in terms of money, sex and power. When Ned lost his
job, he—like many men—pulled away from his family. Pam didn't know
what to say to make him feel better. Ned interpreted her silence as criticism. When they started <u>sniping</u> at each other, both realized something
was wrong.

"Men never talk about it," says Felton-Collins, "but when their wives   8
make more money than they do, they worry about being needed. If his family doesn't need him as a provider, a man wonders if they need him at all."

Pam finally took the initiative. "I told Ned that I felt we were both tip-   9
toeing around on eggshells because money had become such a sensitive
issue," she explains. "It took a lot of encouragement, but Ned gradually
began to open up. He felt he wasn't contributing to the family anymore, so
I told him all the things I'd assumed he knew—like how much we all love
him, what a wonderful husband and father he is. I also described my own
feelings about being the primary breadwinner. He'd thought I enjoyed having the upper hand, when I really hated it."

Pam and Ned also talked about practical matters. After losing his job,   10
Ned stopped paying the bills. That made Pam feel that all their financial
problems had been dumped on her. Once Ned resumed an active role in
managing their money, both felt better. He also volunteered to help with
school sports and other activities. "He saw how much the kids loved having time with him, and that made a difference too," says Pam. "And now
that everything is out in the open, we all have the sense that we'll get
through these tough times together."

"WHOSE MONEY IS IT ANYWAY?"

Before his marriage last year, Jake never thought twice about spend-   11
ing money. "Why not have fun when I'm young?" he said. Now, whenever
Jake spends $50 on a night out with the guys, his wife, Lucy, gets angry.

"How can you be so selfish?" she asks. "We could use that money for a down payment on a house."

"Why should you tell me how to spend my money?" Jake counters.   12

In more than half of all marriages today, both spouses work. Yet many   13
enter marriage with very different notions about what's his, hers and theirs. Jake, for instance, simply assumed he could spend "his" money as he chose; Lucy thought his earnings were "theirs."

Lucy and Jake finally had an overdue talk about their goals and priori-   14
ties. "We both want to buy a house before starting a family," says Jake. "To me, that's down the road a bit. But Lucy thinks we have to start saving now or we'll never make it. She spent her childhood moving from one military post to another with her dad. To her, having a house is the dream of a life-time. When she explained that, I understood why she'd gotten so upset."

Talking, though, is just the first step. According to Alexis Mitchell, a   15
certified financial planner and vice president of Fidelity Investments in Sacramento: "Two people have to negotiate until they reach a decision—and then make a commitment to stick to their agreement."

For Jake, the bottom line was having some money to spend as he   16
pleased. Lucy, on the other hand, wanted a real commitment to shared goals. Their solution involved three separate bank accounts—an individual account for each, plus a joint account. Jake can spend his money without answering to Lucy. She can do the same. But both deposit 75 percent of their take-home pay into the joint account to cover expenses and start sav-ing toward their own home. . . .

"WHY SHOULD I HAVE TO BEG FOR MONEY?"

Jennie worked from the time she graduated from high school until her   17
first child was born. Now a full-time mother of three, she feels she has to plead for money. "If I ask Greg for $20, he wants to know what I'm going to spend it on," she says. "He even checks the receipts to make sure I really did buy diapers."

Greg, a salesman whose <u>commissions</u> have fallen off, feels he's simply   18
being responsible. "Jennie used to blow $20 on makeup every week," he says in self-defense. "We can't afford that kind of spending with three kids."

Babies invariably change the emotional and economic dynamics of a   19
relationship. "A lot of working couples live like financial roommates until they have a child," notes psychologist Arlene Modica Matthews, author of *If I Think about Money So Much, Why Can't I Figure It Out?* "Parenthood makes them feel more bonded to each other."

"Couples who have been very modern and businesslike in handling   20
money may return to old family patterns once they become parents," Mitchell observes. "The husband may have thought in terms of *his* money

Money problems can keep couples apart unless they actively work together to solve them.

and *her* money. When her money stops coming in, he's still thinking it's all *his* money—and he resents spending some of it on her needs."

Mitchell urges new parents to talk about their feelings. Jennie, for 21 example, told Greg that his failure to discuss money matters made her feel that she didn't count anymore. When she accused him of treating her "like a child," Greg remembered that his own father had handled the family finances by controlling every penny. "When I became a father, I guess I thought that was how I had to act," he admitted.

Jennie and Greg decided that both needed to keep track of their 22 money. For three months, they recorded every dollar that came in and how it was spent. That gave them a clear idea of their cash flow. They discussed ways to supplement their income if Greg's commissions continued to drop. For example, Jennie might take care of neighborhood children. They also agreed on a weekly amount for Jennie to receive to cover household expenses. . . .

"WHY CAN'T WE GET OUT OF DEBT?"

Jason and Molly aren't quite broke, but they owe thousands of dollars 23 on their credit cards. Despite promises to stop spending, both continue to find—and charge—items they can't resist. "How could you spend so much on a tennis racquet?" Molly cries when she sees the bills. "Well, look at how much you spent on clothes!" counters Jason.

Jason and Molly are out-of-control spenders. "They're like kids in a   24
candy store," says Mitchell, who finds that such couples often need professional help. Molly and Jason consulted a therapist with experience in solving money problems. As a first step, she advised leaving their credit cards
at home.

Each calculated how much cash was needed each day and carried only   25
that amount. "At first, I was crushed when I'd see great earrings and not be
able to buy them," says Molly, "but when I went back to the store later they
didn't have the same appeal. I began to see that I bought a lot of things
simply to make me feel better." Jason came to a similar realization: He
spent money impulsively when he felt unsure of himself. He'd buy a sports
jacket, for instance, before calling on a new client.

Jason and Molly also made a list of all their <u>assets</u> and <u>liabilities</u>. They   26
agreed to allocate $300 a month to paying off their credit cards before mak-
ing any new purchases. Then they came up with alternative ways to boost
their spirits: weekend drives in the country, free concerts in the park, din-
ners at inexpensive restaurants. "We also learned how to express our feelings directly," says Molly. "Now if I get angry, I tell Jason how I feel rather
than heading for the mall to shop.". . .

Finding solutions [to money conflicts] isn't easy but can result in unex-   27
pected dividends. "If couples learn to deal with money, they can tackle
other issues such as success, independence, trust, commitment, power,"

HOW TO AVOID MONEY CONFLICTS

Many money fights can be avoided by taking these practical steps in
advance:

Don't let a lack of information create misunderstandings. Go over your
    finances together. Prepare a simple financial worth statement so you're
    both aware of debts, assets, investments and obligations.
Discuss your feelings about money. Does having it make you feel inde-
    pendent, secure, successful, loved, powerful? How do you feel when you
    spend money on yourself or give it to others? What worries you the most?
Tackle one financial chore at a time. Don't try to establish a budget and
    make investment decisions all at once.
Recognize the value of unpaid work. A husband in school or a wife raising
    children at home should feel that these contributions are just as vital as
    a salary.
Set financial goals and discuss how you'll meet them. "Management by
    objective is always preferable to management by accident," notes finan-
    cial planner Victoria Felton-Collins.

says Rodney Shapiro, Ph.D., director of family therapy at California Pacific Medical Center in San Francisco. "Once they've worked out their money problems, they have more confidence in their problem-solving skills and more trust in each other. If they can stop fighting about money, they think they can handle anything. They may be right."

RESPOND
Take time to think about what the reading means to you.

Follow-Up Activities   After you've finished reading, use these activities to respond to "Money Fights Can Ruin a Marriage." You may write your answers or prepare them in your mind to discuss in class.

Grab your first impressions.

1. Which of the money fights described could you picture yourself having? Why?

2. In reading about the conflicts each couple faced, did you relate more easily to the person who is the same sex as you? Why or why not?

Work with new words.

Some words in this reading may be unfamiliar to you. Use the methods of Strategies 3 and 4 to explain what the listed words mean.

1. Use context clues.

    a. erratic (Paragraph 1) (use contrast clues)

    _____

    b. delve (Paragraph 3) (use logic clues)

    _____

    c. snide (Paragraph 5) (use logic clues)

    _____

    d. sniping (Paragraph 7) (use logic clues)

    _____

2. Use the dictionary.

    Choose the correct definition of these words as they are used in the context of this reading.

    a. metaphor (Paragraph 3)

    _____

    _____

b. commissions (Paragraph 18)

_____

_____

c. assets (Paragraph 26)

_____

_____

d. liabilities (Paragraph 26)

_____

_____

Ask and answer questions.

1. According to the author, why does losing a job seem more of a blow for men than for women?

2. Jake and Lucy in "Whose Money Is It Anyway?" had different ideas about how they should spend their money. How did they resolve their differences?

3. How can new parents deal effectively with their money if the wife stops working?

4. Jason and Molly in "Why Can't We Get Out of Debt?" were advised to carry only cash—no credit cards—when they left home. What did they discover about themselves when they followed that advice?

5. What does money represent to Jason and Molly? Why is money such a source of conflict not only for them, but for most couples?

Ask and answer your own question.

Write a question of your own. Share your question with others, and work together on an answer.

Answer your umbrella question to state the overall point.

Here is the umbrella question from page 129: "How *do* money fights ruin a marriage?" What important ideas in the reading work together to answer this question? Try to find a summary statement of the main ideas in the reading. The statement will likely answer your umbrella question and state the overall point. Otherwise, make your own summary statement.

Form your final thoughts.

1. How did your parents handle money problems? Do you think you and your spouse handle or will handle money in similar or different ways? Explain.

2. What pieces of advice from the boxed information on page 133 do you think would help you the most? Why?

3. Discuss with others the special money problems young men and women face today, whether they are sharing their finances with another or are on their own.   ■

Get a Close-Up of the New Strategy: Find Topics and Main Ideas

You've had a chance to try **finding topics and main ideas** during and after reading "Money Fights Can Ruin a Marriage." Now, take a closer look at how the new strategy can improve your understanding of the reading's ideas.

Finding Topics and Main Ideas

2 *Find the main idea about each topic.*

As you've seen, your umbrella question helps you find topics and focus your reading on the writer's ideas about the topic. Sometimes, but not always, the writer states main ideas directly.

Stated main idea. A *stated main idea* is expressed directly in a sentence or two in the reading. For example, in Reading 9, the second topic is "fighting about what's his, hers, and theirs." But what does Hales say about that topic? The idea about this type of money fight is stated in these sentences from Paragraph 13:

> In more than half of all marriages today, both spouses work. Yet many enter marriage with very different notions about "what's his, hers and theirs."

The part of the sentence in quotation marks gives the topic. The remainder of these two sentences states the main idea. It explains why this particular type of money fight occurs.

Notice how all the other information in the section relates to this main idea:

- background about the different ideas Jake and Lucy have about spending their money (Paragraphs 11 and 12)

- the couple's discussion about their different goals and priorities (Paragraph 14)

- the need, according to a financial planner, for couples to negotiate their differences (Paragraph 15)

- the negotiated solution: new shared goals and three separate bank accounts: his, hers, and theirs (Paragraph 16)

Unstated main idea. An *unstated main idea* is one you understand without its appearing in one sentence. You get the idea by summing up the important details about a topic. For example, in Reading 9, the first topic is "fighting over money when one spouse loses his or her job." Here's what Hales says about that topic. After stating Ned and Pam's situation, she says, in Paragraph 7:

> Losing a job <u>is a blow to ego</u> as well as to income—<u>especially for men,</u> who define manhood in terms of money, sex and power. <u>When Ned lost his job, he—like many men—pulled away from his family. Pam didn't know what to say</u> to make him feel better. <u>Ned interpreted her silence as criticism.</u>

The beginning of the first sentence—"losing a job"—names this section's type of money fight—the topic for this section. The underlined sentences and phrases explain how this type of money fight occurs. These parts can be summarized to get this unstated main idea:

> The couple misunderstood each other because Ned, feeling the blow to his ego from losing his job, pulled away, and Pam didn't know what to say to help.

You can see how all the other information in the section relates to this main idea:

- background about Ned losing his job and the couple relying on Pam's income (Paragraphs 5 and 6)

- information about men's fears when wives earn more money (Paragraph 8)

■ solutions to the problem resulting from better communication and understanding, so Ned feels appreciated and Pam feels supported (Paragraphs 9 and 10)

Main Ideas and the Overall Point

3 *See how the main ideas relate to the overall point.*

Look again at the way main ideas add up to the overall point. The main idea you just looked at from Reading 9 partially answers how money fights ruin a marriage. Ned and Pam's money fight hurt their marriage when the couple stopped understanding each other because Ned lost his job. Each of the four couples' problems gives a partial and specific answer. The general answer, which covers all their situations, comes in Paragraph 3:

> You must understand how you and your spouse view and use money if you're going to stop fighting about it.

The summary statement is the overall point. It covers all the main ideas about each of the four types of fights.

Marking Topics and Main Ideas

4 *Read with a pencil or pen.*

To help you find and remember main ideas, use the fourth step in Strategy 6, read with a pencil or pen in your hand. You have already been doing this as you use your reader's voice. You jot down your response to an idea or note the answer to a question. You mark unfamiliar words or confusing sentences. This final step of Strategy 6 shows you how marking your books keeps you focused on finding the writer's important ideas.

It's good to start marking these ideas with a pencil, but you may want to switch to a pen for a clearer record. At test time, you'll appreciate having an accurate record of important ideas. Instead of having to reread all the material, you can *review*—look back over—your marking of the important information. The "Time Out for You" at the end of this chapter suggests more tools and methods for effective marking.

Margin notes. This textbook has wide left margins for marking. Notes in the margin—often called *annotations*—give a brief record of a reading's important ideas. You can use the margin to write an important word or phrase. You can also mark important parts with an arrow, asterisk, or other symbol.

Underlining. You can indicate important ideas by *underlining* phrases or a whole sentence or two. Highlighting makes sentences stand out forever. So save the highlighter until you're sure you have identified the important ideas.

Now, look at this sample marking for Reading 9. See how the reading's main ideas—both stated and unstated—are marked. Note also how the overall point is marked.

Sample Marking

READING 9   MONEY FIGHTS CAN RUIN A MARRIAGE

DIANNE HALES

1   Whether couples are rich, poor or somewhere in between, whether they have two steady incomes or one that's erratic, most fight about money. And as money gets tight—which is increasingly common these days—battles over the budget increase.

2   "When couples are forced to set priorities, someone has to give up something—and that's when the fights begin," explains Victoria Felton-Collins, author of *Couples and Money: Why Money Interferes with Love and What to Do About It.* Once money spats flare up, they can turn ugly. "Money is a magnet that draws in all the frustrations in our lives," she observes.

3   It doesn't have to be this way, but you do have to delve beyond the dollars-and-cents dilemmas before you can stop the fights. Says Felton-Collins: "Money is a metaphor for power, freedom, self-esteem and love. *Overall Point* <u>You must understand how you and your spouse view and use money if you're going to stop fighting about it.</u>"

4   Consider how some real couples—who asked that their names be changed—handled these typical situations.

1st $ fight —

"WHAT AM I WORTH IF I LOSE MY JOB?"

5   Despite 15 years' seniority, Ned was fired when his company was sold. At first, he and his wife were thankful they had Pam's salary. But after months of fruitless job hunting, Ned started making snide remarks. "I can't spend a dime without getting her highness's approval," he complained. And Pam grew resentful. "I'm working extra hours just to pay our mortgage, utility and food bills," she said.

6   "When I get home at night, I'd like to feel appreciated."

Main Idea

Losing a job is a blow to ego as well as to income—especially for men, who define manhood in terms of money, sex and power. When Ned lost his job, he—like many men—pulled away from his family. Pam didn't know what to say to make him feel better. Ned interpreted her silence as criticism. When they started sniping at each other, both realized something was wrong. 7

"Men never talk about it," says Felton-Collins, "but when their wives make more money than they do, they worry about being needed. If his family doesn't need him as a provider, a man wonders if they need him at all." 8

imp. detail —

Ned is still needed

Pam finally took the initiative. "I told Ned that I felt we were both tiptoeing around on eggshells because money had become such a sensitive issue," she explains. "It took a lot of encouragement, but Ned gradually began to open up. He felt he wasn't contributing to the family anymore, so I told him all the things I'd assumed he knew—like how much we all love him, what a wonderful husband and father he is. I also described my own feelings about being the primary breadwinner. He'd thought I enjoyed having the upper hand, when I really hated it." 9

imp. detail —

solution

Pam and Ned also talked about practical matters. After losing his job, Ned stopped paying the bills. That made Pam feel that all their financial problems had been dumped on her. Once Ned resumed an active role in managing their money, both felt better. He also volunteered to help with school sports and other activities. "He saw how much the kids loved having time with him, and that made a difference too," says Pam. "And now that everything is out in the open, we all have the sense that we'll get through these tough times together." 10

2nd $ fight —

"WHOSE MONEY IS IT ANYWAY?"

Before his marriage last year, Jake never thought twice about spending money. "Why not have fun when I'm young?" he said. Now, whenever Jake spends $50 on a night out with the guys, his wife, Lucy, gets angry. "How can you be so selfish?" she asks. "We could use that money for a down payment on a house." 11

"Why should you tell me how to spend my money?" Jake counters. 12

Main Idea —

In more than half of all marriages today, both spouses work. Yet many enter marriage with very different notions about what's his, hers and theirs. Jake, for instance, simply assumed he could spend "his" money as he chose; Lucy thought his earnings were "theirs." 13

imp. detail —

diff. ideas about $

Lucy and Jake finally had an overdue talk about their goals and priorities. "We both want to buy a house before starting a family," says Jake. "To me, that's down the road a bit. But Lucy thinks we have to start saving 14 now or we'll never make it. She spent her childhood moving from one military post to another with her dad. To her, having a house is the dream of a lifetime. When she explained that, I understood why she'd gotten so upset."

15   Talking though, is just the first step. According to Alexis Mitchell, a certified financial planner and vice president of Fidelity Investments in Sacramento: "Two people have to negotiate until they reach a decision—and then make a commitment to stick to their agreement."

imp. detail —

solution

3 accounts

16   For Jake, the bottom line was having some money to spend as he pleased. Lucy, on the other hand, wanted a real commitment to shared goals. Their solution involved three separate bank accounts—an individual account for each, plus a joint account. Jake can spend his money without answering to Lucy. She can do the same. But both deposit 75 percent of their take-home pay into the joint account to cover expenses and start saving toward their own home. . . .

3rd $ fight —

"WHY SHOULD I HAVE TO BEG FOR MONEY?"

imp. detail —

Now Greg controls all $

17   Jennie worked from the time she graduated from high school until her first child was born. Now a full-time mother of three, she feels she has to plead for money. "If I ask Greg for $20, he wants to know what I'm going to spend it on," she says. "He even checks the receipts to make sure I really did buy diapers."

18   Greg, a salesman whose commissions have fallen off, feels he's simply being responsible. "Jennie used to blow $20 on makeup every week," he says in self-defense. "We can't afford that kind of spending with three kids."

19   Babies invariably change the emotional and economic dynamics of a relationship. "A lot of working couples live like financial roommates until they have a child," notes psychologist Arlene Modica Matthews, author of *If I Think about Money So Much, Why Can't I Figure It Out?* "Parenthood makes them feel more bonded to each other."

Main Idea —

20   "Couples who have been very modern and businesslike in handling money may return to old family patterns once they become parents," Mitchell observes. "The husband may have thought in terms of *his* money and *her* money. When her money stops coming in, he's still thinking it's all *his* money—and he resents spending some of it on her needs."

imp. detail —

solution

21   Mitchell urges new parents to talk about their feelings. Jennie, for example, told Greg that his failure to discuss money matters made her feel that she didn't count anymore. When she accused him of treating her "like a child," Greg remembered that his own father had handled the family finances by controlling every penny. "When I became a father, I guess I thought that was how I had to act," he admitted.

solution

Jennie and Greg decided that both needed to <u>keep track of their money.</u> For three months, they recorded every dollar that came in and how it was spent. That gave them a clear idea of their cash flow. They <u>discussed ways to supplement their income</u> if Greg's commissions continued to drop. For example, Jennie might take care of neighborhood children. They also agreed on a weekly amount for Jennie to receive to cover household expenses. . . . 22

4th $ fight —

"WHY CAN'T WE GET OUT OF DEBT?"

imp. detail —
credit card debt

Jason and Molly aren't quite broke, but <u>they owe thousands of dollars on their credit cards.</u> Despite promises to stop spending, both continue to find—and charge—<u>items they can't resist.</u> "How could you spend so much on a tennis racquet?" Molly cries when she sees the bills. "Well, look at how much you spent on clothes!" counters Jason. 23

Main Idea —

<u>Jason and Molly are out-of-control spenders.</u> "They're like kids in a candy store," says Mitchell, who finds that <u>such couples often need professional help.</u> Molly and Jason consulted a therapist with experience in solving money problems. As a first step, she advised leaving their credit cards at home. 24

imp. detail —
solution =
cash only

<u>Each calculated how much cash was needed each day and carried only that amount.</u> "At first, I was crushed when I'd see great earrings and not be able to buy them," says Molly, "but when I went back to the store later they didn't have the same appeal. I began to see that I bought a lot of things simply to make me feel better." Jason came to a similar realization: He spent money impulsively when he felt unsure of himself. He'd buy a sports jacket, for instance, before calling on a new client. 25

Jason and Molly also made a list of all their assets and liabilities. They agreed to <u>allocate $300 a month to paying off their credit cards before making any new purchases.</u> Then they came up with <u>alternative ways to boost their spirits:</u> weekend drives in the country, free concerts in the park, dinners at inexpensive restaurants. "We also learned how to express our feelings directly," says Molly. "Now if I get angry, I tell Jason how I feel rather than heading for the mall to shop.". . . 26

more for Overall
Point —

Finding solutions [to money conflicts] isn't easy but can result in unexpected dividends. "If couples learn to deal with money, they can tackle other issues such as success, independence, trust, commitment, power," says Rodney Shapiro, Ph.D., director of family therapy at California Pacific Medical Center in San Francisco. <u>"Once they've worked out their money problems, they have more confidence in their problem-solving skills and more trust in each other.</u> If they can stop fighting about money, they think they can handle anything. They may be right." 27

Apply the New Strategy: Find Topics and Main Ideas

Now that you understand all the steps in Strategy 6, put it into practice with Reading 10, "The Influence of Sports on Male Identity" (or with one of the Additional Readings at the end of Part III, selected by your instructor).

Before reading, **check in.** Then, **ask questions** to get an overview. There are no headings in this reading, so your overview will depend mainly on the title, the introduction, and the conclusion (especially the first sentence). Put these cues together. Try writing the following:

CHECK IN
The title states the subject. How can you relate your experience and feelings to this subject?

Umbrella question: _____

_____

Topics (look for a few topics that relate to your umbrella question):

_____

_____

Answer (predictions about the overall point): (What sorts of influences might there be?) _____

_____

_____

As you read, use a pencil or pen to mark topics and main ideas as well as the overall point.

Words that may be unfamiliar are underlined. Strategy 3, **Use Context Clues,** and Strategy 4, **Find the Right Definition,** will help you understand them.

READING 10   THE INFLUENCE OF SPORTS ON MALE IDENTITY

JAMES M. HENSLIN

This reading comes from the sociology textbook Essentials of Sociology, *by James M. Henslin, a professor of sociology at Southern Illinois University.*

RESPOND
Remember to pause from time to time; relate what you've read to your own experience.

Some sports <u>exalt</u> the "male values" of competition and rough physical contact, <u>akin</u> to violence. Boys who play these sports are thought of as learning to be "real men." Even if they don't play a sport, it is considered appropriate for boys and men to follow sports in order to <u>affirm</u> male cultural values and to display their own masculinity.   1

Sociologist Michael Messner[1] interviewed men who had played professional sports and other men for whom sports provided a central identity during and after high school. A former professional football player, whose two older brothers had gained reputations for success in sports, said: 2

> My brothers were role models. I wanted to prove—especially to my brothers—that I had a heart, you know, that I was a man. . . . And . . . as I got older, I got better and I began to look around me and see, well hey! I'm competitive with these guys, even though I'm younger, you know? 3

Success at sports, then, brings recognition from significant others—and gratifying awareness that one has achieved manly characteristics. This same football player also said, 4

> And then of course all the compliments come—and I began to notice a change, even in my parents—especially in my father—he was proud of that and that was very important to me. . . . He showed me more affection, now that I think of it. 5

The boost in the boy's self-esteem, however, can come at a high cost to others. Messner recounts a haunting scene during his visit to a summer basketball camp headed by a professional coach: 6

> The youngest boys, about eight years old (who could barely reach the basket with their shots) played a brief <u>scrimmage</u>. Afterwards, the coaches lined them up in a row in front of the older boys who were sitting on the grandstands. One by one, the coach would stand behind each boy, put his hand on the boy's head (much in the manner of a priestly <u>benediction</u>), and the older boys in the stands would applaud and cheer, louder or softer, depending on how well or poorly the young boy was judged to have performed. The two or three boys who were clearly the exceptional players looked confident that they would receive the praise they were due. Most of the boys, though, had expressions ranging from puzzlement to thinly disguised terror on their faces as they awaited the judgments of the older boys 7

Cooley's looking-glass self: term for our sense of self developing through internalizing others' reactions to us

The implications of sports go far beyond the game itself. Messner suggests that sports even affect intimate relationships. In the competitive world of sports, being a "winner" means to be accepted by others. To be a loser is to be rejected. Following Cooley's *looking-glass self,* the boys begin to see themselves in this light—if they win, they are better people than if they lose. Accomplishments, then, become the key to relationships. Boys then tend to develop *instrumental* <u>relationships</u> (that is, relationships that are not based on feelings, but on how useful the relationship is—on what you can get out of it). Such an <u>orientation</u>, of course, brings problems, for males try to relate instrumentally to females—who are more likely to have been socialized to construct their identities on meaningful relationships, not on competitive success. 8

Note

[1] Michael Messner. "Boyhood, Organized Sports, and the Construction of Masculinities." *Journal of Contemporary Ethnography,* 18, no. 4 (January 1990):416–444.

Follow-Up Activities   After you've finished reading, use these activities to respond to "The Influence of Sports on Male Identity." You may write your answers or prepare them in your mind to discuss in class.

Grab your first impressions.

1. What sports have you been involved with—either as a participant or as a fan? How do you think your sex has affected your involvement in these sports?

2. If you're a man, what parts of this reading match your own experience? If you're a woman, have you ever developed the "instrumental relationships" boys tend to develop? Explain your answer.

Work with new words.

Some words in this reading may be unfamiliar to you. Use the methods of Strategies 3 and 4 to explain what the listed words mean.

1. Use context clues.

   a. exalt (Paragraph 1) (use logic clues)

   _____

   b. instrumental relationships (Paragraph 8) (don't miss the definition clues!)

   _____

2. Use word parts.

   a. akin (Paragraph 1) (remember the word "kin," meaning related to)

   _____

   b. affirm (Paragraph 1) (see the word "firm" and use logic clues)

   _____

   c. benediction (Paragraph 7) (this word is made up of "bene," meaning good, and the familiar root "dict")

   _____

3. Use the dictionary.

Choose the correct definition of these words as they are used in the context of this reading.

a. scrimmage (Paragraph 7)

_____

b. orientation (Paragraph 8)

_____

Ask and answer questions.

1. According to the reading, what are the "male values" exalted by certain sports, such as football?

2. What did the professional football player say about his reasons for wanting to play football during and after high school? Who were the people he was most anxious to prove something to?

3. What did the coaches at the summer basketball camp do to let the boys know how well they had played? How did most of the boys feel about being judged in this way?

4. What are "instrumental relationships"? How do sports contribute to the tendency for males to develop these types of relationships?

5. According to the sociologist Michael Messner, males are likely to construct their identities on being successful in competition; females are "more likely . . . to construct their identities on meaningful relationships." Why do these differences cause problems for men (and women)?

Ask and answer your own question.

Write a question of your own. Share your question with others, and work together on an answer.

Find the topics and main ideas.

Since there are no headings, use your umbrella question to help divide the reading into a few main topics. Start with Paragraph 1 as the introduction. Paragraph 2 is about the advantages of playing sports for boys who are good at sports. Call that the first topic. Where does that topic change? Where does a third topic begin? Mark in pencil where you see these changes in topic.

A sample marking of this reading follows. It gives only the topics (as margin notes), without main ideas marked. Try marking the main idea for each of these topics (underline sentences and/or add to the margin notes).

Sample Marking

READING 10 THE INFLUENCE OF SPORTS ON MALE IDENTITY

JAMES M. HENSLIN

Intro

Some sports exalt the "male values" of competition and rough physical contact, akin to violence. Boys who play these sports are thought of as learning to be "real men." Even if they don't play a sport, it is considered appropriate for boys and men to follow sports in order to affirm male cultural values and to display their own masculinity.   1

Topic 1 — advantages

Sociologist Michael Messner interviewed men who had played professional sports and other men for whom sports provided a central identity during and after high school. A former professional football player, whose two older brothers had gained reputations for success in sports, said: 2

> My brothers were role models. I wanted to prove—especially to my brothers—that I had a heart, you know, that I was a man. . . . And . . . as I got older, I got better and I began to look around me and see, well hey! I'm competitive with these guys, even though I'm younger, you know?   3

Success at sports, then, brings recognition from significant others—and gratifying awareness that one has achieved manly characteristics. This same football player also said,   4

> And then of course all the compliments come—and I began to notice a change, even in my parents—especially in my father—he was proud of that and that was very important to me. . . . He showed me more affection, now that I think of it.   5

Topic 2 — high cost

The boost in the boy's self-esteem, however, can come at a high cost to others. Messner recounts a haunting scene during his visit to a summer basketball camp headed by a professional coach: 6

> The youngest boys, about eight years old (who could barely reach the basket with their shots) played a brief scrimmage. Afterwards, the coaches lined them up in a row in front of the older boys who were sitting on the grandstands. One by one, the coach would stand behind each boy, put his hand on the boy's head (much in the manner of a priestly benediction), and the older boys in the stands would applaud and cheer, louder or softer, depending on how well or poorly the young boy was judged to have performed. The two or three boys who were clearly the exceptional players looked confident that they would receive the praise they were due. Most of the boys, though, had expressions ranging from puzzlement to thinly disguised terror on their faces as they awaited the judgments of the older boys. . . .   7

Topic 3— effect on intimate relationships

The implications of sports go far beyond the game itself. Messner suggests that sports even affect intimate relationships. In the competitive world of sports, being a "winner" means to be accepted by others. To be a loser is to be rejected. Following Cooley's looking-glass self, the boys   8 begin to see themselves in this light—if they win, they are better people than if they lose. Accomplishments, then, become the key to relationships. Boys then tend to develop *instrumental* relationships (that is, relationships that are not based on feelings, but on how useful the relationship is—on what you can get out of it). Such an orientation, of course, brings problems, for males try to relate instrumentally to females—who are more likely to have been socialized to construct their identities on meaningful relationships, not on competitive success.

 Answer your umbrella question to state the overall point.

Here is an example of an effective umbrella question: "How do sports influence male identity?" What important ideas in the reading work together to answer this question? Try to find a summary statement of the main ideas in the reading. The statement will likely answer your umbrella question and state the overall point. Otherwise, make your own summary statement.

 Form your final thoughts.

1. What do you find positive about the qualities encouraged by playing sports? Can sports also encourage negative qualities? Explain your answer.

2. Nowadays, many girls are taking part in competitive sports, such as soccer and basketball. Will this increased participation in sports make such girls more likely to develop the male type of "instrumental relationships" described by Michael Messner? Why or why not?

3. Discuss as a group of men and women the problems you've had due to the different ways men and women tend to view relationships.   ■

Chapter 6 Summary

How does Strategy 6 help you *use your reader's voice to be an active reader?*

Finding topics and main ideas improves your understanding of any reading. The strategy gives steps for finding the important ideas that relate most closely to the writer's overall point. As you mark these ideas, you use your reader's voice to respond to them in your own way.

How does the *find topics and main ideas* strategy work?

You use your umbrella question from your overview as a guide in finding a few main topics. As you read, you find main ideas about each topic, and these main ideas act as partial answers to your umbrella question. A summary statement of the main ideas gives the reading's overall point and a complete answer to the umbrella question. You use your own system for marking the main topics, main ideas, and the overall point.

STRATEGY 6: FIND TOPICS AND MAIN IDEAS

1 Use your umbrella question to help find main topics.

2 Find the main idea about each topic.

3 See how the main ideas relate to the overall point.

4 Read with a pencil or pen.

Are you familiar with the meaning of these terms?

annotations: notes you write in margins to go along with underlining

main idea: general or overall idea about a main topic; it helps explain the overall point

margin notes: words, phrases, or symbols written in the margin next to a sentence or sentences you want to respond to in some way

review: go over again to study and remember

stated main idea: idea expressed directly in a sentence or two in the reading

topic: what a part of a reading is about

underlining: using pencil or pen to draw a line under important phrases or sentences

unstated main idea: idea understood without its appearing in one sentence; can be given as a summary statement of important details

How is the strategy working for you so far?

Explain which parts of **finding topics and main ideas** you've found most helpful in the readings you've practiced with. Which parts have been least helpful?

TIME OUT FOR YOU

HOW CAN YOU MARK IDEAS
IN YOUR BOOKS?

Marking ideas in your books helps you stay involved with what the writer is saying. You also improve your understanding—and your recall—of a reading when you find and mark the ideas that support or explain the writer's message. Over time you'll develop your own system for marking ideas. Try out these methods and tools to see what works best for you.

Underline Ideas with a Pencil or Pen

Either a pencil or pen can be a good, all-around tool. You can underline twice for emphasis or circle important words or phrases. With a pencil or pen, you can easily switch from underlining to writing margin notes.

Highlight Ideas

A highlighter can be satisfying to use. One stroke makes a sentence stand out. But use a highlighter along with a pencil or pen, so you can make notes as well as highlight. Remember, too, that each yellow or pink stroke is permanent, so be sure to highlight only the ideas you've identified as important.

Write Margin Notes

When you write notes in the margin—often called annotations—you make a comment, ask a question, or summarize an idea. By adding margin notes to your underlining or highlighting, your marking will be more meaningful, especially for later study.

Use Symbols, Color, and Numbers

Marking is more effective when it helps display important ideas and relationships. Here are some ways to give visual emphasis to ideas:

- *Circle* a word or phrase to make it stand out from other underlining.

- Use *arrows* to show the relationship between ideas.

- Use an *asterisk* (*) beside the overall point of a reading.

- Use a *different colored highlighter* or pen to indicate the overall point.

- *Number* details to remind you how many there are and to help you remember them.

Use Abbreviations for Your Annotations

Abbreviations can save time and space. Use some common ones, listed below, or make up your own.

Some Commonly Used Abbreviations

ex = example	et al = Latin for "and other things"
reas = reasons	info = information
def = definition	vs = versus
intro = introduction	$ = money
¶ = paragraph	# = number
concl = conclusion	> more than
diffs = differences	< less than
amt = amount	= equals

Your underlining and margin notes should make sense when you read them on their own. That way you don't have to reread all the material later on. Develop your own system for marking ideas. You'll increase your understanding of what you read and give yourself a head start when it's time to review.

CHAPTER 7

FIND THE SUPPORT

Strategy 6, **Find Topics and Main Ideas,** guides you to the most important ideas of a reading, and helps you see how these ideas relate to the reading's overall point. Strategy 7, **Find the Support,** gives you a more detailed understanding of a reading. Thus, your response to the reading can be more complete.

Try the New Strategy: Find the Support

Strategy 7, **Find the Support,** shows how certain details support main ideas, just as main ideas support a reading's overall point. *Support* for an idea refers to various ways of explaining, demonstrating, or backing up that idea. Supporting details can be *examples, facts,* or *quotations.* With Strategy 7, you can see how main ideas and details work together to support the writer's overall point.

STRATEGY 7: FIND THE SUPPORT

1 Find details that support main ideas.

2 Look for different types of supporting details.

3 Look for ideas in specific paragraphs.

Before reading "How Men and Women Communicate in Relationships," **check in.** Then, **ask questions** about the title and other cues. Note especially the headings, introduction, and conclusion (can communication improve between men and women?). Put these cues together. Try writing the following:

Umbrella question: _____

_____

Topics (note the headings): _____

_____

Predictions about the overall point (How can men and women overcome differences in the way they communicate?): _____

_____

_____

As you read, use a pencil or pen to mark topics and main ideas as well as the overall point.

Words that may be unfamiliar are underlined. Strategy 3, **Use Context Clues,** and Strategy 4, **Find the Right Definition,** will help you understand them.

READING 11   HOW MEN AND WOMEN
COMMUNICATE IN RELATIONSHIPS

REBECCA J. DONATELLE

This reading comes from the chapter called "Healthy Relationships" in the textbook Access to Health, *by Rebecca J. Donatelle, a professor of public health at Oregon State University.*

Are men really from Mars° and women from Venus° when it comes to trying to communicate with one another, as is suggested by the popular press? If they are not planets apart, how far apart are they, and what are the implications of the <u>disparities</u>? In her book *You Just Don't Understand: Women and Men in Conversation,* psychologist Deborah Tannen described many basic differences in conversational styles between men and women that make communication between genders° confusing and difficult.[1] ... Tannen is not alone in her research. In fact, communication patterns between women and men have been studied for generations, with similar results.   1

Recent research <u>validates</u> much of Tannen's work and indicates that women are more expressive, more relationship oriented, and more con-   2

"Mars . . . Venus": refers to popular 1992 book *Men Are from Mars; Women Are from Venus*

gender: sexual identity, as expressed in each culture or society

cerned with creating and maintaining intimacy; men tend to be more instrumental°, task-oriented, and concerned with gathering information or with establishing and maintaining social status or power.[2] Unlike women, men tend to believe that they are not supposed to show emotions and are brought up to believe that "being strong" is often more important than having close friendships. As a result, according to research, only 1 male in 10 has a close male friend to whom he <u>divulges</u> his innermost thoughts.[3]. . .

instrumental: involved in getting things done and having influence

EXPRESSING FEELINGS

Although men tend to talk about intimate issues with women more fre-   3
quently than with men, women still complain that men do not communi-cate enough about what is really on their minds. This may reflect the powerfully different <u>socialization</u> processes experienced by women and men, which influence their communication styles. Throughout their lives, females are offered opportunities to practice sharing their thoughts and feelings with others. In contrast, males receive strong <u>societal</u> messages to withhold their feelings. The classic example of this training in very young males is the familiar saying "big boys don't cry." Males learn very early that certain emotions are not to be shared, with the result that they are more information-focused and businesslike in their conversations with females than females are. Understandably, such differences in communication styles contribute to misunderstandings and conflict between the sexes. . . .

Although men are often perceived as being less emotional than   4
women, the question remains whether men really feel less or just have more difficulty expressing their emotions. In one study, when men and women were shown scenes of people in distress, the men exhibited little outward emotion, whereas the women communicated feelings of concern and distress. However, physiological measures of emotional <u>arousal</u> (such as heart rate and blood pressure) indicated that the male subjects were actually as affected emotionally as the female subjects but <u>inhibited</u> the expression of their emotions, whereas the women openly expressed them. In other studies, men and women responded very differently to the same test.[4]

When men are angered, they tend to interpret the cause of their anger   5
as something or someone in their environment and are likely to turn their anger outward in an aggressive manner. Women, on the other hand, tend to see themselves as the source of the problem and turn their anger inward, thereby <u>suppressing</u> direct expression of it.[5] Such differences in expressing anger can easily lead to breakdowns in communication between men and women.

TECHNIQUES FOR BETTER COMMUNICATION

Communication in intimate relationships between two adults is often a source of difficulty and can lead to an inability to solve problems and dissatisfaction with the relationship. The following techniques can help improve communication between couples:[6]

1. **Leveling** refers to sending your partner a clear, simple, and honest message. The purposes of leveling are (1) to make communication clear; (2) to make clear the expectations partners have of each other; (3) to clear up pleasant and unpleasant feelings and thoughts from past incidents; (4) to make clear what is <u>relevant</u> and what is irrelevant; and (5) to become aware of the things that draw you together or push you apart. 　　　　　6

2. **Editing,** or <u>censoring</u> remarks that may be hurtful or are irrelevant, is another useful skill that improves couple communication. Often, when people are upset, they let everything fly, bringing up old issues and incidents that cause pain and put a partner on the defensive. Editing means taking the time and making the effort not to say <u>inflammatory</u> things. Leveling and editing help establish genuine communication characterized by caring and sensitivity.

3. **Documenting** refers to giving specific examples of issues under discussion. Documenting helps you avoid gross generalizations that tend to be accusatory, such as "You always" and "You never." If you provide specific examples of when and how an incident occurred, your partner will gain a concrete understanding of the issue. In documenting, you can also include specific suggestions for changing or improving the situation.

4. **Validating** means letting a partner know that although you may not agree with his or her point of view, you still respect the person's

Leveling	The communication of a clear, simple, and honest message.
Editing	The process of censoring comments that would be intentionally hurtful or irrelevant to the conversation.
Documenting	Giving specific examples of issues being discussed.
Validating	Letting your partner know that although you may not agree with his or her point of view, you still respect the fact that he or she thinks or feels that way.

thoughts and feelings ("I don't agree with you, but I can see how you might view things that way"). This does not mean that you are giving in to your partner; you are simply recognizing that your opinions differ.

IMPROVING COMMUNICATION BETWEEN MEN AND WOMEN

Can communication between men and women be improved? Under-   7
standing gender differences in communication patterns, rather than casting blame at each other, may be the first step toward bettering communication between men and women.

Tannen suggests that expecting persons of the other sex to change   8
their style of communication is not an effective means of dealing with the gender gap. Instead, learning to interpret messages while explaining your own unique way of communicating may be more useful. Both men and women want to be heard and understood in their conversations. Working to understand the different ways in which males and females use language will help achieve the goal of clear and honest communication.

Notes

[1] D. Tannen, *You Just Don't Understand: Women and Men in Conversation* (New York: William Morrow, 1990).

[2] S. L. Michaud and R. M. Warner, "Gender Differences in Self-Reported Response in Troubles Talk," *Sex Roles: A Journal of Research* 37 (1997): 528.

[3] M. McGill, *The McGill Report on Male Intimacy* (New York: Holt, Rinehart and Winston, 1985), 87–88.

[4] C. Morris, *Understanding Psychology* (Englewood Cliffs, N.J.: Prentice Hall, 1993).

[5] *Ibid.*

[6] M. Brenton, *Sex Talk* (New York: Stein and Day, 1972); J. Gottman, C. Notarius, and H. Markman, *A Couple's Guide to Communication* (Champaign, Ill: Research Press, 1976).

Follow-Up Activities   After you've finished reading, use these activities to respond to "How Men and Women Communicate in Relationships." You may write your answers or prepare them in your mind to discuss in class.

Grab your first impressions.

1. What differences have you noticed in the ways men and women communicate? Do your observations match the ideas in this reading? Explain your answer.

2. What ideas from this reading could you use to communicate better with someone of the opposite sex?

Work with new words.

Some words in this reading may be unfamiliar to you. Use the methods of Strategies 3 and 4 to explain what the listed words mean.

1. Use context clues.

    a. disparities (Paragraph 1) (use logic clues, such as "how far apart")

    _____

    b. validates (Paragraph 2) (use logic clues)

    _____

    c. divulges (Paragraph 2) (use logic clues)

    _____

    d. arousal (Paragraph 4) (use the examples in the parentheses)

    _____

2. Use word parts.

    a. socialization and societal (Paragraph 3) (note how suffixes change the familiar words "social" and "society")

    _____

    b. suppressing (Paragraph 5) (the prefix "sub" changes to "sup" before a word beginning with "p")

    _____

    c. inflammatory (Paragraph 6) (look for the word "flame")

    _____

3. Use the dictionary.

    Choose the correct definition of these words as they are used in the context of this reading.

    a. inhibited (Paragraph 4)

    _____

    b. relevant (Paragraph 6)

    _____

    c. censoring (Paragraph 6) (refer to Reading 7, "Movie Censorship")

    _____

Ask and answer questions.

1. Research shows that women tend to be more interested in developing and taking care of relationships than men. What are men more interested in?

2. What did the study referred to in Paragraph 4 indicate about men's emotions? Are men really less emotional, or are they just less able to express their emotions? Explain your answer.

3. What are the differences in the ways men and women respond to anger?

4. What are the four techniques given for improving communication between men and women? Give an example of how you might use one of these techniques to improve communication.

5. Donatelle refers in Paragraph 3 to the "powerfully different socialization processes experienced by women and men." What are these processes? How do they affect men's and women's communication?

 Ask and answer you own question.

Write a question of your own. Share your question with others, and work together on an answer.

 Find the topics and mark main ideas.

Try finding topics and marking main ideas in Reading 11. Then compare your work with the sample marking that follows.

Sample Marking

 READING 11   HOW MEN AND WOMEN COMMUNICATE IN RELATIONSHIPS

REBECCA J. DONATELLE

Are men really from Mars and women from Venus when it comes to   1
trying to communicate with one another, as is suggested by the popular press? If they are not planets apart, how far apart are they, and what are the implications of the disparities? In her book *You Just Don't Understand: Women and Men in Conversation,* psychologist Deborah Tannen described many basic differences in conversational styles between men and women that make communication between genders confusing and difficult. . . . Tannen is not alone in her research. In fact, communication patterns between women and men have been studied for generations, with similar results.

Overall Point—
women

men

Recent research validates much of Tannen's work and indicates that   2
women are <u>more expressive</u>, more <u>relationship oriented</u>, and more <u>con-</u>
<u>cerned with creating and maintaining intimacy;</u> <u>men</u> tend to be <u>more</u>
<u>instrumental</u>, <u>task-oriented</u>, and <u>concerned with gathering information</u> or
with <u>establishing and maintaining social status or power</u>. <u>Unlike women,</u>
<u>men</u> tend to believe that they are <u>not supposed to show emotions</u> and
are brought up to believe that <u>"being strong" is often more important than</u>
<u>having close friendships</u>. As a result, according to research, only 1 male
in 10 has a close male friend to whom he divulges his innermost
thoughts.[3] . . .

Men & Women   **EXPRESSING FEELINGS**   *Differently*

Although men tend to talk about intimate issues with women more fre-   3
quently than with men, women still complain that men do not communicate enough about what is really on their minds. This may reflect the
powerfully different socialization processes experienced by women and
men, which influence their communication styles. <u>Throughout their lives,</u>
<u>females are offered opportunities to practice sharing their thoughts and</u>
<u>feelings with others. In contrast, males receive strong societal messages to</u>
<u>withhold their feelings.</u> The classic example of this training in very young
males is the familiar saying "big boys don't cry." Males learn very early that
certain emotions are not to be shared, with the result that they are more
information-focused and businesslike in their conversations with females
than females are. <u>Understandably, such differences in communication</u>
<u>styles contribute to misunderstandings and conflict between the sexes.</u> . . .

Main Idea

supports
(feel less? or express
less?)

Although men are often perceived as being less emotional than   4
women, the <u>question remains whether men really feel less or just have</u>
<u>more difficulty expressing their emotions.</u> In one study, when men and
women were shown scenes of people in distress, the men exhibited little
outward emotion, whereas the women communicated feelings of concern
and distress. However, physiological measures of emotional arousal (such
as heart rate and blood pressure) indicated that the male subjects were
actually as affected emotionally as the female subjects but <u>inhibited</u> the
expression of their emotions, whereas the women openly expressed
them. In other studies, men and women responded very differently to the
same test.

anger—
men—outward
women—inward

<u>When men are angered</u>, they tend to interpret the cause of their anger   5
as something or someone in their environment and are likely to <u>turn their</u>
<u>anger outward in an aggressive manner</u>. <u>Women</u>, on the other hand, tend
to see themselves as the source of the problem and <u>turn their anger inward,</u>

thereby <u>suppressing direct expression of it.</u> Such differences in expressing anger can easily lead to breakdowns in communication between men and women.

TECHNIQUES FOR BETTER COMMUNICATION

Communication in intimate relationships between two adults is often a   6
source of difficulty and can lead to an inability to solve problems and dissatisfaction with the relationship.

<u>The following techniques can help improve communication between</u>   7
<u>couples:</u>

Main Idea

major detail

minor details
(purposes)

1. **Leveling** <u>refers to sending your partner a clear, simple, and honest message.</u> The purposes of leveling are (1) to make communication clear; (2) to make clear the expectations partners have of each other; (3) to clear up pleasant and unpleasant feelings and thoughts from past incidents; (4) to make clear what is <u>relevant</u> and what is irrelevant; and (5) to become aware of the things that draw you together or push you apart.

2. **Editing,** <u>or censoring remarks that may be hurtful or are irrelevant, is</u> <u>another useful skill that improves couple communication.</u> Often, when people are upset, they let everything fly, bringing up old issues and incidents that cause pain and put a partner on the defensive. Editing means taking the time and making the effort not to say inflammatory things. Leveling and editing help establish genuine communication characterized by caring and sensitivity.

3. **Documenting** <u>refers to giving specific examples of issues under discussion.</u> Documenting helps you avoid gross generalizations that tend to be accusatory, such as "You always" and "You never." If you provide specific examples of when and how an incident occurred, your partner will gain a concrete understanding of the issue. In documenting, you can also include specific suggestions for changing or improving the situation.

4. **Validating** <u>means letting a partner know that although you may not</u> <u>agree with his or her point of view, you still respect the person's</u> <u>thoughts and feelings</u> ("I don't agree with you, but I can see how you might view things that way"). This does not mean that you are giving in to your partner; you are simply recognizing that your opinions differ.

*summary—
major
details
(techniques)*

Leveling	The communication of a clear, simple, and honest message.
Editing	The process of censoring comments that would be intentionally hurtful or irrelevant to the conversation.
Documenting	Giving specific examples of issues being discussed.
Validating	Letting your partner know that although you may not agree with his or her point of view, you still respect the fact that he or she thinks or feels that way.

IMPROVING COMMUNICATION BETWEEN MEN AND WOMEN

Can communication between men and women be improved? Understanding gender differences in communication patterns, rather than casting blame at each other, may be the first step toward bettering communication between men and women.   8

Tannen suggests that expecting persons of the other sex to change their style of communication is not an effective means of dealing with the gender gap. Instead, learning to interpret messages while explaining your own unique way of communicating may be more useful. Both men and women want to be heard and understood in their conversations. <u>Working to understand the different ways in which males and females use language will help achieve the goal of clear and honest communication.</u>   9

Main Idea—

 Answer your umbrella question to state the overall point.

Here is an example of an effective umbrella question: "How do men and women communicate in relationships?" But, if we add "How do men and women communicate *differently* in relationships?" the question covers the main ideas more clearly. Note that the sample marking for Reading 11 points to Paragraph 2 as the overall point that answers that question. Can you form a statement using your own words that summarizes the overall point?

 Form your final thoughts.

1. Discuss in a group of men and women the ideas you agree with from the reading and those you disagree with. How much is the response of each member of your group dependent on his or her sex?

2. In Paragraph 2, Donatelle refers to "instrumental" relationships, the relationship referred to in Reading 10, "The Influence of Sports on Male Iden-

tity." Does your experience match the distinction made in both readings between instrumental relationships, typical of men, and expressive relationships, typical of women? Explain your answer.

3. How can men and women improve their communication with one another? Discuss the suggestions given in the reading, as well as other ideas those in your group can offer.   ■

Get a Close-Up of the New Strategy: Find the Support

You've had a chance to try **finding the support** during and after reading "How Men and Women Communicate in Relationships." Now take a closer look at how the new strategy can improve your understanding of the reading's ideas.

Main Ideas and Supporting Details

1 *Find details that support main ideas.*

You've already learned that each main idea supports—explains or demonstrates—a reading's overall point. Strategy 7 shows how each main idea is itself supported by certain details, called *supporting details*.

General and specific levels of support. Main ideas and details work as different levels of support for the writer's overall point. Before looking at these levels of support, it's important to understand the terms *general* and *specific*.

- *General* refers to a large category (for example, fruit or vehicles)

- *Specific* refers to a particular type or part within the larger category (for example, fruit includes bananas, grapes, and apples; vehicles include cars, buses, and planes)

A general idea is one that covers or includes many others. Remember that the overall point can be thought of as an "umbrella idea," because it covers all the other ideas in the reading. In contrast, a main idea is more specific. It refers to just one part of the overall point. However, a main idea is more general than a supporting detail because it covers, or includes, several supporting details.

The chart here shows the relationship between the overall point and the different levels of support.

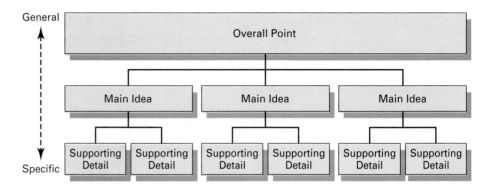

Subheadings for supporting details. Headings in a reading indicate main topics that support the overall point. In the same way, *subheadings* indicate specific details that support a main topic. Details that support a main topic are often called *subtopics*. Subheadings for these subtopics are smaller than headings. They are often in a different color or are indented, like the subheadings under the section "Techniques for Better Communication" in Reading 11, on page 156.

The main idea for this topic is stated in the first sentence of Paragraph 7: "The following techniques can help improve communication between couples." The first subheading, "Leveling," shows that the paragraph under it is a supporting detail. It will support the main idea by explaining the first technique.

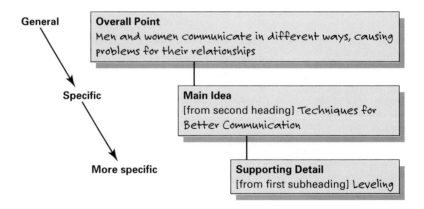

Major and minor details. The paragraph about leveling also demonstrates the difference between major and minor details. A *major detail* supports the main idea directly. The first sentence of that paragraph defines the technique of leveling, so it is a major detail. A *minor detail* is even more specific; it supports the major detail. For example, each specific purpose of leveling given after the first sentence is a minor detail. Each explains more about leveling.

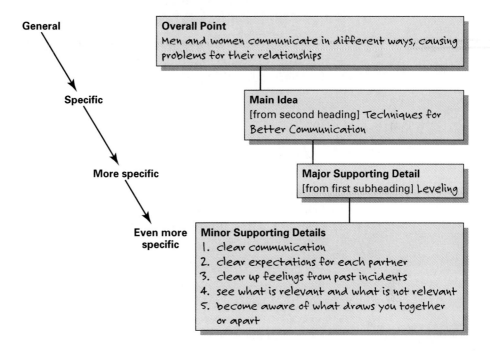

Now try to distinguish between the major and minor details in the next technique Reading 11 describes. Take a look at the paragraph with the subheading "Editing." The major detail there defines that term. Then three minor details support—or explain—that definition. What are they?

Supporting details without subheadings. Subheadings are common in textbooks, but much less common in other readings. Without subheadings, you have to first watch for stated and unstated main ideas. Take note of a stated main idea—a sentence that expresses a general statement about a main topic. Then look for specific details that support that idea. These are the major details. These major details are supported, in turn, by the minor details.

If you don't spot a stated main idea, find details that relate directly to the main topic. They are major details. A summary statement of these details would state the main idea for that topic.

Finding the main idea and supporting details. Try finding the main idea and supporting details in Paragraphs 3–5, the section headed "Expressing Feelings," from Reading 11, on page 155.

- Main topic: The heading names the topic, "Expressing Feelings." Because of your umbrella question, you would add "'men and women' expressing feelings 'differently'."

- Main idea: A likely main idea statement about the topic appears as the last sentence in Paragraph 3: "Understandably, such differences in communication styles contribute to misunderstandings and conflict between the sexes."

- Major and minor details: Find the major details that support that main idea. This summary of each of Paragraphs 3–5 shows that each one gives specific details related to the main idea. But see if you can tell why Paragraph 4 provides a minor detail, rather than a major one.

Paragraph 3 (major detail): Men and women are socialized very differently, with women learning to express feelings and men learning to suppress them, and these differences cause misunderstandings.

Paragraph 4 (minor detail): "The question remains whether men really feel less" or, as one study indicates, they "just have more difficulty expressing their emotions."

Paragraph 5 (major detail): Men turn anger outward, but women turn anger inward; these differences lead to "breakdowns in communication."

Paragraph 4 is a minor detail because it supports the major detail in Paragraph 3 about men learning to suppress emotions. It refers to a specific study about whether men don't feel—or simply suppress—their emotions. Note that Paragraph 5 adds a brand new major detail about anger.

Testing the main idea. To make sure you've identified a main idea sentence, *test* it. *Testing a main idea sentence* means examining it closely to see if it is a general statement that covers—or includes—all the supporting details related to the topic. We said that a likely main idea sentence for the topic "men and women expressing feelings differently" is the last sentence in Paragraph 3. Here is the last sentence: "Understandably, such differences in communication styles contribute to misunderstandings and conflict between the sexes." You can see that the sentence does cover both of the major details from Paragraphs 3–5: (1) men suppress emotions more than women do, but (2) men express anger more.

Types of Supporting Details

2 *Look for different types of supporting details.*

You'll find many different types of details used to support a more general idea. Each type makes a writer's ideas clearer or more convincing. Here are some types of supporting details:

Examples. Examples give specific situations or cases to demonstrate a general idea.

Explanations. To explain, or give an *explanation,* means to give details that clarify or give reasons to support an idea.

Descriptive details. These are details about people, places or things. *Descriptions* tell how someone or something looks, sounds, or feels.

Facts. A *fact* can be proven or confirmed by going to a reliable source. Facts are used to explain, give background, or provide evidence for an idea.

Quotations. Appropriate *quotations*—the exact words someone else, often an expert, has said or written—are used to back up or clarify an idea.

Ideas in Paragraphs

3 *Look for ideas in specific paragraphs.*

The steps for finding main ideas and supporting details in a whole reading are the same ones you use to find the main idea and supporting details in a single paragraph. Each paragraph usually makes sense if you read it with the reading's umbrella question and main topics in mind. But if a paragraph needs clarification, apply these same steps.

Topics. First, find the topic of the paragraph—what the paragraph is about. In other words, what topic do all the sentences point to? Try finding the topic of Paragraph 8 in Reading 11. (The sentences have been numbered for easy reference.)

> (1) Tannen suggests that expecting persons of the other sex to change their style of communication is not an effective means of dealing with the gender gap. (2) Instead, learning to interpret messages while explaining your own unique way of communicating may be more useful. (3) Both men and women want to be heard and understood in their conversations. (4) Working to understand the different ways in which males and females use language will help achieve the goal of clear and honest communication.

Each sentence in this paragraph points to this topic: "improving communication between males and females."

Supporting details and stated main ideas. The first three sentences of Paragraph 8 provide specific supporting details. Each explains or clarifies the more general, fourth sentence, so that sentence is the stated main idea about the topic (improving communication between males and females). When a sentence states the main idea of a paragraph, as that sentence does, it is often called the paragraph's *topic sentence.* This term may be familiar to you from writing classes in which you create topic sentences that state the main ideas of your paragraphs. Topic sentences are often—but not always—the first sentence in a paragraph.

Supporting details and unstated main ideas. Not every paragraph has a stated main idea (topic sentence). For paragraphs that do not, you can sum up the supporting details to make your own statement of the main idea.

Identify the topic in Paragraph 14 of Reading 9, "Money Fights Can Ruin a Marriage." This paragraph comes under the heading, "Whose Money Is It Anyway?"

> (1) Lucy and Jake finally had an overdue talk about their goals and priorities. (2) "We both want to buy a house before starting a family," says Jake. (3) "To me, that's down the road a bit. (4) But Lucy thinks we have to start saving now or we'll never make it. (5) She spent her childhood moving from one military post to another with her dad. (6) To her, having a house is the dream of a lifetime. (7) When she explained that, I understood why she'd gotten so upset."

Each sentence in the paragraph points to one topic: "talking about the couple's goals and priorities." The first sentence introduces the topic but doesn't give an idea of how their talk goes. The rest of the sentences give the specific details of their talk: first what they agree on, then what they disagree about, and finally Lucy's explanation of why the house is so important—the explanation that makes Jake understand her need to save now.

Here's how you could sum up the supporting details as a main idea:

> When Lucy and Jake talked over their goals and priorities, Jake discovered why Lucy has a stronger need than he does to start saving for a house right away.

Apply the New Strategy: Find the Support

Now that you understand Strategy 7, put it into practice with Reading 12, "The Men We Carry in Our Minds" (or with one of the Additional Readings at the end of Part III, selected by your instructor).

Before reading, **check in**. Then **ask questions**. There are no headings in this reading, so your overview will depend mainly on the title and these cues: the notes before the reading and the introduction (Paragraph 1). Note, too, the first sentences of the next two or three paragraphs. Put these cues together. Try writing the following:

Umbrella question: _____

_____

Topics (look for a few topics that relate to your umbrella question):

_____

_____

Predictions about the overall point (What types of men will Sanders discuss?): _____

_____

_____

As you read, **find the support** for main ideas. Scott Russell Sanders uses many descriptive details as well as examples and explanations to support his main ideas. Use a pencil or pen to mark some supporting details, as well as topics and main ideas and the overall point.

THE MEN WE CARRY IN OUR MINDS

SCOTT RUSSELL SANDERS

This reading is excerpted from an essay in Scott Russell Sanders' book of essays, The Paradise of Bombs *(1987). Sanders, a professor of English at Indiana University, has published several books of fiction and nonfiction. In this reading, he explains why it took him some time to understand why women might think men have, in his words, "all the joys and privileges of the earth."*

RESPOND
Remember to connect your own experience to what the writer says.

Memphis: city in Tennessee

boll-weevil: beetle that damages cotton

"twin poles": extreme opposites of types of men

Words that may be unfamiliar are underlined. **Use Context Clues** and **Find the Right Definition** will help you understand them.

The first men, besides my father, I remember seeing were black con- 1
victs and white guards, in the cottonfield across the road from our farm on the outskirts of Memphis? I must have been three or four. The prisoners wore dingy gray-and-black zebra suits, heavy as canvas, sodden with sweat. Hatless, stooped, they chopped weeds in the fierce heat, row after row, breathing the acrid dust of boll-weevil° poison. The overseers wore dazzling white shirts and broad shadowy hats. The oiled barrels of their shotguns flashed in the sunlight. Their faces in memory are utterly blank. Of course those men, white and black, have become for me an emblem of racial hatred. But they have also come to stand for the twin poles° of my early vision of manhood—the brute toiling animal and the boss.

When I was a boy, the men I knew labored with their bodies. They were 2
marginal farmers, just scraping by, or welders, steelworkers, carpenters; they swept floors, dug ditches, mined coal, or drove trucks, their forearms ropy with muscle; they trained horses, stoked furnaces, built tires, stood on assembly lines wrestling parts onto cars and refrigerators. They got up before light, worked all day long whatever the weather, and when they came home at night they looked as though somebody had been whipping them. In the evenings and on weekends they worked on their own places, tilling gardens that were lumpy with clay, fixing broken-down cars, hammering on houses that were always too drafty, too leaky, too small.

hernia: displacement of an organ, such as the intestine, often due to physical strain

ulcer: sore, in this case inside the stomach

The bodies of the men I knew were twisted and maimed in ways visi- 3
ble and invisible. The nails of their hands were black and split, the hands tattooed with scars. Some had lost fingers. Heavy lifting had given many of them finicky backs and guts weak from hernias°. Racing against conveyor belts had given them ulcers°. Their ankles and knees ached from years of standing on concrete. Anyone who had worked for long around machines was hard of hearing. They squinted, and the skin of their faces was creased like the leather of old work gloves. There were times, studying them, when I dreaded growing up. Most of them coughed, from dust or cigarettes, and most of them drank cheap wine or whiskey, so their eyes looked bloodshot and bruised. The fathers of my friends always seemed older than the mothers. Men wore out sooner. Only women lived into old age.

GIs: men enlisted in the U.S. army

limbo: state of uncertainty

braves . . . the hunt: Native American hunters and warriors

As a boy I also knew another sort of men, who did not sweat and break down like mules. They were soldiers, and so far as I could tell they scarcely worked at all. During my early school years we lived on a military base, an <u>arsenal</u> in Ohio, and every day I saw GIs° in the guardshacks, on the stoops of barracks, at the wheels of olive drab Chevrolets. The chief fact of their lives was boredom. Long after I left the Arsenal I came to recognize the sour smell the soldiers gave off as that of souls in limbo°. They were all waiting—for wars, for transfers, for leaves, for promotions, for the end of their hitch—like so many braves° waiting for the hunt to begin. Unlike the warriors of older tribes, however, they would have no say about when the battle would start or how it would be waged. Their waiting was broken only when they practiced for war. They fired guns at targets, drove tanks across the churned-up fields of the military reservation, set off bombs in the wrecks of old fighter planes. I knew this was all play. But I also felt certain that when the hour for killing arrived, they would kill. When the real shooting started, many of them would die. This was what soldiers were *for,* just as a hammer was for driving nails.

Warriors and toilers: those seemed, in my boyhood vision, to be the chief destinies for men. They weren't the only destinies, as I learned from having a few male teachers, from reading books, and from watching television. But the men on television—the politicians, the astronauts, the generals, the <u>savvy</u> lawyers, the philosophical doctors, the bosses who gave orders to both soldiers and laborers—seemed as removed and unreal to me as the figures in tapestries. I could no more imagine growing up to become one of these cool, potent creatures than I could imagine becoming a prince.

A nearer and more hopeful example was that of my father, who had escaped from a red-dirt farm to a tire factory, and from the assembly line to the front office. Eventually he dressed in a white shirt and tie. He carried himself as if he had been born to work with his mind. But his body, remembering the earlier years of slogging work, began to give out on him in his fifties, and it quit on him entirely before he turned sixty-five. Even such a partial escape from man's fate as he had accomplished did not seem possible for most of the boys I knew. They joined the Army, stood in line for jobs in the smoky plants, helped build highways. They were bound to work as their fathers had worked, killing themselves or preparing to kill others.

A scholarship enabled me not only to attend college, a rare enough feat in my circle, but even to study in a university meant for the children of the rich. Here I met for the first time young men who had assumed from birth that they would lead lives of comfort and power. And for the first time I met women who told me that men were guilty of having kept all the joys

4

5

6

7

and privileges of the earth for themselves. I was <u>baffled</u>. What privileges? What joys? I thought about the maimed, dismal lives of most of the men back home. What had they stolen from their wives and daughters? The right to go five days a week, twelve months a year, for thirty or forty years to a steel mill or a coal mine? The right to drop bombs and die in war? The right to feel every leak in the roof, every gap in the fence, every cough in the engine, as a wound they must mend? The right to feel, when the lay-off comes or the plant shuts down, not only afraid but ashamed?

I was slow to understand the deep <u>grievances</u> of women. This was   8 because, as a boy, I had envied them. Before college, the only people I had ever known who were interested in art or music or literature, the only ones who read books, the only ones who ever seemed to enjoy a sense of ease and grace were the mothers and daughters. Like the menfolk, they fretted about money, they scrimped and made-do. But, when the pay stopped coming in, they were not the ones who had failed. Nor did they have to go to war, and that seemed to me a blessed fact. By comparison with the narrow, ironclad days° of fathers, there was an <u>expansiveness</u>, I thought, in

ironclad days: days controlled by rigid work schedules

the days of mothers. They went to see neighbors, to shop in town, to run errands at school, at the library, at church. No doubt, had I looked harder at their lives, I would have envied them less. It was not my fate to become a woman, so it was easier for me to see the <u>graces</u>. Few of them held jobs outside the home, and those who did filled thankless roles as clerks and waitresses. I didn't see, then, what a prison a house could be, since houses seemed to me brighter, handsomer places than any factory. I did not realize—because such things were never spoken of—how often women suffered from men's bullying. I did learn about the wretchedness of abandoned wives, single mothers, widows; but I also learned about the wretchedness of lone men. Even then I could see how exhausting it was for a mother to cater all day to the needs of young children. But if I had been asked, as a boy, to choose between tending a baby and tending a machine, I think I would have chosen the baby. (Having now tended both, I know I would choose the baby.)

So I was baffled when the women at college accused me and my sex of   9 having cornered the world's pleasures. I think something like my bafflement has been felt by other boys (and by girls as well) who grew up in dirt-poor farm country, in mining country, in black ghettos, in Hispanic barrios°,

Hispanic barrios: Spanish-speaking neighborhoods

in the shadows of factories, in Third World nations—any place where the fate of men is as grim and bleak as the fate of women. Toilers and warriors. I realize now how ancient these identities are, how deep the tug° they exert

deep the tug . . . the undertow: pull for these men toward feeling the same identities they had in the past

on men, the undertow of a thousand generations. The miseries I saw, as a boy, in the lives of nearly all men I continue to see in the lives of many—the

body-breaking toil, the <u>tedium</u>, the call to be tough, the humiliating powerlessness, the battle for a living and for territory.

When the women I met at college thought about the joys and privi-   10
leges of men, they did not carry in their minds the sort of men I had known
in my childhood. They thought of their fathers, who were bankers, physicians, architects, stockbrokers, the big wheels of the big cities. These
fathers rode the train to work or drove cars that cost more than any of my
childhood houses. They were attended from morning to night by female
helpers, wives and nurses and secretaries. They were never laid off, never
short of cash at month's end, never lined up for welfare. These fathers
made decisions that mattered. They ran the world.

The daughters of such men wanted to share in this power, this glory.   11
So did I. They yearned for a say over their future, for jobs worthy of their
abilities, for the right to live at peace, unmolested, whole. Yes, I thought,
yes yes. The difference between me and these daughters was that they saw
me, because of my sex, as destined from birth to become like their fathers,
and therefore as an enemy to their desires. But I knew better. I wasn't an
enemy, in fact or in feeling. I was an <u>ally</u>. If I had known, then, how to tell
them so, would they have believed me? Would they now?

Follow-Up Activities   After you've finished reading, use these activities to
respond to "The Men We Carry in Our Minds." You may write your answers or
prepare them in your mind to discuss in class.

Grab your first impressions.

1. What kinds of men did you know when you were growing up? How were
   they similar to or different from the men Sanders knew as a child?

2. How are the lives of women you know difficult or unfairly limited? How
   are men's lives difficult and unfairly limited?

Work with new words.

Some words in this reading may be unfamiliar to you. Use the methods
of Strategies 3 and 4 to explain what the listed words mean.

1. Use context clues.

   a. savvy (Paragraph 5) (use logic clues)

   _____

   b. graces (Paragraph 8) (use example clues)

   _____

    c. ally (Paragraph 11) (use contrast clues)

    _____

2. Use word parts.

    a. marginal (Paragraph 2) (see the word "margin," meaning "edge")

    _____

    b. expansiveness (Paragraph 8) (has the same root as "expand")

    _____

    c. tedium (Paragraph 9) (has the same root as "tedious")

    _____

3. Use the dictionary.

    Choose the correct definition of these words as they are used in the context of this reading.

    a. emblem (Paragraph 1)

    _____

    b. toiling (Paragraph 1)

    _____

    c. maimed (Paragraph 3)

    _____

    d. arsenal (Paragraph 4)

    _____

    e. baffled (Paragraph 7)

    _____

    f. grievances (Paragraph 8)

    _____

Ask and answer questions.

1. Who were the two groups of men Sanders first remembers observing? Explain what he means when he says these two groups came "to stand for the twin poles of my early vision of manhood—the brute toiling animal and the boss"?

2. Sanders describes how men's work ruined their bodies and their general health. What are some specific details that show how and why these men "wore out"?

3. What is Sanders' explanation for his original belief that women had an easier time than men? What difficulties does he later recognize in their lives?

4. In college many women told Sanders that, "men were guilty of having kept all the joys and privileges of the earth for themselves." What kinds of men were they referring to? How did these men contrast with the kinds of men Sanders had known?

5. What did Sanders have in common with the women he met at the university?

 Ask and answer your own question.

Write a question of your own. Share your question with others, and work together on an answer.

 Find the topics and mark main ideas and supporting details.

You may want to use the following suggestions to clarify your sense of the reading's topics, main ideas, and supporting details.

Since Reading 12 has no headings, use the umbrella question to divide the reading into a few main topics. Call Paragraph 1 an introduction. Paragraph 2 is about men as laborers—the first topic. Where does that topic change? You might consider Paragraph 4 a new topic—men as soldiers. But try from there on to find no more than three more main topics. Mark main ideas and supporting details for each topic. Compare your marking with the sample that follows.

Sample Marking

READING 12   THE MEN WE CARRY IN OUR MINDS

SCOTT RUSSELL SANDERS

Intro:

2 types of men

The first men, besides my father, I remember seeing were <u>black convicts</u> and <u>white guards</u>, in the cottonfield across the road from our farm on the outskirts of Memphis. I must have been three or four. The prisoners wore dingy gray-and-black zebra suits, heavy as canvas, sodden with sweat. Hatless, stooped, they chopped weeds in the fierce heat, row after row, breathing the acrid dust of boll-weevil poison. The overseers wore dazzling white shirts and broad shadowy hats. The oiled barrels of their shotguns flashed in the sunlight. Their faces in memory are utterly blank. Of course those men, white and black, have become for me an emblem of racial hatred. <u>But they have also come to stand for the twin poles of my early vision of manhood—the brute toiling animal and the boss.</u>   1

Main Idea ——————→   When I was a boy, the men I knew labored with their bodies. They were   2

Laborers   marginal farmers, just scraping by, or welders, steelworkers, carpenters;
they swept floors, dug ditches, mined coal, or drove trucks, their forearms

exs.   ropy with muscle; they trained horses, stoked furnaces, built tires, stood on
assembly lines wrestling parts onto cars and refrigerators. They got up
before light, worked all day long whatever the weather, and when they

their   came home at night they looked as though somebody had been whipping

work   them. In the evenings and on weekends they worked on their own places,
tilling gardens that were lumpy with clay, fixing broken-down cars, hammering on houses that were always too drafty, too leaky, too small.

The bodies of the men I knew were twisted and maimed in ways visi-   3
ble and invisible. The nails of their hands were black and split, the hands
tattooed with scars. Some had lost fingers. Heavy lifting had given many of
them finicky backs and guts weak from hernias. Racing against conveyor

physical   belts had given them ulcers. Their ankles and knees ached from years of

damage   standing on concrete. Anyone who had worked for long around machines
was hard of hearing. They squinted, and the skin of their faces was creased
like the leather of old work gloves. There were times, studying them, when
I dreaded growing up. Most of them coughed, from dust or cigarettes, and
most of them drank cheap wine or whiskey, so their eyes looked bloodshot and bruised. The fathers of my friends always seemed older than the
mothers. Men wore out sooner. Only women lived into old age.

As a boy I also knew another sort of men, who did not sweat and break   4
down like mules. They were soldiers, and so far as I could tell they scarcely

Main Idea   worked at all. During my early school years we lived on a military base, an

Soldiers   arsenal in Ohio, and every day I saw GIs in the guardshacks, on the stoops

wait to kill   of barracks, at the wheels of olive drab Chevrolets. The chief fact of their

or die   lives was boredom. Long after I left the Arsenal I came to recognize the
sour smell the soldiers gave off as that of souls in limbo. They were all
waiting—for wars, for transfers, for leaves, for promotions, for the end of
their hitch—like so many braves waiting for the hunt to begin. Unlike the
warriors of older tribes, however, they would have no say about when the
battle would start or how it would be waged. Their waiting was broken
only when they practiced for war. They fired guns at targets, drove tanks
across the churned-up fields of the military reservation, set off bombs in
the wrecks of old fighter planes. I knew this was all play. But I also felt certain that when the hour for killing arrived, they would kill. When the real
shooting started, many of them would die. This was what soldiers were *for,*
just as a hammer was for driving nails.

Main Idea ——————→   Warriors and toilers: those seemed, in my boyhood vision, to be the   5
chief destinies for men. They weren't the only destinies, as I learned from

having a few male teachers, from reading books, and from watching television. But the men on television—the politicians, the astronauts, the generals, the savvy lawyers, the philosophical doctors, the bosses who gave orders to both soldiers and laborers—seemed as removed and unreal to me as the figures in tapestries. I could no more imagine growing up to become one of these cool, potent creatures than I could imagine becoming a prince.

father's "partial escape"

A nearer and more hopeful example was that of my father, who had   6
escaped from a red-dirt farm to a tire factory, and from the assembly line to the front office. Eventually he dressed in a white shirt and tie. He carried himself as if he had been born to work with his mind. But his body, remembering the earlier years of slogging work, began to give out on him in his fifties, and it quit on him entirely before he turned sixty-five. Even <u>such a partial escape from man's fate as he had accomplished did not seem possible for most of the boys I knew</u>. They joined the Army, stood in line for jobs in the smoky plants, helped build highways. They were bound to work as their fathers had worked, killing themselves or preparing to kill others.

<u>A scholarship enabled me not only to attend college, a rare enough</u>   7
<u>feat in my circle, but even to study in a university meant for the children of</u>
<u>the rich</u>. Here I met for the first time young men who had assumed from birth that they would lead lives of comfort and power. And for the first time <u>I met women who told me that men were guilty of having kept all the joys and privileges</u> of the earth for themselves. <u>I was baffled</u>. What privileges?

Main Idea— male privilege? confusing because of men & women he knew

What joys? I thought about the maimed, dismal lives of most of the men back home. What had they stolen from their wives and daughters? The right to go five days a week, twelve months a year, for thirty or forty years to a steel mill or a coal mine? The right to drop bombs and die in war? The right to feel every leak in the roof, every gap in the fence, every cough in the engine, as a wound they must mend? The right to feel, when the lay-off comes or the plant shuts down, not only afraid but ashamed?

<u>I was slow to understand the deep grievances of women</u>. This was   8
<u>because, as a boy, I had envied them</u>. Before college, the only people I had ever known who were interested in art or music or literature, the only ones who read books, the <u>only ones who ever seemed to enjoy a sense of ease and grace were the mothers and daughters</u>. Like the menfolk, they fretted about money, they scrimped and made-do. But, when the pay stopped coming in, they were not the ones who had failed. Nor did they have to go to war, and that seemed to me a blessed fact. <u>By comparison with the narrow, ironclad days of fathers, there was an expansiveness, I thought, in the days of mothers</u>. They went to see neighbors, to shop in town, to run errands at school, at the library, at church. No doubt, had I looked harder at

Why women's lives seemed better

*Why
women's lives
seemed ———→
better*

their lives, I would have envied them less. It was not my fate to become a woman, so it was easier for me to see the <u>graces</u>. Few of them held jobs outside the home, and those who did filled thankless roles as clerks and waitresses. I didn't see, then, what a prison a house could be, since houses seemed to me brighter, handsomer places than any factory. <u>I did not realize</u>—because such things were never spoken of—how <u>often women suffered from men's bullying</u>. I did learn about the wretchedness of abandoned wives, single mothers, widows; but I also learned about the wretchedness of lone men. Even then I could see how exhausting it was for a mother to cater all day to the needs of young children. <u>But if I had been asked, as a boy, to choose between tending a baby and tending a machine</u>, I think I would have <u>chosen the baby</u>. (Having now tended both, I know I would choose the baby.)

So I was baffled when the women at college accused me and my sex of   9
having cornered the world's pleasures. I think something like my bafflement has been felt by other boys (and by girls as well) who grew up in dirt-poor farm country, in mining country, in black ghettos, in Hispanic barrios, in the shadows of factories, in Third World nations—any place where the fate of men is as grim and bleak as the fate of women. Toilers and warriors. I realize now how ancient these identities are, how deep the tug they exert on men, the undertow of a thousand generations. The miseries I saw, as a boy, in the lives of nearly all men I continue to see in the lives of many—the body-breaking toil, the <u>tedium</u>, the call to be tough, the humiliating powerlessness, the battle for a living and for territory.

*Suggests Overall
Point
———→
men in their
minds*

When the women I met at college thought about the joys and privi-   10
leges of men, they did not carry in their minds the sort of men I had known in my childhood. They thought of their fathers, who were bankers, physicians, architects, stockbrokers, the big wheels of the big cities. These fathers rode the train to work or drove cars that cost more than any of my childhood houses. They were attended from morning to night by female helpers, wives and nurses and secretaries. They were never laid off, never short of cash at month's end, never lined up for welfare. These fathers made decisions that mattered. They ran the world.

*but "his
men"
———→
made him
want same
power women
wanted*

The <u>daughters of such men wanted to share in this power, this glory.</u>   11
<u>So did I.</u> They yearned for a say over their future, for jobs worthy of their abilities, for the right to live at peace, unmolested, whole. Yes, I thought, yes yes. The difference between me and these daughters was that they saw me, because of my sex, as destined from birth to become like their fathers, and therefore as an enemy to their desires. But I knew better. I <u>wasn't an enemy, in fact or in feeling. I was an ally</u>. If I had known, then, how to tell them so, would they have believed me? Would they now?

Answer your umbrella question to state the overall point.

Here is an example of an effective umbrella question: "What kinds of men do we carry in our minds?" After completing the reading, we might add to that question, "and why does it matter to us?" Note that the sample marking for Reading 12 shows sentences in Paragraph 10 that suggest the overall point. Form your own summary statement based on the sentences.

Form your final thoughts.

1. Scott Russell Sanders was born in 1945. Based on your experiences—and those of your parents—how have men's and women's roles changed since the time of his childhood?

2. At the end of the reading Sanders says he is not an "enemy to [the] desires" of women, but an ally. Discuss whether you agree or disagree with him.

3. Sanders grew up in a community "where the fate of men is as grim and bleak as the fate of women." Discuss whether you agree or disagree with Sanders when he says that people growing up in such communities have a hard time understanding women's sense of injustice.

Chapter 7 Summary

How does Strategy 7 help you *use your reader's voice to be an active reader?*

Strategy 7, **Find the Support,** gives you a clearer sense of a reading at every level—from general ideas to specific details. As you get a firmer grasp of the writer's ideas, you have more to say in response to them.

How does the *find the support* strategy work?

This strategy shows how specific, supporting details explain, demonstrate, or back up a more general idea. With this strategy you can identify the details that support main ideas in a single paragraph as well as in a reading as a whole.

STRATEGY 7: FIND THE SUPPORT

1 Find details that support main ideas.

2 Look for different types of supporting details.

3 Look for ideas in specific paragraphs.

Are you familiar with the meaning of these terms?

descriptions: details that tell how someone or something looks, sounds, or feels

examples: instances that give specific situations or cases to demonstrate a general idea

explanations: clarifications or reasons given to support an idea

fact: statement that can be proven or confirmed

general: refers to a large category (for example, fruit)

major detail: detail that directly supports the main idea

minor detail: more specific detail that supports a major detail

quotation: the exact words used by another writer or speaker

specific: refers to a particular type or part within a larger category (for example, type of fruit, including bananas, grapes, apples)

subheading: heading that names a subtopic

subtopic: a specific topic that supports a more general topic

support: various ways of explaining, demonstrating, or backing up a main idea

supporting detail: specific detail used to support a more general idea

testing a main idea sentence: examining the sentence to see if it covers all the supporting details

topic sentence: the stated main idea of a paragraph

How is the strategy working for you so far?

Explain which parts of **finding the support** you've found most helpful in the readings you've practiced with. Which parts have been least helpful?

TIME OUT FOR YOU

HOW CAN YOU HANDLE THE
STRESS OF TAKING TESTS?

No one looks forward to walking into a classroom on the day of a test. Even when you're well prepared, taking a test is bound to cause some stress. It can even make your mind go blank on a question you know the answer to. But you can learn to handle that stress so it doesn't get in the way of your performance on the test.

Practice Simple Relaxation Techniques

As part of your test preparation, learn a few techniques to help you relax during a test. Here are some simple ones to try.

Breathe!

When we're feeling stressed, we're apt to take shorter breaths. But that's just when we need more oxygen to relax and get our brains in gear. Focus on the air going in and out of your lungs for a minute or so. That focus reminds you to breathe in a comfortable way: take a few deep breaths, and then just breathe in a normal, relaxed way. The breathing eases tension throughout your body.

Smile

It's strange to say, but the act of smiling tells our brains and our bodies that we're okay. Try it now. See if a smile activates a slight relaxation of tension in you.

Let go of tension

Focus on the areas in your body where you feel tense. For one area at a time, breathe, and let go of the tension in that part. It often helps to consciously tense that part first. For example, lift up your shoulders, tense them, and then relax them. Do you notice the release of tension?

Stretch

You don't have to reach for the ceiling to relax by stretching. Just pull your shoulders up and back, or stretch your arms down at your sides. Lift your legs off the floor a bit, and stretch them out in front of you. Stretching one part of your body eases tension everywhere.

Handle Stress throughout the Test

You'll experience less stress if you come prepared to the test, knowing the material and having relaxation techniques for reducing tension. In addition, here are some guidelines for tackling any test from start to finish.

Get into your test routine

On the day of the test, get to class on time so you don't add to your stress by missing anything the teacher says before the test. On the other hand, don't get there so early that you hear a lot of panicky "pre-test" talk from other students. Once in your seat, start your test routine, a set of things you do that put you into the right frame of mind for the test. Here are some things that help at this stage:

- Remind yourself that jittery feelings are to be expected at the beginning of a test, and remember they'll lessen as you get into the work itself.

- Use a relaxation technique now, and remember it for later during the test.

- Use margins of the test paper—or scratch paper, if it's allowed—to jot down any fact or formula that you're afraid of forgetting.

- Listen to any directions the instructor gives.

Be focused and efficient during the test

Don't use your test time to worry about the grade you'll get. Focus on the specific questions you're working on. Here are suggestions for a good routine once you begin the test:

- Glance over the whole test to see what each part is worth and to judge how much time each part will require.

- Read the instructions for each part carefully before writing any answers.

- To gain more confidence, do the easiest items first, and mark the more difficult items to come back to later.

- Give yourself positive, not negative feedback ("You're doing fine," not "You idiot, you should know that!").

- Pace yourself, so you put in more time on the items that are worth more.

Come to a good finish

The end of the test is another time when it pays to be focused and efficient. You may start rushing in order to leave the stressful test situation. But rushing can lead to careless mistakes. Slow down as much as you can. If you do finish early, don't dash off. Instead, make it part of your routine to do the following:

- Check for errors, such as marking the wrong box, leaving out an important word or number, or overlooking a question.

- Avoid changing answers unless you're sure you've made a mistake, because your first instinct is usually best.

- If you still have time, you might add a bit more information to an answer or guess at some answers for possible credit.

- Hand in your test, and walk out the door feeling you've done your best!

CHAPTER **8**

LOOK FOR PATTERNS OF THOUGHT

Strategy 6, **Find Topics and Main Ideas,** and Strategy 7, **Find the Support,** help you understand the general and specific ideas of a reading. Strategy 8, **Look for Patterns of Thought,** helps you recognize how these ideas are presented, so your reader's voice, in response, is more confident.

Introduction to the New Strategy: Look for Patterns of Thought

Patterns of thought are structures our minds use as we think, talk, read, or write. One of the easiest patterns to recognize is *examples*. Note the example in this everyday comment: "That restaurant has terrible service! For example, no one waited on us for over half an hour!" Another common pattern, *comparison and contrast*, can be seen in this response: "Yes, but the restaurant next door is even worse!" You already saw in Strategy 7, **Find the Support,** that writers use examples as supporting details. But any pattern of thought—examples, comparison and contrast, and others—can be used to supply supporting details. Any pattern can also be used to organize a main idea or the overall point of a reading. Noticing common patterns as you read helps you see the relationship among main ideas, supporting details, and the overall point.

STRATEGY 8: LOOK FOR PATTERNS OF THOUGHT

1 Be alert to common patterns of thought.

2 Use these patterns to find main ideas and supporting details.

3 Watch for transitions from one thought to the next.

Six Common Patterns

1 *Be alert to common patterns of thought.*

Strategy 3, **Use Context Clues,** showed you how the patterns of *examples, comparison and contrast,* and *definition* help you use context to define a word. You can also use these and other common patterns of thought to help you understand the writer's ideas. Three other common patterns of thought are *cause-and-effect reasoning, sequence,* and *location.* Special signal words and phrases often indicate a specific pattern. Become familiar with these words and phrases. They are listed in the margin for each pattern.

Signal words and phrases for examples

for example
e.g.
such as
to illustrate
for instance
to be specific
that is to say
namely

Examples. As you learned in Strategy 7, **Find the Support,** an example is one type of supporting detail. An example shows a specific instance of the main idea, so the idea is easier to understand. Examples help clarify any *generalization,* or statement of a general idea. See how the "classic example" in Paragraph 3 from Reading 11, "How Men and Women Communicate in Relationships," makes the first sentence—a general statement—come to life.

> . . . males receive strong societal messages to withhold their feelings. The classic example of this training in very young males is the familiar saying "big boys don't cry."

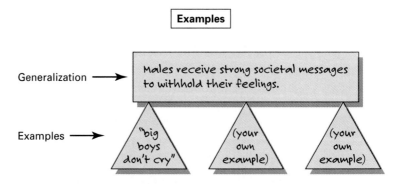

Examples support a generalization. What other examples of messages can you think of that tell males they should withhold their feelings?

Often a longer example—sometimes called an *illustration*—is used to demonstrate a generalization. An illustration is used in Paragraph 4 of Reading 13, "When Not Asking for Directions Is Dangerous to Your Health." That paragraph gives a specific story that illustrates the danger referred to in the title. It tells how a woman and her father came close to crashing their small plane when her father wouldn't ask for directions because he didn't "want them [in the control tower] to think I'm lost."

Signal words and phrases for comparison and contrast

For comparison:
as
like
similarly
in a similar way
compared with
in a like manner

For contrast:
but
yet
however
while
whereas
on the other hand
in contrast to
contrary to
although

Comparison and contrast. When *comparing* you look for similarities; when *contrasting* you look for differences. We use each pattern separately, but they frequently work together. Much of Reading 11, "How Men and Women Communicate in Relationships," is based on the pattern of contrast. It shows the differences between men's and women's ways of communicating. Can you identify supporting details that show contrast in this paragraph from Reading 11?

Recent research validates much of Tannen's work and indicates that women are more expressive, more relationship oriented, and more concerned with creating and maintaining intimacy; men tend to be more instrumental, task-oriented, and concerned with gathering information or with establishing and maintaining social status or power. Unlike women, men tend to believe that they are not supposed to show emotions and are brought up to believe that "being strong" is often more important than having close friendships. As a result, according to research, only 1 male in 10 has a close male friend to whom he divulges his innermost thoughts.

Did you take note of all these contrasting details?

Men	Women
instrumental (getting things done)	expressive
task-oriented	relationship-oriented
concerned with gathering information, establishing and maintaining social status or power	concerned with creating and maintaining intimacy
not supposed to show emotion	supposed to show emotion
being strong more important	having close friendships more important

Signal words and phrases for definition

that is
that is to say
or
to define this
to say what this means
namely

Signal words and phrases for classification

category
elements of
characteristics
features
types
kinds
parts

Definition and classification. *Definition* answers the question "What is it?" It explains the meaning of a word or idea. A long, detailed definition may be used to explain a new term or take a new look at a familiar term. A definition often includes *classification,* a pattern that shows how a word or idea fits into a larger category. Classification answers the question "What type of . . . ?" For example, in Reading 11, the author gives a definition of a particular use of the word "editing."

> Editing, or censoring remarks that may be hurtful or are irrelevant, is another useful skill that improves couple communication. Often, when people are upset, they let everything fly, bringing up old issues and incidents that cause pain and put a partner on the defensive. Editing means taking the time and making the effort not to say inflammatory things. Leveling and editing help establish genuine communication characterized by caring and sensitivity.

In this paragraph, the first sentence gives a phrase that explains the term: "censoring remarks that may be hurtful or are irrelevant." Then, the sentence gives the classification or category the word belongs in: useful skills that improve couple communication. Find two other patterns that give more details about "editing" in the rest of the paragraph.

An example is found in the sentence about letting "everything fly." A comparison is found in the last sentence. There leveling and editing are shown to be similar in that both "help establish genuine communication characterized by caring and sensitivity."

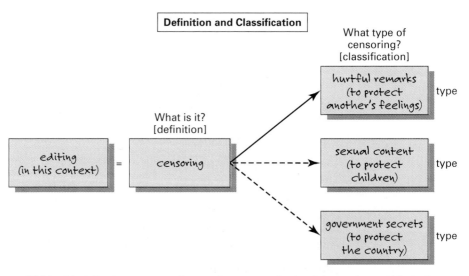

"Editing" is defined as one type of censoring—not saying hurtful remarks—within the larger category of censoring. The dotted lines point to other types of censoring.

Signal words and phrases for cause-and-effect reasoning

for this reason
because
to explain
as a result
consequently
hence
therefore
thus
then

Cause-and-effect reasoning. Cause-and-effect reasoning gives logical reasons that answer the question "why" or "how." A *cause* is the reason for something happening; an *effect* is the result or outcome.

See how this pattern works in this excerpt from Paragraph 2 of Reading 13, "When Not Asking for Directions Is Dangerous to Your Health."

> Of all the examples of women's and men's characteristic styles that I discussed in *You Just Don't Understand,* the one that (to my surprise) attracted the most attention was the question "Why don't men like to stop and ask for directions?" . . . And my explanation seems to have rung true: that men are more likely to be aware that asking for directions, or for any kind of help, puts them in a one-down position.

Tannen asks the "why" question: "Why don't men like to stop and ask directions?" Then she answers why, giving the cause—her "explanation"—in the last sentence.

In Paragraph 5, a pilot tells Tannen about an effect of this unwillingness of small-plane pilots to ask for help. According to him, the effect is "more than a few small-plane crashes."

Here is a summary of Reading 13's cause-and-effect reasoning (specifically related to men who pilot small planes):

Cause-and-Effect Reasoning

Cause: Not wanting to be put in a "one-down" position

↓

Effect [new cause]: Not wanting to ask directions

↓

Next Effect [new cause]: Getting lost and running out of gas

↓

Final Effect: (unless lucky) Plane crashes

A cause brings about an effect. That effect may in turn become a cause for further effects, as in this instance.

Sequence. The *sequence* pattern gives details in a certain order. Sequence is important when telling what happened in a story or in history. You can see the sequence pattern in Reading 1, "Poppa and the Spruce Tree," when Cuomo tells the story of how his father, with the help of his two sons, rescued their 40-foot spruce tree after a storm. Cuomo begins the sequence of events when he and his brother come home and see the spruce, "defeated." The brothers' hearts sink, "but not Poppa's." Cuomo then relates, step by step, how the three get the tree standing upright and replanted. Note in this last part of the story how the details are given in the order of what they did:

> With the rain still falling, Poppa dug away at the place where the roots were, making a muddy hole wider and wider as the tree sank lower and lower toward security. Then we shoveled mud over the roots and moved boulders to the base to keep the tree in place. Poppa drove stakes in the ground, tied rope from the trunk to the stakes, and maybe two hours later looked at the spruce, the crippled spruce made straight by ropes, and said, "Don't worry, he's gonna grow again. . . ."

Sequence (Time Order)

Poppa widens hole for tree	Boys shovel mud over roots	They move boulders to tree base	Poppa stakes the tree	Poppa looks at tree	He says "Don't worry"
First	Next	Next	Next	2 hours later	Finally

Telling what happened in a story or in history presents details in sequence—the order in which events took place.

Sequence also matters when explaining how something works (for example, the stages of labor a mother goes through in delivering a baby) and when explaining how to do something as a series of steps. For example, typical advice for taking tests depends on a certain sequence that helps you get the test under control. Here are the first few steps:

> Look over the entire test first to see how much each section is worth. Read the directions carefully and ask questions if anything is confusing. Then, jot down any memory aids, such as formulas or facts you're worried about forgetting.

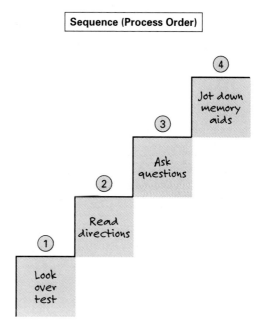

A process for doing something is often given as a sequence of steps to follow. Here you see the first steps to take when beginning a test.

Often items in a sequence are numbered. If not, as in the preceding example, try numbering the steps yourself to make them easier to remember.

Signal words and phrases for location

above
around
behind
below
next to
opposite
within
elsewhere
beyond
close by
adjacent to

Location. The *location* pattern places details in space. As you saw in Strategy 7, descriptive details are one type of support. Location is used when it is important to show where these descriptive details are. For example, before telling about the rescue of the spruce tree, Cuomo tells about the important move his family made from an apartment to their own house.

> We had just moved to Holliswood, New York, from our apartment behind the store. We had our own house for the first time; it had some land around it, even trees. One, in particular, was a great blue spruce that must have been 40 feet tall.

The pattern of location helps place the descriptive details so we can see first the apartment "behind" the store, then the house, with land "around" it.

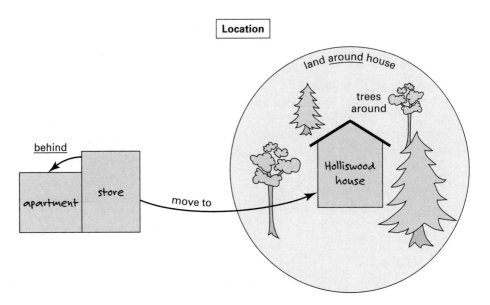

Cuomo uses the pattern of location to show the descriptive details of his former home in an apartment and his move to Holliswood.

Patterns and Main Ideas

2 Use these patterns to find main ideas and supporting details.   These common patterns can help you find the main ideas that support the overall point. Watch for patterns as you go through steps from Strategy 6, **Find Topics and Main Ideas.**

Dividing the reading into main topics. If a reading has headings, see if the headings fit a pattern in relation to the overall point. For example, the title of Reading 9, "Money Fights Can Ruin a Marriage," turns into the question "How do money fights ruin a marriage?" The question suggests a cause-and-effect reasoning pattern. Each of the headings points to a specific fight—a specific cause—for trouble in a marriage.

Patterns can also be helpful in a reading without headings. For example, in Reading 10, "The Influence of Sports on Male Identity," the title points to the pattern of cause-and-effect reasoning, because the word "influence" is another word for "effect." A useful umbrella question emphasizes the pattern: "What are the effects of sports on male identity?" As part of your answer, you might divide that reading into three main topics, each dealing with a different effect of sports on male identity: (1) the effect of success on boys who win recognition, (2) the effect of lack of success on boys who don't perform as well, (3) the effect of the idea of "winning" on men's relationships.

Finding main ideas about topics. Patterns can also help you identify a main idea about a topic. The second topic of Reading 10 is the effect of lack of success on boys who don't perform as well. What is the main idea about that topic? Keep in mind the cause-and-effect reasoning pattern from your umbrella question, and see what the writer says about this specific effect. Note this sentence that introduces Paragraph 6: "The boost in the boy's self-esteem, however, can come at a high cost to others." The phrase "high cost to others" is another way of saying "bad effect on others." So, this sentence expresses the writer's main idea as part of the cause-and-effect reasoning pattern.

Finding supporting details about a main idea. Let patterns help you as you read for details that support a main idea. In Reading 12, "The Men We Carry in Our Minds," the unstated main idea of Paragraphs 7–9 can be expressed this way:

> In college, Sanders' female classmates complained about men keeping power away from women, and their complaints made him think of his own experience of the contrast between men and women.

You can see the pattern of comparison and contrast in the middle of Paragraph 7 when Sanders contrasts his classmates' view of the privileges of men with his own experience of men's hardships. Then he gives supporting details that show the contrast between the men and women he knew. Here are supporting details from Paragraph 8:

- He saw only women—never men—having time for art, music, literature.

- Like men, women worried about money, but they weren't failures if the pay stopped.

- Unlike men, women didn't have to go to war.

- Women had more freedom than men—to go to visit neighbors, to go the library.

- He didn't see that houses could be prisons, because they seemed so much better than any factory.

This clear pattern of comparison and contrast throughout Paragraphs 7–9 pulls together all the supporting details, so they demonstrate why Sanders' view of men and women was so different from that of his wealthy classmates.

Be flexible as you use Strategy 8, **Look for Patterns of Thought.** Patterns—especially the pattern of examples—can help you understand a difficult reading. But what you read doesn't always fall neatly into one pattern. Instead, you'll often find combinations of patterns.

Transitions

3 *Watch for transitions from one thought to the next.*

A *transition* is a word or phrase that makes a bridge, or link, from one thought to the next. Transitions give you a signal as to what the new thought will be.

Transitions and patterns of thought. The new thought may fit one of the six common patterns you've just learned. For example, the word "consequently" is a signal word for cause-and-effect reasoning. In this example see how it acts as a transition—a bridge—leading to the next thought: the effect of wearing helmets on children's well-being.

> Many more children now wear helmets for biking and skateboarding. Consequently there are fewer children who experience head injuries.

The most likely words and phrases for transitions to all six common patterns are the same signal words and phrases listed in the margin next to each pattern on pages 186–191. Thus "for instance," "for example," or "to be specific" are transitions to an example pattern; "to say what this means" or "to define this" are transitions to a definition pattern; "beyond," "around," or "elsewhere" are transitions to a location pattern, and so on. You'll find a listing of signal words for all common patterns in the summary table on page 202.

Transitions to more information. Other words and phrases are used to mark different types of transitions. These transitions signal that the new information will say more about the preceding thought through *clarification, addition,* or *summary.* Note the definitions and examples for each of these types.

Signal words and phrases for clarification

in other words
clearly
in fact
certainly
obviously
without a doubt
of course

Clarification   Clarification makes a previous statement clearer by saying it in other words or discussing it further. In the example, "of course" signals the new thought.

> Children who have been taught to play the piano tend to do better in math. Of course, they must have played for a sufficient period of time.

Signal words and phrases for addition

in addition
also
as well as
finally
furthermore
moreover
besides
what's more

Signal words and phrases for summary

in brief
in short
in conclusion
to sum up
to summarize
on the whole
thus

Addition   Addition provides extra information that goes along with the previous idea. In the example, "also" signals additional information.

> You'll need to bring your own swimsuit and towels. Also, don't forget swim goggles for underwater swimming.

Summary   Summary reviews or sums up preceding details. In the example, "in short" indicates a summary of details in the preceding sentence.

> Swimming is good for increasing stamina, flexibility, and strength, and it does not stress the joints. In short, it is an excellent all-around exercise.

Making the most of transitions. The little words and phrases that act as transitions can give your reading a big boost. They alert you to what's coming next. Here are a few examples of the way transitions help you spot important ideas.

- A transition for summary, such as "in short" or "to sum up" may point you to the conclusion—and possibly the overall point—of the reading.

- Transition words for sequence, such as "first," "next," and "finally" can lead you to the main topics of a reading.

- The simple word for contrast, "but," at the beginning of a paragraph signals a new direction of ideas, possibly a whole new topic.

- Transition words for comparison, such as "similarly," "in a similar way," or "in a like manner," remind you to compare the new thought to the one you just read.

Try the New Strategy: Look for Patterns of Thought

Now that you understand Strategy 8, put it into practice with Reading 13, "When Not Asking for Directions Is Dangerous to Your Health" (or with one of the Additional Readings at the end of Part III, selected by your instructor).

CHECK IN
Keep in mind the Part III theme (men and women, boys and girls).
Are there differences between men and women when it comes to asking for directions? How can you relate your experience and feelings to this subject?

Before reading, **check in.** Then, **ask questions.** There are no headings, so your overview will depend mainly on the title, the introduction, and the conclusion. Note words and phrases in the title and other cues that suggest a cause-and-effect reasoning pattern for your umbrella question and predicted overall point. Try writing the following:

Umbrella question: _____

_____

Topics: _____

_____

Predictions about the overall point: _____

_____

As you read, **look for patterns of thought.** See how cause-and-effect reasoning organizes this reading. In addition, see how comparison and contrast and examples are used for main ideas and/or supporting details. Use a pencil or pen to mark some supporting details, as well as main ideas and the overall point.

READING 13 ## WHEN NOT ASKING FOR DIRECTIONS IS DANGEROUS TO YOUR HEALTH

DEBORAH TANNEN

This reading comes from Talking from 9 to 5: Men and Women in the Workplace *(1994), by Deborah Tannen, a professor of linguistics at Georgetown University in Washington, D.C. She is the author of the widely read book* You Just Don't Understand: Women and Men in Conversation *(1990), as well as many other books about communication.*

If conversational-style differences lead to troublesome outcomes in work as well as private settings, there are some work settings where the outcomes of style are a matter of life and death. Health-care professionals are often in such situations. So are airline pilots. 1

Words that may be unfamiliar are underlined. **Use Context Clues** and **Find the Right Definition** will help you understand them.

Of all the examples of women's and men's characteristic styles that I discussed in *You Just Don't Understand,* the one that (to my surprise) attracted the most attention was the question "Why don't men like to stop and ask for directions?" Again and again, in the responses of audiences, talk-show hosts, letter writers, journalists, and conversationalists, this question seemed to <u>crystallize</u> the frustration many people had experienced in their own lives, And my explanation seems to have rung true: that 2

one-down position: an inferior position.

men are more likely to be aware that asking for directions, or for any kind of help, puts them in a one-down position.

With regard to asking directions, women and men are keenly aware of the advantages of their own style. Women frequently observe how much time they would save if their husbands simply stopped and asked someone instead of driving around trying in vain to find a destination themselves. But I have also been told by men that it makes sense not to ask directions because you learn a lot about a neighborhood, as well as about navigation, by driving around and finding your own way.

But some situations are more risky than others. A Hollywood talk-show producer told me that she had been flying with her father in his private airplane when he was running out of gas and uncertain about the precise location of the local landing strip he was heading for. Beginning to panic, the woman said, "Daddy! Why don't you radio the control tower and ask them where to land?" He answered, "I don't want them to think I'm lost." This story had a happy ending, else the woman would not have been alive to tell it to me.

Some time later, I repeated this <u>anecdote</u> to a man at a cocktail party—a man who had just told me that the bit about directions was his favorite

3

4

5

RESPOND

Remember to relate these ideas to your own experience.

Women and men approach the issue of asking for directions differently.

FAA: Federal Aviation Administration

part of my book, and who, it turned out, was also an amateur pilot. He then went on to tell me that he had had a similar experience. When learning to fly, he got lost on his first solo flight. He did not want to <u>humiliate</u> himself by tuning his radio to the FAA° emergency frequency and asking for help, so he flew around looking for a place to land. He spotted an open area that looked like a landing field, headed for it—and found himself <u>deplaning</u> in what seemed like a deliberately hidden landing strip that was mercifully deserted at the time. Fearing he had stumbled upon an enterprise he was not supposed to be aware of, let alone poking around in, he climbed back into the plane, relieved that he had not gotten into trouble. He managed to find his way back to his home airport as well, before he ran out of gas. He maintained, however, that he was certain that more than a few small-plane crashes have occurred because other amateur pilots who did not want to admit they were lost were less lucky. In light of this, the amusing question of why men prefer not to stop and ask for directions stops being funny.

The <u>moral</u> of the story is not that men should immediately change and   6
train themselves to ask directions when they're in doubt, any more than women should immediately stop asking directions and start <u>honing</u> their navigational skills by finding their way on their own. The moral is flexibility: Sticking to habit in the face of all challenges is not so smart if it ends up getting you killed. If we all understood our own styles and knew their limits and their alternatives, we'd be better off—especially at work, where the results of what we do have <u>repercussions</u> for co-workers and the company, as well as for our own futures.

Follow-Up Activities   After you've finished reading, use these activities to respond to "When Not Asking for Directions Is Dangerous to Your Health." You may write your answers or prepare them in your mind to discuss in class.

Grab your first impressions.

1. What did you find most surprising in this reading?

2. How does your experience compare to what Tannen says about men not liking to ask for directions? What differences have you noticed in the way men and women handle getting help when they're lost or having problems in other situations?

Work with new words.

Some words in this reading may be unfamiliar to you. Use the methods of Strategies 3 and 4 to explain what the listed words mean.

1. Use context clues.

    a. anecdote (Paragraph 5) (use logic clues and the example from the pre-
       ceding paragraph)

    _____

    b. moral (Paragraph 6) (use logic clues; note the special use of the word)

    _____

    c. honing (Paragraph 6) (use logic clues)

    _____

2. Use word parts.

    a. crystallize (Paragraph 2) (see the word "crystal"; remember "-ize" indi-
       cates a verb)

    _____

    b. deplaning (Paragraph 5) (combines prefix "de-" and "plane")

    _____

3. Use the dictionary.

    Choose the correct definition of these words as they are used in the con-
    text of this reading.

    a. humiliate (Paragraph 5)

    _____

    b. repercussions (Paragraph 6)

    _____

Ask and answer questions.

1. What is Tannen's explanation for why men don't ask for directions? Why
   do men say it makes sense not to ask for directions?

2. Why did the amateur pilot Tannen talked to get back in his plane immediately after landing?

3. What did this same pilot say was the cause of some small-plane crashes?

4. What advice does Tannen give to men and women on this subject? What
   does she mean when she says, "The moral is flexibility"?

5. At the beginning of the reading, Tannen mentions health care as another
   work setting "where the outcomes of style are a matter of life and death."
   How could fear of asking for help be "a matter of life and death" in the
   health-care field?

Ask and answer your own question.

Write a question of your own. Share your question with others, and work together on an answer.

Look for patterns of thought.

Use patterns to help find topics and mark main ideas and supporting details in Reading 13. The following questions will help you. The first one is done for you.

1. How does cause-and-effect reasoning in Paragraph 1 suggest what the overall point may be? *These phrases—"lead to troublesome outcomes" and "outcomes of style are a matter of life and death"—relate to the title; the "outcomes" are the effects of not asking for directions.*

2. How does comparison and contrast organize the ideas for a first topic, made up of Paragraphs 2 and 3? What differences are explored in those paragraphs?

   _____

   _____

3. Paragraph 2 also uses the pattern of cause-and-effect reasoning to give supporting details about men's attitudes. What words and phrases identify this pattern?

   _____

   _____

4. What is the pattern that organizes Paragraphs 4 and 5 into one topic? What is the topic?

   _____

   _____

5. How would you state the main idea for the topic in Paragraphs 4 and 5? Your predictions about the overall point show that cause-and-effect reasoning organizes this reading, so state this idea as an effect.

   _____

   _____

6. What is the pattern of Paragraph 6, the conclusion? Explain your answer.

   _____

   _____

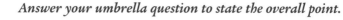

Answer your umbrella question to state the overall point.

The word "when" from the title produces a useful umbrella question. In this case, "when" is not just asking for the time something took place. Instead it asks "in what situations," or "when *is* it dangerous not to ask for directions?" The question uses cause-and-effect reasoning because it implies dangerous effects. Tannen does not answer this question in one statement. Try to form your own summary statement that answers your umbrella question and states the overall point.

Form your final thoughts.

1. Discuss as a group of men and women Tannen's finding that the reason men are more reluctant to ask for directions is because they don't want to be put in a "one-down position." Do you agree or disagree with the finding? Explain your answer.

2. Did this reading encourage you to modify your attitude about asking for directions—or for any kind of help? If so, how? If not, why not?   ■

Chapter 8 Summary

How does Strategy 8 help you *use your reader's voice to be an active reader?*

Looking for patterns of thought helps keep your mind active. As you notice common patterns, you gain clarity about the writer's ideas and feel more confident to voice your own response.

How does the *look for patterns of thought* strategy work?

The strategy reminds you to look for common patterns of thought. Patterns often help you **find topics and main ideas** and **find the support.** Six common patterns are: examples and illustration, comparison and contrast, definition and classification, cause-and-effect reasoning, sequence, and location. Descriptions of each pattern are given in the table on page 202.

Here are the three steps for Strategy 8.

STRATEGY 8: LOOK FOR PATTERNS OF THOUGHT

1 Be alert to common patterns of thought.

2 Use these patterns to find main ideas and supporting details.

3 Watch for transitions from one thought to the next.

In addition to the patterns of thought, are you familiar with the meaning of these terms?

patterns of thought: structures our minds use as we think, talk, read, or write

transition: a word or phrase that serves as a bridge or link from one thought to the next

Summary Table of Patterns of Thought

Note: Numbers in parentheses refer to pages in this chapter where the pattern is discussed.

Pattern	Description	Signal Words and Phrases
Generalization with examples and illustrations	Show specific instances of a general idea. (186)	for example, e.g., such as, to illustrate, for instance, to be specific, that is to say, namely
Comparison	Gives similarities between two or more things. (187)	as, like, similarly, in a similar way, compared with, in a like manner
Contrast	Gives differences between two or more things. (187)	but, yet, however, while, whereas, on the other hand, in contrast to, contrary to, although
Definition	Explains the meaning of a word or an idea. (188)	that is, that is to say, or, to define this, to say what this means, namely

Classification	Shows how a word or idea belongs within a larger category. (188)	category, elements of, characteristics, features, types, kinds, parts
Cause-and-effect reasoning	Explains why or how one event brings about another. (189)	for this reason, because, to explain, as a result, consequently, hence, therefore, thus, then
Sequence (for time order)	Gives events in the order in which they took place in time. (190)	first, before, after, afterward, at last, during, now, at that time, since, until
Sequence (for process order)	Gives items in the order in which they should be done. (190–191)	first, second, third, next, the next step, further, then, before, after that, finally, last
Location	Places details in space. (191–192)	above, around, behind, below, next to, opposite, within, elsewhere, beyond, close by, adjacent to

Summary Table of Transitions to More Information

Note: Numbers in parentheses refer to pages in this chapter where the type of transition is discussed.

Type of transition	Description	Signal Words and Phrases
Clarification	Makes a statement clearer by saying it in other words or discussing it further. (194)	in other words, clearly, in fact, certainly, obviously, without a doubt, of course
Addition	Provides more information. (195)	in addition, also, as well as, finally, furthermore, moreover, besides, what's more
Summary	Gives a brief, condensed statement of the preceding ideas. (195)	in brief, in short, in conclusion, to sum up, to summarize, on the whole, thus

How is the strategy working for you so far?

Explain which parts of **looking for patterns of thought** you've found most helpful in the readings you've practiced with. Which parts have been least helpful?

TIME OUT FOR YOU

HOW CAN YOU PREDICT TEST QUESTIONS?

You can spend a lot of time reviewing for a test and still not do well. When that happens it's often because you didn't know enough about what the test would be like. Here are some guidelines for predicting test questions so your studying will pay off.

Use Your Class Notes and Other Materials

Your class notes should include anything the instructor says about the type of questions (multiple-choice or short answer, for example) and the amount and type of information to be covered. In addition, use any quizzes or other graded material to get a sense of the kinds of questions the instructor likes to ask. The material covered also might reappear in a different form on the test.

Ask Your Instructor

Most instructors are glad to answer your questions about the test. What topics will be emphasized? What level of detail will you be expected to remember? How can you best spend your review time?

Be Alert to Test Directions and Types of Test Questions

On the day of the test, don't miss points by neglecting to read directions carefully. Here are some points about multiple-choice and true/false questions that may help you raise your test score.

Multiple-choice questions

- Read the first part of the question carefully. Sometimes this part gives important clues. Note the word "ones," for example, in "Which ones of the following are causes of drug dependency?" The plural shows that you need to choose more than one answer.

- Try to complete the statement before looking at the choices; that way you're less likely to be confused by all the choices.

- Watch out for questions that are stated in the negative. For example, the question about drug dependency might say: "Which ones of the following are *not* causes of drug dependency?" You may need to take note of the choice that is a cause of drug dependency, but be sure you write down the answers that are not causes.

- Be sure to read every choice completely before selecting one. Answers may be quite similar, but only one is correct (unless there are directions that tell you to choose more than one).

- Watch for words used as qualifiers, such as "sometimes," "never," "all," or "most." These are key words that can change the meaning of a statement. For example, here's the beginning of a statement: "Traffic accidents occur. . . ." Which of these two choices ends that statement correctly?

   a. ". . . because people sometimes disobey the rules of the road."

   b. ". . . because people always disobey the rules of the road."

  The first choice (a) is correct because people do sometimes disobey the rules of the road. The second choice (b) is incorrect. It is not true that people "always" disobey the rules of the road.

- If you don't know the answer, make an educated guess. Select the answer that seems likely to be right. Or look for two answers that are similar (similar words or quantities, for example), and choose one of these.

True/false questions

Read each statement completely. Keep yourself from making careless mistakes by going too fast.

- Note any word or phrase that is false. One false part makes the whole statement false.

- Watch for words used as qualifiers, as you do in reading multiple-choice questions. Words that are absolutes, such as "all," "never," and "always," often make a statement false.

Go Through a "Trial Run"

Put yourself through a trial run before the test. You can test yourself using questions from the book and your notes. Cover up the answers or, better still, make your own flash cards, putting a question on one side of an index card and the answer on another. If possible, arrange to study with a student or group of students from your class. You can share the work of coming up with possible questions, and your trial run will be more enjoyable and effective.

PART III

ADDITIONAL READINGS ON
MEN AND WOMEN,
BOYS AND GIRLS

The readings that follow will give you further practice in using the strategies from Parts I, II, and III with a variety of readings on the theme of men and women, boys and girls.

READING III-A **TEACHING SEX ROLES**

JANET GONZALEZ-MENA AND JANET EMERITA

This reading comes from a child development textbook, The Child in the Family and the Community, *by Janet Gonzales-Mena and Janet Emerita. In this excerpt the authors show how language and role models influence children's ideas about the roles males and females are expected to play in our society.*

Before reading "Teaching Sex Roles," **check in.** *Then,* **ask questions** *about the title and other cues. Note especially the headings and subheadings and the introduction. Put these cues together. Try writing the following:*

CHECK IN
Look for the subject in the first paragraph as well as the title. How can you relate your experience and feelings to this subject?

Umbrella question: _____

_____

Topics (note the headings):_____

_____

Predictions about the overall point: _____

_____

_____

As you read, use the new strategies—Strategies 6–8—to find topics, main ideas, and supporting details. Here the writers use examples, explanations, facts, and quotations to support main ideas. Use a pencil or pen to mark some supporting details, as well as topics, main ideas, and the overall point.

Parents can take note of some of the practices [for expanding sex roles   1
that] early childhood professionals are using and support those practices while adding to them at home. At-home parents can also take note about arranging play dates, buying toys, setting up a nonsexist° environment, and encouraging broader sex roles.

nonsexist: not based on prejudice or discrimination against one sex, usually women

THE POWER OF LANGUAGE

Words that may be unfamiliar are underlined. **Use Context Clues** and **Find the Right Definition** will help you understand them.

Language has an influence on sex role development. Language shapes perceptions.   2

Job Titles

If you talk about firemen, policemen, and chairmen, you set an expectation that these jobs are filled by men and that it's an exception when there's a "woman policeman." Better to make these titles non-gender-specific. That can be accomplished by using the terms *fire fighter, police officer,* and *chair* or *chairperson.* Children will get the message that either sex may fill these roles.   3

Some titles are already non-gender-specific—for example *teacher, doctor,* and *president.* However, children may consider them as gender-specific because of their own experience. There's the story of the English girl who asked her mother, "What are they going to call the new prime minister now that Mrs. Thatcher's gone?"   4

"By his name, of course," answered the mother.   5

"But what's his *title?*" persisted the child.   6

"Prime minister," answered the mother.   7

"But that's a woman's title!" said the child.   8

Interruption and Power

Studies of "conversational politics" have found that people use language to show their power, as one person exerts control over another. For example, men tend to interrupt women more than the reverse. Interruption is an important indicator of relative power and importance. Children learn these interruption patterns early from their parents. Parents, teachers, and other early childhood professionals need to be aware of these patterns so when they see them occurring they can put a stop to them. That's not easy to do when you're an involved party, but it's possible. It's easier to look for the patterns when they occur between boys and girls and then intervene, insisting that the girls get their say. Empowerment of girls is important if there is to be sex equity.   9

Assertive Language

assertive: being firm and confident but not necessarily aggressive

Female parents and teachers can also help empower girls by teaching them to use assertive° language. To do this, they need to model such language themselves. Women who live or work with girls can pay attention to   10

What do these toys show about the sex roles these three-year-olds are already taking on?

RESPOND
How much does your response to these ideas depend on your sex?

how often they end a sentence with a question that <u>dilutes</u> the message. For example, "I want you to sit down in your car seat, OK?" or "It's time for lunch; will you come in now?"

Females can model assertive language by cutting down the number of 11 times they <u>hedge</u> with phrases such as *sort of* and *I guess.* They can also quit being ultrapolite. For example, "Your shoes are sort of muddy. It'd be really nice if you took them off before you walk on the rug. I'd sure appreciate it." That way of talking is very courteous, but it depends on the goodwill of the listener to be effective. When being polite gives the message that the speaker is powerless, it's a good idea to find more assertive ways to speak. It's more powerful for a person to say what she means—to be direct and informative. That's what men do, and that's why they are more likely to be listened to than women. For example, a direct way to deal with the muddy shoes is this: "Please take off your muddy shoes. They'll dirty the rug." Or: "Muddy shoes belong on the mat by the door." Or if necessary: "If you walk on the rug with muddy shoes, you're going to have to clean it."

THE POWER OF ROLE MODELS

. . . Modeling is an important method of teaching sex roles. Children   12
imitate the important people in their lives, so when girls see their mothers
act helpless in the face of a flat tire or their female preschool teachers
wait for a man to appear on the scene to unclog toilets or fix the broken
handle on the cupboard, they pick up silent messages about women's
capabilities. When a boy sees his father hand his mother a needle and
thread and a shirt with a missing button, he gets a silent message about
men's capabilities.

When children see their father reading the newspaper while their   13
mother fixes dinner, then watching the news on TV while she cleans up
after dinner, they get silent messages about sex roles. They come to see
some activities as for women only and some for men only. They see a
sexually determined power differential. In a household where tasks are
shared, children get a broader idea of capabilities as well as appropri-
ateness.

A good deal of modeling comes from television. Power Rangers, a   14
children's television program widely criticized for its violence, at least has
both boy and girl rangers. However, the "bad guy" is an evil old woman.
Powerful elderly females as evil is a <u>stereotype</u> that has been with us for
centuries. The witch-hunts of the past show how such a negative stereotype can be used to oppress, even kill. Some older feminists facing the
negative stereotype of being feminine and old have decided to redefine
themselves as "crones"—the old woman as powerful, knowledgeable, and
wise, but not evil.

Books can leave strong stereotypical images. In early readers, Dick   15
was always busy fixing something, while Mother, Jane, and Sally stood
helplessly looking on. Dick and Father were active in a variety of ways.
Mother, Jane, and Sally were <u>passive</u> except in the kitchen. It seems as
though times should have changed by now, but as late as 1986, when
books read to kindergartners were analyzed, the main character was male
over 70% of the time. Still today it is easy to see that children's books are
more often about boys than girls, male animals instead of female ones.
You can also easily find females being dependent more often than independent and poor <u>damsels</u> needing help.

Follow-Up Activities   After you've finished reading, use these activities to
respond to "Teaching Sex Roles." You may write your answers or prepare them
in your mind to discuss in class.

Grab your first impressions.

1. What are some of your early memories of learning about sex roles? What part (or parts) of this reading came closest to your own experiences?

2. How do you think the young children you know today are learning sex roles? Is their experience similar to what you learned as a child or different? Explain your answer.

Work with new words.

Some words in this reading may be unfamiliar to you. Use the methods of Strategies 3 and 4 to explain what the listed words mean.

1. Use context clues.

   a. exerts (Paragraph 9) (use logic clues)

   _____

   b. dilutes (Paragraph 10) (use logic clues)

   _____

   c. passive (Paragraph 15) (note the contrast with "active" in the preceding sentence)

   _____

2. Use word parts.

   a. intervene (Paragraph 9) (note the prefix "inter-" and use logic clues)

   _____

   b. empowerment (Paragraph 9) (note the word "power")

   _____

   c. equity (Paragraph 9) (note the beginning of the word, suggesting "equal," and use logic clues)

   _____

3. Use the dictionary.

   Choose the correct definition of these words as they are used in the context of this reading.

   a. perceptions (Paragraph 2)

   _____

b. hedge (Paragraph 11)

_____

c. stereotype (Paragraph 14)

_____

d. damsels (Paragraph 15)

_____

Ask and answer questions.

1. What suggestions do the authors give for non-gender-specific job titles? Why is it important for children to get used to non-gender-specific job titles?

2. Interrupting is one way a person "exerts control over another," and studies indicate that "men tend to interrupt women more than the reverse." What can adults do to teach boys and girls to interact in more equal ways?

3. What is an example you can give of an ultrapolite message asking someone to do something? How could you change the message to be more "direct and informative"?

4. What are some examples from the reading of teachers or parents acting in stereotypically female or male ways?

5. How can parents provide children with role models that demonstrate an expanded view of roles for males and females?

 Ask and answer your own question.

Write a question of your own. Share your question with others, and work together on an answer.

Look for patterns of thought.

Find the sentence or sentences that demonstrate the specific pattern listed for each of these paragraphs. Explain briefly how the pattern is used.

1. Paragraph 10: examples

_____

_____

2. Paragraph 11: comparison and contrast

_____

_____

3. Paragraph 12: cause-and-effect reasoning

_____

_____

_____

Find the topics and mark main ideas and supporting details.

Use patterns to help find topics and mark main ideas and supporting details in Reading III-A.

 Answer your umbrella question to state the overall point.

Here is an example of an effective umbrella question: "How can we teach children broader sex roles, that is, less limited roles for girls/women and boys/men?" What main ideas in the reading work together to answer this question? Try to find a summary statement of main ideas in the reading. The statement will likely answer your umbrella question and state the overall point. Or form your own summary statement.

 Form your final thoughts.

1. Which ideas from the reading about raising children do you find most important?

2. How might you modify your behavior or your language in order to demonstrate less limited sex roles for children? If you don't need to change your language or behavior, explain why.   ■

READING III-B HORRORS! GIRLS WITH GAVELS!
WHAT A DIFFERENCE A DAY MAKES!

ANNA QUINDLEN

This reading was first published as one of Anna Quindlen's regular columns in the April 15, 2002, issue of Newsweek *magazine. The title refers to Take Our Daughters to Work Day, originated by the Ms. Foundation for Women. In 2003, the foundation changed the program to Take Our Daughters and Sons to Work*

Day. The foundation made the change so that both boys and girls—and their community—can think about how future work situations can allow both mothers and fathers enough time for raising a family.

CHECK IN
The notes before the reading help you understand the title. How can you relate your experience and feelings to this subject?

Before reading "Horrors! Girls with Gavels! What a Difference a Day Makes!" **check in.** *Then* **ask questions** *about the title and other cues: especially the notes before the reading and the introduction. Put these cues together. Try writing the following:*

Umbrella question: _____
_____

*Topics:*_____
_____

Predictions about the overall point: _____
_____
_____

RESPOND
Remember to pause from time to time to comment and ask the writer a question.

As you read, **find the support** *for main ideas. Quindlen uses examples, explanations, descriptive details, and facts as support for her main ideas. Use a pencil or pen to mark some supporting details, as well as topics and main ideas and the overall point.*

Not long ago I spoke at a meeting sponsored by a company's women's networking group. Like most other American corporations, this one had a lot of women in entry-level jobs, a fair number of women in middle management and a few women in the top ranks, in a pyramid configuration° that has become commonplace.

configuration: shape

Commonplace, too, was the response of the majority males at the top to this particular evening event. It <u>rankled</u>, this meeting, closed to them in the same way the ranks of management had once been closed to their distaff counterparts°. It rankled, even for one night. Apparently none of them saw it as a learning experience, the possibility of imagining for just a few hours what it had been like to be female for many, many years.

Words that may be unfamiliar are underlined. **Use Context Clues** and **Find the Right Definition** will help you understand them.

distaff counterparts: female equivalents

This immediately called to mind Take Our Daughters to Work Day, which comes around . . . at the end [of April]. . . . It's amazing how, almost from its <u>inception</u>, the opponents were all over it, complaining that it sent a bad message about female victimhood, that it was based on false research about girls and low self-esteem, above all that it was <u>gender-biased</u>, that the boys were not invited. The same people who weren't the least bit bothered when boys got the only decent school sports programs—or, for that matter, the entire Supreme Court—were flipping out about a bunch of 13-year-old girls eating in the corporate cafeteria for one afternoon.

Take Our Daughters to Work Day began in April 1992.

"What will we tell the boys?" parents agonized. I never had a bit of trouble explaining: I just remind them that the Senate is still 87 percent

1

2

3

4

male. Boys have issues and problems, too, but they're not the same as the ones girls have. We just don't start from the same place; otherwise it wouldn't be called "helping" when a man performs tasks in his own home, or "baby-sitting" when he looks after his own children. That's why the most famous remark about Take Our Daughters to Work Day is the one from Eleanor Holmes Norton°; when asked why there was no such day for boys, she said it was for the same reason there's no White History Month.

Eleanor Holmes Norton: African-American Congresswoman, Democrat from Washington, D.C.

Women still agonize over balancing work and family; lots of guys still   5
assume they'll balance work and family by getting married. Boys don't have to be introduced to the office. They're old acquaintances. In a survey done for the Ms. Foundation for Women about changing roles, 61 percent of the respondents said they believe men and women are treated differently in the workplace. You can talk all you want about improved <u>access</u> for women now, but it's a recent development, and it still stops several steps from most executive suites°. . . .

executive suites: offices for the top-level managers of a business

There's a photograph from one Take Our Daughters to Work Day on   6
my desk that sums it all up for me. The daughter is mine. She has a huge grin on her face, and a gavel in her hand, and standing behind her is a female federal judge. The judge is wearing a pink sweater; my daughter is wearing the judge's robes. And when I look at that picture I wonder if the judge and I were thinking the same thing, looking at that girl: that the chance of either of us hearing "woman" and "judge" in the same sentence when we were her age was just about nil°. Today there are 199 women judges in the federal system; when I was 11, there were three. Present at the revolution: that's what I feel every time I look at that photograph. Every time a girl plays Little League, every time a father assumes his daughter is as likely to go to college as his son, every time no one looks twice at a female cop or <u>balks</u> at a female surgeon, it's a moment in history, <u>radical</u> and ordinary both at the same time.

nil: zero

Critics say that we should talk to girls about their marvelous opportuni-   7
ties instead of taking them out of school and promoting that pesky "<u>feminist</u> agenda" once a year. Pooh. Gavels speak louder than words. Besides, kids are always getting pulled out of school to go to Monticello° or chocolate factories or Six Flags. How come there's an uproar only when the field trip takes girls to a place in which girls were fairly recently unheard of, unwelcome? I remember fondly my daughter toddling around my office during the first Take Our Daughters to Work Day 10 years ago with a pencil in her fist, roaring, "I'm working!" whenever anyone tried to talk to her. There are girls now who are second-generation Takers, who went to work themselves when they were teenagers, and are now inviting others. The

Monticello: the home of Thomas Jefferson in Virginia

Ms. Foundation for Women has found a group of those women who say the event had a major impact on their lives, on the way they saw themselves and envisioned their futures. One day seems a <u>scant</u> investment for that sort of return.

But it will be a long time before we can truly judge the full effects of the program, just as it has taken us decades to appreciate the effects of the feminist revolution°. The assumption of access based on ability and not on gender that seemed <u>utopian</u> when we were young has become the guiding principle of the mainstream, even when it is honored only in the breach°. Take Our Daughters to Work Day is as much about our successes as it is about our continued <u>striving</u>. How could it not be? Our successes have remade the world. Welcome to it, girls. The boys may complain. But that will teach you something, too.

8

feminist revolution: gains toward equal rights for women, especially those made during the 1970s

breach: breaking or violation

honored only in the breach: even when people don't act according to this "guiding principle," they don't deny its correctness

Follow-Up Activities   After you've finished reading, use these activities to respond to "Horrors! Girls with Gavels! What a Difference a Day Makes!" You may write your answers or prepare them in your mind to discuss in class.

Grab your first impressions.

1. Do you agree with Quindlen's reasons for not including sons as well as daughters in the Take Our Daughters to Work Day? If so, why? If not, why not?

2. Does your response to the reading depend on whether you are male or female? Explain your answer.

Work with new words.

Some words in this reading may be unfamiliar to you. Use the methods of Strategies 3 and 4 to explain what the listed words mean.

1. Use context clues.

   a. inception (Paragraph 3) (use logic clues)

   _____

   b. access (Paragraph 5) (use logic clues)

   _____

   c. balks (Paragraph 6) (use logic clues)

   _____

    d. radical (Paragraph 6) ("both at the same time" suggests that "radical" contrasts with "ordinary")

_____

    e. scant (Paragraph 7) (use logic clues)

_____

2. Use the dictionary.

   Choose the correct definition of these words as they are used in the context of this reading.

    a. rankled (Paragraph 2)

_____

    b. biased (part of "gender-biased") (Paragraph 3)

_____

    c. feminist (Paragraph 7)

_____

    d. utopian (Paragraph 8)

_____

    e. striving (Paragraph 8)

_____

Ask and answer questions.

1. How does the term "pyramid configuration" demonstrate the way women were spread throughout the company where Quindlen spoke?

2. What were the three major complaints made by the opponents of Take Our Daughters to Work Day?

3. What are some details Quindlen uses to explain why Take Our Daughters to Work Day is not unfair to boys?

4. What makes the photograph of Quindlen's daughter and the judge so significant?

5. In the last paragraph, Quindlen states: "The assumption of access based on ability and not on gender that seemed utopian when we were young has become the guiding principle of the mainstream, even when it is honored only in the breach." How could you break up that sentence and restate it in your own words? Use the definitions in the margin on page 216 to help you.

Ask and answer your own question.

Write a question of your own. Share your question with others, and work together on an answer.

Look for patterns of thought.

Find the sentence or sentences that demonstrate the specific pattern listed for each of these paragraphs. Explain briefly how the pattern is used.

1. Paragraphs 2 and 3: comparison and contrast

    _____

    _____

2. Paragraph 5: comparison and contrast

    _____

    _____

3. Paragraph 6: example (illustration) and comparison and contrast

    _____

    _____

    _____

4. Paragraph 7: cause-and-effect reasoning

    _____

    _____

Find the topics and mark main ideas and supporting details.

Use patterns to help find topics and mark main ideas and supporting details in Reading III-B.

Answer your umbrella question to state the overall point.

A first try at an effective umbrella question might be: "Why do people say 'horrors' about having a special day to take daughters to work?" After reading, a more effective question seems to be: "Why *should* there be a special day to take daughters to work?" Try to find a summary statement of main ideas in the reading. The statement will likely answer your umbrella question and state the overall point. Or form your own summary statement.

Form your final thoughts.

1. What parts of the reading made the strongest impression on you—either positive or negative? Explain why.

2. The jobs Quindlen refers to are professional—business, politics, law, and her own profession of newspaper and magazine writing. Do you think the value of Take Your Daughters to Work Day depends on the type of job a parent does? Explain your answer.

3. Why does the Ms. Foundation for Women now want to include sons in its program? What's the difference between its reason for including sons and the original program's opponents' reason for including them? How do you think Quindlen feels about the Ms. Foundation's change?   ■

READING III-C **ONLY DAUGHTER**

SANDRA CISNEROS

This reading, by Sandra Cisneros, comes from Latina: Women's Voices from the Borderlands *(1995), edited by Lillian Castillo-Speed. Cisneros is well known for her poetry and fiction, especially* The House on Mango Street *(1984). Here she tells the story of how her father came to terms with his only daughter's career as a writer.*

CHECK IN

Consider the title and the first paragraph to find the subject. How can you relate your experience and feelings to this subject?

Before reading "Only Daughter," **check in.** Then, **ask questions** about the title and other cues. There are no headings in this reading, so your overview will depend mainly on these cues: the introduction (paragraphs 1 and 2) and the conclusion (the last three or four paragraphs). Put these cues together. Try writing the following:

Umbrella question: _____

_____

Topics: _____

_____

Predictions about the overall point: _____

_____

_____

As you read, **find the support** for main ideas. Cisneros uses examples, explanations, and descriptive details as support for her main ideas. Use a pencil or pen to mark some supporting details, as well as topics and main ideas and the overall point.

Once, several years ago, when I was just starting out my writing career, I was asked to write my own contributor's note for an anthology I was part of. I wrote: "I am the only daughter in a family of six sons. *That* explains everything."

Well, I've thought about that ever since, and yes, it explains a lot to me, but for the reader's sake I should have written: "I am the only daughter in a *Mexican* family of six sons." Or even: "I am the only daughter of a Mexican father and a Mexican-American mother." Or: "I am the only daughter of a working-class family of nine." All of these had everything to do with who I am today.

RESPOND
What feelings—as well as thoughts—does this reading bring up for you?

I was/am the only daughter and *only* a daughter. Being an only daughter in a family of six sons forced me by circumstance to spend a lot of time by myself because my brothers felt it beneath them to play with a *girl* in public. But that aloneness, that loneliness, was good for a would-be writer. It allowed me time to think and think, to imagine, to read and prepare myself.

Being only a daughter for my father meant my destiny would lead me to become someone's wife. That's what he believed. But when I was in the fifth grade and shared my plans for college with him, I was sure he understood. I remember my father saying, *"Que bueno, mi'ja°,* that's good." That meant a lot to me, especially since my brothers thought the idea hilarious. What I didn't realize was that my father thought college was good for girls—good for finding a husband. After four years in college and two more in graduate school, and still no husband, my father shakes his head even now and says I wasted all that education.

"mi'ja," short for "mi hija": my daughter

Words that may be unfamiliar are underlined. **Use Context Clues** and **Find the Right Definition** will help you understand them.

In <u>retrospect</u>, I'm lucky my father believed daughters were meant for husbands. It meant it didn't matter if I majored in something silly like English. After all, I'd find a nice professional eventually, right? This allowed me the liberty to putter about <u>embroidering</u> my little poems and stories without my father interrupting with so much as a "What's that you're writing?"

But the truth is, I wanted him to interrupt. I wanted my father to understand what it was I was scribbling, to introduce me as "My only daughter, the writer." Not as "This is only my daughter. She teaches." *Es maestra*—teacher. Not even *profesora.*

In a sense, everything I have ever written has been for him, to win his approval even though I know my father can't read English words, even though my father's only reading includes the brown-ink *Esto* sports magazines from Mexico City and the bloody *¡Alarma!* magazines that feature yet another sighting of *La Virgen de Guadalupe* on a tortilla or a wife's revenge on her philandering° husband by bashing his skull in with a *molcajete* (a kitchen mortar made of volcanic rock). Or the *fotonovelas,* the little picture

philandering: having many love affairs

paperbacks with tragedy and <u>trauma</u> erupting from the characters' mouths in bubbles.

My father represents, then, the public majority. A public who is disinterested in reading, and yet one whom I am writing about and for, and privately trying to <u>woo</u>.   8

When we were growing up in Chicago, we moved a lot because of my father. He suffered bouts of <u>nostalgia</u>. Then we'd have to let go of our flat, store the furniture with mother's relatives, load the station wagon with baggage and bologna sandwiches and head south. To Mexico City.   9

We came back, of course. To yet another Chicago flat, another Chicago neighborhood, another Catholic school. Each time, my father would seek out the parish priest in order to get a tuition break, and complain or boast: "I have seven sons."   10

He meant *siete hijos,* seven children, but he translated it as "sons." "I have seven sons." To anyone who would listen. The Sears Roebuck employee who sold us the washing machine. The short-order cook where my father ate his ham-and-eggs breakfasts. "I have seven sons." As if he deserved a medal from the state.   11

My papa. He didn't mean anything by that mistranslation, I'm sure. But somehow I could feel myself being erased. I'd tug my father's sleeve and whisper: "Not seven sons. Six! and *one daughter.*"   12

When my oldest brother graduated from medical school, he fulfilled my father's dream that we study hard and use this—our heads, instead of this—our hands. Even now my father's hands are thick and yellow, <u>stubbed</u> by a history of hammer and nails and twine and coils and springs. "Use this," my father said, tapping his head, "and not this," showing us those hands. He always looked tired when he said it.   13

Wasn't college an investment? And hadn't I spent all those years in college? And if I didn't marry, what was it all for? Why would anyone go to college and then choose to be poor? Especially someone who had always been poor.   14

Last year, after ten years of writing professionally, the financial rewards started to trickle in. My second National Endowment for the Arts Fellowship. A guest professorship at the University of California, Berkeley. My book, which sold to a major New York publishing house.   15

At Christmas, I flew home to Chicago. The house was throbbing, same as always: hot tamales and sweet tamales hissing in my mother's pressure cooker, and everybody—my mother, six brothers, wives, babies, aunts, cousins—talking too loud and at the same time. Like in a Fellini° film, because that's just how we are.   16

Fellini: Italian movie director

Chicano: adopted in the 1960s and 1970s as a term of ethnic pride for Mexican-Americans

I went upstairs to my father's room. One of my stories had just been translated into Spanish and published in an anthology of Chicano° writing and I wanted to show it to him. Ever since he recovered from a stroke two years ago, my father likes to spend his leisure hours horizontally. And that's how I found him, watching a Pedro Infante° movie on Galavisión and eating rice pudding. 17

Pedro Infante: Mexican movie star of the 1940s and 1950s

There was a glass filled with milk on the bedside table. There were several vials of pills and balled Kleenex. And on the floor, one black sock and a plastic urinal that I didn't want to look at but looked at anyway. Pedro Infante was about to burst into song, and my father was laughing. 18

Tepeyac, the colonia: a hillside settlement near Mexico City

I'm not sure if it was because my story was translated into Spanish, or because it was published in Mexico, or perhaps because the story dealt with Tepeyac°, the *colonia* my father was raised in and the house he grew up in, but at any rate, my father punched the mute button on his remote control and read my story. 19

I sat on the bed next to my father and waited. He read it very slowly. As if he were reading each line over and over. He laughed at all the right places and read lines he liked out loud. He pointed and asked questions: "Is this So-and-so?" "Yes," I said. He kept reading. 20

When he was finally finished, after what seemed like hours, my father looked up and asked: "Where can we get more copies of this for the relatives?" 21

Of all the wonderful things that happened to me last year, that was the most wonderful. 22

Follow-Up Activities   After you've finished reading, use these activities to respond to "Only Daughter." You may write your answers or prepare them in your mind to discuss in class.

Grab your first impressions.

1. What part or parts of the reading did you like best? Why?

2. How does this reading relate to the culture you grew up in? Were girls treated very differently from boys in your experience? Explain your answer.

Work with new words.

Some words in this reading may be unfamiliar to you. Use the methods of Strategies 3 and 4 to explain what the listed words mean.

1. Use context clues.

   a. embroidering (Paragraph 5) (use logic clues to see the what the word means in this sentence)

   _____

   b. stubbed (Paragraph 13) (use logic clues to see the what the word means in this sentence)

   _____

2. Use the dictionary.

   Choose the correct definition of these words as they are used in the context of this reading.

   a. retrospect (Paragraph 5)

   _____

   b. trauma (Paragraph 7)

   _____

   c. woo (Paragraph 8)

   _____

   d. nostalgia (Paragraph 9)

   _____

Ask and answer questions.

1. What new details about herself does Cisneros think she should add to her original contributor's note for an anthology? Why are these details important?

2. What did Cisneros gain from the fact that her brothers didn't want "to play with a *girl* in public"?

3. What did her father hope college would do for his sons? What did he hope it would do for his daughter?

4. What did Cisneros' father do and say that showed her how much he appreciated her story?

5. Why does Cisneros say her father represents the "public majority" she is trying to woo?

Ask and answer your own question.

Write a question of your own. Share your question with others, and work together on an answer.

Look for patterns of thought.

Find the sentence or sentences that demonstrate the specific pattern listed for each of these paragraphs. Explain briefly how the pattern is used.

1. Paragraph 3: definition (the word "only" is defined in two ways here; what are the two different ways?)

   _____

   _____

2. Paragraph 4: cause-and-effect reasoning, examples, and comparison and contrast

   _____

   _____

3. Paragraph 7: examples

   _____

   _____

4. Paragraph 12: cause-and-effect reasoning

   _____

   _____

5. Paragraph 13: comparison and contrast

   _____

   _____

Find the topics and mark main ideas and supporting details.

Use patterns to help find topics and mark main ideas and supporting details in Reading III-C.

 Answer your umbrella question to state the overall point.

A first try at an effective umbrella question might be: "What does it feel like to be 'an only daughter'?" What do you need to add to the question to include the other meaning of "only" as in "only a daughter"? Can you form a statement using your own words that answers this question and summarizes the overall point?

Form your final thoughts.

1. Cisneros' father had a different goal for her than she had for herself. What kinds of differences are there between what your parents want for you and what you want for your own future?

2. How has your relationship with either parent been affected by your sex? What kinds of differences have you noticed between the way you and your siblings (or friends) of the opposite sex were brought up?

 3. In a group of men and women, discuss the ways in which this reading relates to other readings from Part III. ■

PART III REVIEW
UNDERSTANDING MAIN IDEAS

You've completed Part III. Now take some time to look back at both the theme and the strategies introduced in this part.

Theme: Men and Women, Boys and Girls

The theme of Part III is the experience of being a man—or boy—or woman—or girl—in today's society. Write down or discuss with others in class the ideas you found most interesting on this theme. Which were your favorite readings? Why?

_____

_____

_____

_____

_____

Strategies: Find Topics and Main Ideas, Find the Support, and Look for Patterns of Thought

In Part III you learned how to find main ideas and the details that support them. You also saw how to use common patterns of thought to help you in identifying main ideas and supporting details. Look at the chart on the next page to remind yourself when you use the three new strategies, **Find Topics and Main Ideas, Find the Support,** and **Look for Patterns of Thought.** The new strategies are in white.

PART III REVIEW

Using Strategies Throughout the Reading Process

GET STARTED Begin with strategies that help you think about the subject and find out about what the writer will say.

- Check in
- Ask questions

READ Use strategies that help you read with greater understanding, interpret the language, and respond with your own questions and ideas.

- Use context clues
- Find the right meaning
- Ask questions
- Find topics and main ideas
- Find the support
- Look for patterns of thought
- Respond

FOLLOW UP End with strategies that help you look more closely at the language and ideas in the reading, assess your understanding, and respond in a thoughtful way.

- Find the right meaning
- Ask questions
- Find topics and main ideas
- Find the support
- Look for patterns of thought
- Respond

How Are the Strategies Working for You?

Answer the following questions to help you evaluate what you have learned. Then compare your answers with other students, and ask your instructor for ideas on how to get more out of the strategies.

1. How much time are these strategies taking? (Remember that all strategies take more time while you're learning them, but because they will help you understand more easily, they will save you time later.)

_____

_____

_____

2. Overall, how helpful have the strategies been in increasing your ability to understand and enjoy what you read?

_____

_____

_____

3. What can you do to make the strategies work better for you?

_____

_____

_____

PART IV

REMEMBERING AND INTERPRETING

WITH READINGS ON WORKING IN AMERICA

Work takes a big chunk out of the lives of most Americans. Today, most American workers spend more hours on the job than their parents did in the past and significantly more hours than workers in Western Europe do currently. In fact, if you're like most American college students, you've already put in many hours of part-time work. As a college student, you're preparing for satisfying work in the future. But you're also learning to balance work and your personal life as you combine a job and an education.

Readings in Part IV look at different aspects of working in America. Some readings focus on the individual worker finding meaning and facing challenges at work. Others focus more on the workforce as a whole. They look at how work fits in the larger context of social and economic changes in American society. As you read, think of your own experience of working and your ideas about the work you'd like to do. To think about this theme, look over these questions.

- Other than money, what gives you satisfaction in doing a job?
- What types of jobs have you enjoyed the most? Which ones do you think you'd like to try?
- What causes you problems in doing a job? What gets you through those hard times at work?
- How do you think you'll be able to balance your future work life and your personal life?

The strategies you've learned so far have helped you develop your reader's voice; you now **respond** with more confidence. So, in Part IV, after each reading you'll practice "grabbing your first impressions" on your own.

In Part IV—Remembering and Interpreting—you'll also see how strategies you've already learned provide a foundation for the new strategies. Building on Part III strategies for understanding main ideas, the new strategies expand your recall and understanding of the writer's ideas. Strategy 9, **Write to Remember,** allows you to make a brief record of main ideas. The last two strategies of the book deepen your interpretation of a reading. Strategy 10, **Make Inferences,** helps you figure out certain ideas. With Strategy 11, **Analyze the Information,** you can interpret writers' reasons for writing and their uses of facts and opinions.

CHAPTER 9

WRITE TO REMEMBER

Strategy 9, **Write to Remember,** builds on the Part III strategies for understanding main ideas. This new strategy shows you how to put main ideas on paper in the form of a map or simple outline of ideas or as a brief written summary. Working with the writer's ideas in this way helps imprint them in your mind so you can remember them later. The strategy also develops your reader's voice as you find your own ways of expressing the writer's ideas.

Try the New Strategy: Write to Remember

Strategy 9 gives you steps for mapping ideas. A *map* of ideas is a skeleton of a reading's organization of ideas. One familiar format for mapping is a simple *outline*. An outline is a vertical listing that shows the overall point and main ideas. Other formats for mapping display the overall point and main ideas in a more visual way. Strategy 9 also shows how to write a brief *summary*—a paragraph that accurately restates the writer's main ideas, using your own words. Putting the ideas into an outline, other type of map, or summary makes them clearer and easier to remember.

STRATEGY 9: WRITE TO REMEMBER

1 Map the main ideas and overall point.

2 Write a summary based on your map or marked reading.

CHECK IN

Before reading "The Effects of Work on Motivation," **check in.** Then **ask questions,** using appropriate cues, especially headings, the introduction, and the conclusion. Ask your umbrella question and predict the topics and overall point. As you read, use all appropriate strategies for understanding main ideas. **Look for Patterns of Thought** is especially helpful. Note how cause-and-effect reasoning—suggested in the title—helps organize many of the ideas in the reading.

While reading "The Effects of Work on Motivation," take a pencil and a blank sheet of paper and sketch a rough outline of the reading. Write the overall point at the top of the page, and list the main ideas under it. You will find details about making outlines and maps following the reading.

READING 14 | ## THE EFFECTS OF WORK ON MOTIVATION

CAROLE WADE AND CAROL TAVRIS

Carole Wade is a professor of psychology at Dominican College in California. Carol Tavris is the author of The Mismeasure of Woman *and has coauthored several books with Carole Wade, including* Invitation to Psychology *(2001), the textbook from which this reading comes.*

RESPOND
Remember to relate your own experience to the psychologists' findings.

Psychologists who study achievement motivation ask, "How does having an internal motive to achieve affect a person's chances of success?" But others reverse the question, asking, "How does a person's chances of success affect the motive to achieve?" Achievement, they find, does not depend solely on internal expectations, values, and motives—that is, on enduring, unchanging qualities of the individual. It also depends on conditions of the work you do.   1

WORKING CONDITIONS

Several specific aspects of the work environment are known to increase   2
job involvement, work motivation, and job satisfaction (S. Brown, 1996; Kohn & Schooler, 1983):

■ The work provides a sense of meaningfulness.

■ Employees have control over many aspects of their work—for example, they can set their own hours and make decisions.

For underlined words, **Use Context Clues** and **Find the Right Definition.**

■ Tasks are varied rather than repetitive.

■ The company maintains clear and <u>consistent</u> rules for its workers.

- Employees have supportive relationships with their superiors and co-workers.

- Employees receive useful feedback about their work, so they know what they have accomplished and what they need to do to improve.

- The company offers opportunities for its employees' growth and development.

Companies that <u>foster</u> these conditions tend to have more productive   3
and satisfied employees, and this is true in countries as diverse as the Netherlands, Hungary, and Bulgaria (Roe et al., 1998). Workers tend to become more creative in their thinking and feel better about themselves and their work than they do if they feel stuck in routine, boring jobs that give them no control or flexibility over their daily tasks (Karasek & Theorell, 1990; Locke & Latham, 1990). Conversely, when people with high power or achievement motivation are put in situations that frustrate their desire and ability to express these motives, they become dissatisfied and stressed, and their power and achievement motives decline (Jenkins, 1994).

Did you notice anything missing from that list of beneficial working   4
conditions? Where is money, supposedly the great motivator? Actually, work motivation is related not to the amount of money you get, but to how and when you get it. The strongest motivator is *incentive pay,* bonuses that

Like employees, students can have poor working conditions that affect their motivation. They may have to study in crowded quarters or may have small siblings who interrupt or distract them.

are given upon completion of a goal rather than as an automatic raise (Locke et al., 1981). Incentive pay increases people's feelings of <u>competence</u> and accomplishment ("I got this raise because I deserved it"). This doesn't mean that people should accept low pay so they will like their jobs better, or that they should never demand cost-of-living raises!

OPPORTUNITIES TO ACHIEVE: GETTING THE JOB

Another important working condition that affects achievement is hav-   5
ing the *opportunity* to achieve. When someone does not do well at work, others are apt to say it is the individual's own fault because he or she lacks the internal drive to "make it." But what the person may really lack is a fair chance to make it, and this is especially true for those who have been sub-jected to systematic <u>discrimination</u>, such as women and ethnic minorities. At one time, for example, women were said to be less successful than men in the workplace because women had an internalized "fear of success." Yet as opportunities for women improved and sex discrimination was made illegal, this apparent "motive" vanished.

Similarly, when the <u>proportion</u> of men and women in an occupation   6
changes, so do people's motivations to work in that field (Kanter, 1977/ 1993). Many occupations are still highly <u>segregated</u> by gender; there are few male secretaries or female auto mechanics. As a result, many people form gender <u>stereotypes</u> of the requirements of such careers: "Female" jobs require kindness and nurturance, "male" jobs require strength and smarts. These stereotypes, in turn, <u>stifle</u> many people's <u>aspirations</u> to enter a nontraditional career (Cejka & Eagly, 1999). As job segregation breaks down, however, people's motivations change. When law and bartending were almost entirely male professions, few women aspired to become lawyers or bartenders. Now that women make up a large percentage of both occupations, their motivation to become lawyers or bartenders has changed rapidly.

OPPORTUNITIES ON THE JOB

Once in a career, people may become more motivated to advance up   7
the ladder or less so, depending on how many rungs they are permitted to climb. Men *and* women who work in jobs with no <u>prospect</u> of promotion tend to play down the importance of achievement, fantasize about quitting, and emphasize the social benefits of their jobs instead of the intellectual or financial benefits (Kanter, 1977/1993). Consider the comments of a man who realized in his mid–30s that he was never going to be promoted to top

management and who scaled down his ambitions accordingly (Scofield, 1993). As organizational psychologists would predict, he began to emphasize the benefits of not achieving; "I'm freer to speak my mind," "I can choose not to play office politics." He had time, he learned, for coaching Little League and could stay home when the kids were sick. "Of course," he wrote, "if I ever had any chance for upward corporate mobility it's gone now. I couldn't take the grind. Whether real or imagined, that glass ceiling has become an invisible shield."

Women and members of minority groups are especially likely to encounter a real "glass ceiling" in management—a barrier to promotion that is so subtle as to be transparent, yet strong enough to prevent advancement. Researchers can determine that a company has a glass ceiling when a woman or minority person's educational level, work experience, and professional accomplishments do not predict advancement as they do for white men (Graham, 1994; Valian, 1998). [8]

As you can see, work motivation and satisfaction depend on the right fit between qualities of the individual and conditions of the work. Increasingly, in a global economy dependent on an ethnically <u>diverse</u> workforce, companies face the challenge of how best to structure the work environment so that employees will be productive and satisfied, striving to do their best rather than feeling <u>apathetic</u>, resentful, or burned out. [9]

References

Brown, Steven P. (1996). A meta-analysis and review of organizational research on job involvement. *Psychological Bulletin, 120,* 235–153.

Cejka, Mary Ann, & Eagly, Alice H. (1999). Gender-stereotypic images of occupations correspond to the sex segregation of employment. *Personality and Social Psychology Bulletin, 25,* 413–423.

Graham, Sandra (1994). Motivation in African Americans. *Review of Educational Research, 64,* 55–117.

Jenkins, Sharon Rae (1994). Need for power and women's careers over 14 years: Structural power, job satisfaction, and motive change. *Journal of Personality and Social Psychology, 66,* 155–165.

Kanter, Rosabeth M. (1977/1993). *Men and women of the corporation.* New York: Basic Books.

Karasek, Robert, & Theorell, Tores (1990). *Healthy work: Stress, productivity, and the reconstruction of working life.* New York: Basic Books.

Kohn, Melvin, & Schooler, Carmi (1983). *Work and personality: An inquiry into the impact of social stratification.* Norwood, NJ: Ablex.

Locke, Edwin A., & Latham, Gary P. (1990). Work, motivation and satisfaction: Light at the end of the tunnel. *Psychological Science, 1,* 240–246.

Locke, Edwin A.; Shaw, Karyll; Saari, Lise; & Lathan, Gary (1981). Goal-setting and task performance: 1969–1980. *Psychological Bulletin, 90,* 125–152.

Roe, R. A.; Zinovieva, I. L.; Dienes, E.; & Ten Horn, L. A. (1998). Test of a model of work motivation in the Netherlands, Hungary and Bulgaria. Paper presented at the annual meeting of the International Association for Cross-Cultural Psychology, Bellingham, WA.

Scofield, Michael (1993, June 6). About men: Off the ladder. *New York Times Magazine*, p. 22.

Valian, Virginia (1998). *Why so slow? The advancement of women.* Cambridge, MA: MIT Press.

Follow-Up Activities   After you've finished reading, use these activities to respond to "The Effect of Work on Motivation." You may write your answers or prepare them in your mind to discuss in class.

Grab your first impressions.

You've practiced responding in Parts I–III by answering questions to "grab your first impressions." Now **respond** on your own. Say what you like and dislike; relate your personal experiences to the reading; consider what more you want to know.

Work with new words.

Some words in this reading may be unfamiliar to you. Use the methods of Strategies 3 and 4 to explain what the listed words mean.

1. Use context clues.

   a. foster (Paragraph 3) (use logic clues)

   _____

   b. segregated (Paragraph 6) (use logic clues)

   _____

   c. stereotypes (Paragraph 6) (use example clues)

   _____

   d. aspirations (Paragraph 6) (use logic clues)

   _____

2. Use word parts.

   a. discrimination (Paragraph 5) (the prefix "dis-" helps recall the word's meaning) _____

   b. prospect (Paragraph 7) (note the prefix "pro-" and the root "spect")

   _____

c. apathetic (Paragraph 9) (note the prefix "a-" and the root "path")

_____

3. Use the dictionary.

   Choose the correct definition of these words as they are used in the context of this reading.

   a. consistent (Paragraph 2)

   _____

   b. competence (Paragraph 4)

   _____

   c. proportion (Paragraph 6)

   _____

   d. stifle (Paragraph 6)

   _____

   e. diverse (Paragraph 9)

   _____

Ask and answer questions.

1. What happens when a person who has strong "achievement motivation" has to work in a situation that doesn't allow for independence and control over his or her own work?

2. What is "incentive pay"? What effect does it have on work motivation?

3. Which groups of people have been systematically prevented in the past from having the opportunity to achieve?

4. What are the stereotypes of the requirements for "female" jobs? What are the stereotypes of the requirements for "male" jobs? What is the effect of these stereotypes on men's and women's aspirations for entering a nontraditional career?

5. How might an employee appear to demonstrate low achievement motivation to his or her boss? What working condition (or conditions) might be the actual cause of the employee's problem behavior?

 ### Ask and answer your own question.

Write a question of your own. Share your question with others and work together on an answer.

Answer your umbrella question to state the overall point.

Here is an example of an effective umbrella question: "What is the effect of working conditions on motivation?" Can you find the sentence in the reading that answers this question and states the overall point?

Form your final thoughts.

1. What kind of working conditions have you experienced at a job (or jobs)? Discuss with others how you were affected by positive and negative working conditions.

2. In your experience so far, what helps you succeed at a job? Is it your "achievement motivation," the working conditions, or a combination of the two? Explain your answer.   ■

Get a Close-Up of the New Strategy: Write to Remember

You've had a chance to think about and discuss Reading 14. You also tried making a rough outline of the reading's overall point and main ideas. Now learn more about how the new strategy can improve your understanding and recall of a reading's ideas.

Mapping Main Ideas

1 *Map the main ideas and overall point.*

Mapping builds on Strategy 6, **Find Topics and Main Ideas.** Once you've found the main ideas and overall point, you take them into your mind and then write them down on a blank sheet of paper. The act of placing ideas on paper helps you remember them. In addition, seeing the ideas displayed gives you a mental image that stays in your memory. For more ways to work with information in order to remember it, see the "Time Out for You" at the end of this chapter.

Formats for mapping. You can use a variety of formats for making a map of ideas. Three common types are demonstrated in this chapter: a simple outline—like the one you tried for Reading 14—with the overall point at the top and the main ideas listed under it—a *cluster map* and a *box map.*

Here is a sample of a simple outline for Reading 14.

Informal Outline: "The Effects of Work on Motivation"

(Overall point) Achievem. not just depend. on internal motives, but also on work conditions.

    Intro (gives overall point) (¶1)

    1. Working condits. (like more say, more feedback, etc.) make employees satisfied, creative (¶2–4)

       * Incentive pay = better (adds sense of control)

    2. Opportunities to get job = another imp. work condition (¶5–6)

    3. Once in job, motivation depends on prospects for "climbing ladder" (¶7–9)

       *Women & minorities encounter "glass ceiling"

In a cluster map (see page 242) the overall point is placed in the center, with the main ideas branched around it. In a box map (see page 243), the overall point is placed at the top of the page with all the main ideas spaced horizontally below it. The umbrella diagram that follows (see page 243) reminds you that the overall point in a box map is placed like an umbrella to cover all the main ideas of the reading.

Become familiar with each of these types of maps, so you can decide which one works best for you. As you follow the steps for mapping Reading 14, see how you might modify your own rough outline of the reading.

Note form. For mapping in any format, it's best to write in a shortened *note form,* as you do when taking notes in class or writing margin notes. Your notes should communicate only the essential meaning. To shorten and simplify the wording, follow these suggestions:

- Use abbreviations.

- Leave out unnecessary function words (such as "a," "the," "of").

- Leave out unnecessary verbs (such as "is," "are").

- Leave out examples and extra definitions or explanations.

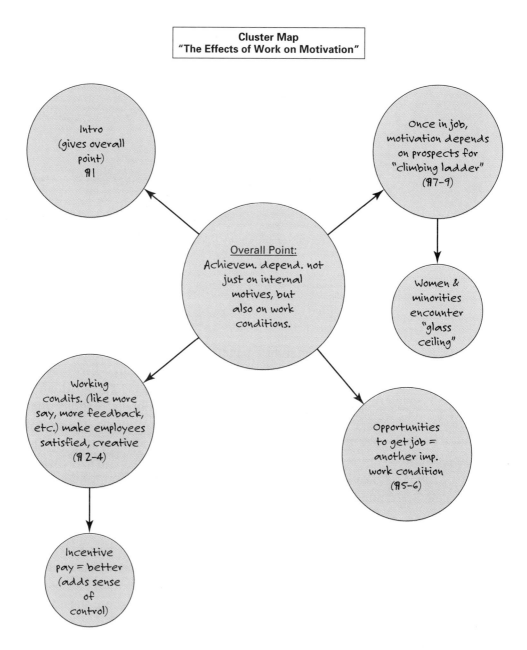

**Cluster Map
"The Effects of Work on Motivation"**

Intro
(gives overall
point)
¶1

Once in job,
motivation depends
on prospects for
"climbing ladder"
(¶7-9)

Overall Point:
Achievem. depend. not
just on internal
motives, but
also on work
conditions.

Women &
minorities
encounter
"glass
ceiling"

Working
condits. (like more
say, more feedback,
etc.) make employees
satisfied, creative
(¶ 2-4)

Opportunities
to get job =
another imp.
work condition
(¶5-6)

Incentive
pay = better
(adds sense
of
control)

Placing overall point and main ideas. Whatever format you choose, be sure it creates a visual image of how the reading is divided into main ideas, each related to the overall point.

You may have found the overall point stated in the reading, or you may have put together your own summary statement of the overall

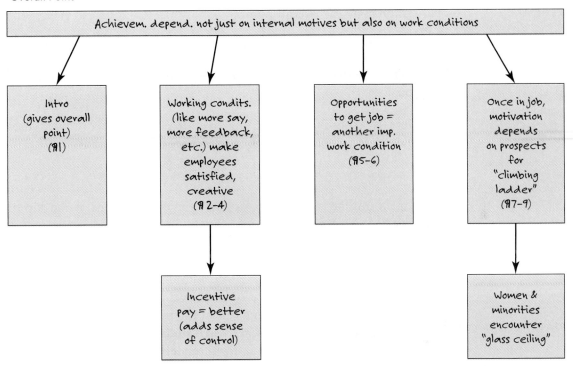

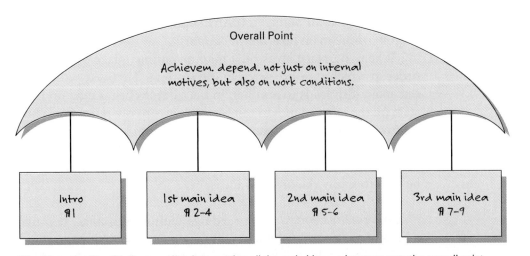

Like this umbrella, with the overall point covering all the main ideas, a box map puts the overall point at the top of the page and spreads it out to cover all the main ideas.

point. In either case, for a cluster map, place a note form of the statement in the center of the page, and circle it. For example, in "The Effects of Work on Motivation," the following sentences in the first paragraph state the overall point:

> Achievement, [psychologists] find, does not depend solely on internal expectations, values, and motives—that is, on enduring, unchanging qualities of the individual. It also depends on conditions of the work you do.

Here is a note version of the overall point. Notice how it uses abbreviations and leaves out unnecessary words and details.

Achievem. depend. not just on internal motives, but also on work conditions.

For an outline or a box map, place the overall point at the top of the page.

For a cluster map, place the main ideas around the overall point to show how they support it. These ideas come out from the central circle like branches. If you need more information on your map, add supporting details to one or more of the main ideas. Put the supporting detail on another branch coming out of the main idea it relates to.

For an outline, main ideas are listed under the overall point. Each main idea is *indented*—moved in from the left margin—to show it supports the overall point. Any supporting detail that is added is placed just below the main idea it supports, and is indented further in from the left margin. For a box map, the main ideas are attached to the bottom of the overall point box. Any supporting detail is attached to the bottom of the main idea box it supports.

When you place ideas on a map or outline, place them in the same order in which they are given in the reading. That way, you show how one main idea leads to another. In the sample cluster map on page 242, start on the left and move counterclockwise to the right. For a box map follow the same order, placing main ideas from left to right. For an outline list the main ideas in order vertically from top to bottom. It also helps to include paragraph numbers on your map or outline, so you'll be sure to know the order of ideas.

Mapping before marking. In readings without headings, you may find it helpful to sketch a rough map of the main topics before marking them in your book. Think what your umbrella question might be, and then sketch on your map or outline the possible main topics. See if the topics lead to answers for your umbrella question. You'll see such a preliminary cluster map for Reading 15 below. Note that in this rough map, the central circle has a question mark. The overall point isn't yet clear. Once you've found the main topics, mark them in your book. Then, for each topic, find the main idea, and, finally, find the overall point.

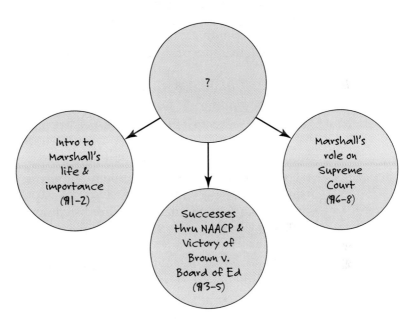

**Preliminary Stage for Cluster Map
"Thurgood Marshall: The Brain of the Civil Rights Movement"**

?

Intro to Marshall's life & importance (¶1–2)

Successes thru NAACP & Victory of Brown v. Board of Ed (¶3–5)

Marshall's role on Supreme Court (¶6–8)

Summarizing

2 Write a summary based on your map or marked reading.

Like mapping, summarizing gets you involved with a reading so you understand and remember more of what you've read. To write a summary, you reduce a reading to its main ideas, stated in your own words. Base your summary on your map of main ideas or on the ideas you marked in your book. That way, you will be sure to include all the important parts of the reading.

Organizing the ideas. The summary should demonstrate the relationship between the overall point, main ideas, and supporting details. If you made a map of ideas, you already have the organization of ideas for your summary. If not, watch for the relationship of the ideas in your marked reading. In either case, follow these guidelines for organizing the ideas.

- Start with the overall point, even if the point doesn't come at the beginning of the reading; that way you show how the overall point "covers" all the other ideas.

- Except for the overall point, follow the order of ideas in the reading.

- Include each main idea.

- Include important supporting details, each one following the main idea it supports.

Paraphrasing. Notes, such as margin notes or notes for your map, leave out all but the essential words. But for a summary to flow easily from one idea to the next, you need complete sentences. A *complete sentence* has to have a subject and a verb. In addition, your sentences may also need extra words and phrases to make the summary clearer. For example, here is a note about the second main idea from the map on page 242:

Opportunities to get job=another imp. work condition

To turn that note into a complete sentence, you need a verb in place of the equal sign. The additional words and phrases help clarify the meaning:

Opportunities to get a job in the first place make up another important working condition.

As you write down the main ideas for your summary, you are *paraphrasing* them. Paraphrasing means translating others' words into your own words. You can be sure you understand the ideas when you can express them in words you feel comfortable with. So when paraphrasing for a summary, try putting the writer's ideas into your everyday language. Here are some guidelines for paraphrasing:

- Write two or more shorter sentences in place of one long one.

- Use a different word order.

■ Choose familiar words that mean the same thing as the original words.

For example, here is an important supporting detail from Paragraph 4 of "The Effect of Work on Motivation," followed by an informal paraphrase of the idea.

> The strongest motivator is *incentive pay,* bonuses that are given upon completion of a goal rather than as an automatic raise.
>
> *Incentive pay means getting extra money when you've completed a goal. That kind of pay motivates people more than raises that come automatically.*

Notice the changes in the paraphrase. It has two sentences, changed word order, and more familiar words ("extra money" for "bonuses" and "motivates people more" instead of "the strongest motivator"). But as you restate ideas in your own words, try not to change the meaning. Don't add new details or leave out important details.

Quoting. Sometimes, even as you paraphrase, it is helpful to quote directly from the reading. You might use a quotation—the exact words used by the writer—when an idea is expressed in an especially effective way. For example, this sentence from Paragraph 7 provides an important supporting detail very clearly: "Once in a career, people may become more motivated to advance up the ladder or less so, depending on how many rungs they are permitted to climb." The quotation helps you imagine a ladder with a variable number of rungs a person is allowed to climb up. This "picture" demonstrates the effect of having opportunities—or not having them—on a person's motivation.

Any time you do use a writer's exact words, be sure you use quotation marks at the beginning and end of the words you've copied to show you are quoting. Also, check to see that you've copied the words exactly.

Setting aside your own ideas. Summarizing a reading helps you clarify the writer's ideas and makes those ideas easier to remember. For this reason, when you summarize, set aside your own ideas. The summary should contain only the writer's ideas. Your personal thoughts and feelings remain important as part of your response to a reading. But keep your response separate from the summary.

Practice Exercise

Write your own summary of Reading 14, based on one of the maps of the reading on pages 242–243.

Is the summary below like the one you wrote? See how the notes from the maps have been made into complete sentences. Notice how the relationship between main ideas and supporting details is expressed verbally instead of visually. The underlining shows the slight changes and added words that make ideas clearer and more complete. Finally, see how quotations are used when the original wording is especially effective.

Sample Summary of "The Effects of Work on Motivation"

Workers' achievement depends on the conditions of work as well as on internal motivation (an individual's unchanging qualities such as values and expectations). There are many different kinds of working conditions that make employees feel satisfied and more creative. Some of these conditions are employees having more say in what they do and getting more feedback about their work. Incentive pay is better than automatic raises because it adds to the employees' sense of control ("I got this raise because I deserved it"). Opportunities to get a job in the first place make up another important working condition. Once in a job, workers' motivation depends a lot on whether the prospects for climbing up the ladder are good or bad. "Women and members of minority groups are especially likely to encounter a real 'glass ceiling' in management" that prevents them from advancing.

Apply the New Strategy: Write to Remember

Before reading "Thurgood Marshall: The Brain of the Civil Rights Movement," Reading 15, **check in.** Then **ask questions,** using appropriate cues, especially the notes before the reading and the introduction. Ask your umbrella question, and predict the topics and overall point. As you read, use all appropriate strategies for understanding main ideas. **Look for Patterns of Thought** is especially helpful. Note the pattern of sequence in the story of Marshall's life and cause-and-effect reasoning in the discussion of his effect on American society.

As you read, try sketching a rough outline or a preliminary map (like the one for Reading 14 on page 241.) Active writing while reading will help you remember what you've read.

READING 15 ## THURGOOD MARSHALL: THE BRAIN
OF THE CIVIL RIGHTS MOVEMENT

ADAM COHEN

This reading by Adam Cohen first appeared in a 1999 issue of Time *magazine. Thurgood Marshall's career demonstrates how possibilities for all Americans opened up during his lifetime—"the grandson of a slave, he became the first black Justice of the U.S. Supreme Court." His career is also an example of work that is a "calling," a vocation with purpose. For Marshall the profession of law was never a mere job. It was his way of working for justice for all Americans.*

For underlined words, **Use Context Clues** and **Find the Right Definition.**

N.A.A.C.P: National Association for the Advancement of Colored People (founded in 1909)

Thurgood Marshall got his start traveling the South in a beat-up 1929   1
Ford with a colleague, banging out legal papers in the car on a manual typewriter. Taking on <u>Jim Crow</u>, the South's <u>entrenched</u> <u>regime</u> of racial <u>segregation</u>, was dangerous work. When Marshall made the rounds of black schools in Mississippi, documenting their shacklike buildings and <u>paltry</u> textbooks, the state N.A.A.C.P.° president arranged to have a hearse filled with armed men follow Marshall's car for protection.

RESPOND

Notice any connections between your previous knowledge and the new information.

Marshall went on to become one of the most important lawyers of the   2
20th century. He was the architect of one of America's most radical transformations: the removal of legal racism, root and branch, from the nation's leading institutions. Just as important, Marshall's personal journey—the grandson of a slave, he became the first black Justice of the U.S. Supreme Court—was a shining example of the more open society he dedicated his life to achieving.

Howard Law School: historically black institution

hung up a shingle: began his law practice

He was born in Baltimore, Md., in 1908, when it was still a sleepy   3
Southern town, and he attended its segregated schools. After graduating from Howard Law School°—the University of Maryland's law school didn't admit blacks—Marshall hung up a shingle° in his hometown and did volunteer legal work for the local N.A.A.C.P. One of his early cases challenged pay gaps in education—black elementary school teachers in Maryland earned $621 a year, while white janitors made $960. Marshall's mother was one of those underpaid teachers.

Working full time for the N.A.A.C.P., Marshall persuaded the Supreme   4
Court to integrate Missouri's all-white law school. He also got it to strike down Texas' whites-only primary elections. And he <u>prevailed</u> on the court to stop Virginia from ordering blacks traveling through on interstate buses to move to the back of the bus. But Marshall's greatest victory was in *Brown v. Board of Education.* That landmark ruling, handed down on May 17, 1954, held that "separate but equal" public schools for blacks and whites violated the Constitution. It caused a firestorm as the South vowed "massive resistance" to school integration. When Marshall appeared on NBC's *Youth Wants to Know,* Georgia stations replaced the show with a taped address by segregationist Governor Herman Talmadge.

Marshall never doubted that his side would <u>prevail</u> in the end. "You   5
can say all you want," Marshall told a black newspaper publisher not long
after *Brown* was decided, "but those white crackers are going to get tired
of having Negro lawyers beating them every day in court." In time Marshall would persuade the court to extend the *Brown* principles to public
accommodations ranging from public housing to beaches.

In 1961 President Kennedy appointed Marshall to the Second Circuit   6
Court of Appeals° in New York. Four years later, President Johnson named
him Solicitor General—the government's top Supreme Court lawyer—and
in 1967 Johnson spoke of "the right thing to do, the right time to do it, the
right man and the right place" and named Marshall to the Supreme Court.

Marshall penned some of the court's most important decisions, includ-   7
ing a sweeping 1969 ruling upholding people's right to possess pornography in their home and a 1972 decision striking down the death penalty
because of the <u>inconsistent</u> way in which it was applied by judges and
juries. He brought an iconoclastic perspective° to the cloistered world of
the high court. When fellow Justices struck down racial quotas in medical-
school admissions, Marshall took issue with those who said poor whites
should be given the same help as blacks. "There's not a white man in this
country who can say he never benefited from being white," Marshall said.
He could be bitingly <u>acerbic</u>, falling into slave dialect and calling the other
Justices "Massa." In 1980, when the University of Maryland Law School
dedicated its new library to him, Marshall wouldn't attend the ceremony.
The school was just "trying to <u>salve</u> its conscience for excluding the
Negroes," he said. As the court grew colder to civil rights, he did little to
hide his bitterness. In one of his last opinions before his retirement in 1991,
Marshall complained that "power not reason is the new currency of this
court's decision making." He died on Jan. 24, 1993.

The Constitution, Marshall once declared, was "<u>defective</u> from the   8
start" because it permitted slavery. But he also recognized that its "true
miracle" was not how it was <u>conceived</u>, but how it <u>evolved</u>. He forced the
nation to evolve along with it.

Court of Appeals: hears appeals of decisions of lower courts

"iconoclastic perspective . . . high court": independent and rebellious views challenged more sheltered world of court

Follow-Up Activities   After you've finished reading, use these activities to
respond to "Thurgood Marshall: The Brain of the Civil Rights Movement." You
may write your answers or prepare them in your mind to discuss in class.

Grab your first impressions.

You've practiced responding in Parts I–III by answering questions to
"grab your first impressions." Now **respond** on your own. Say what you like

and dislike; relate your personal experiences to the reading; consider what more you want to know.

Work with new words.

Some words in this reading may be unfamiliar to you. Use the methods of Strategies 3 and 4 to explain what the listed words mean.

1. Use context clues.

   a. Jim Crow (Paragraph 1) (don't miss the definition clue)

   _____

   b. prevailed/prevail (Paragraphs 4 and 5) (use logic clues, and see the slightly different meanings depending on the context)

   _____

   c. salve (Paragraph 7) (use logic clues)

   _____

   d. defective (Paragraph 8) (use logic clues)

   _____

2. Use word parts.

   a. entrenched (Paragraph 1) (see the word "trench" and use logic clues)

   _____

   b. inconsistent (Paragraph 7) (see how the prefix changes the meaning of "consistent," or "constant")

   _____

   c. evolved (Paragraph 8) (related to the word "evolution" meaning "development")

   _____

3. Use the dictionary.

   Choose the correct definition of these words as they are used in the context of this reading.

   a. regime (Paragraph 1)

   _____

   b. segregation (Paragraph 1)

   _____

c. paltry (Paragraph 1)

_____

d. acerbic (Paragraph 7)

_____

e. conceived (Paragraph 8)

_____

Ask and answer questions.

1. What was Marshall documenting as he rode through Mississippi? What made his work so dangerous that the N.A.A.C.P. arranged for protection for him?

2. What made Marshall's personal journey a "shining example" of the more open society he worked for during his lifetime?

3. What was one of Marshall's early victories in working for the N.A.A.C.P.?

4. What was the Supreme Court decision known as *Brown v. Board of Education?* What further changes based on the "*Brown* principles" did Marshall persuade the court to make?

5. What does Cohen mean in Paragraph 7 by "iconoclastic perspective"? Why does he say Marshall brought this perspective to the "cloistered world of the high court." Give an example of Marshall's iconoclastic perspective.

 ### *Ask and answer your own question.*

Write a question of your own. Share your question with others, and work together on an answer.

Sample Marking

▮READING 15▮ THURGOOD MARSHALL: THE BRAIN OF THE CIVIL RIGHTS MOVEMENT

ADAM COHEN

Thurgood Marshall got his start traveling the South in a beat-up 1929   1
Ford with a colleague, banging out legal papers in the car on a manual typewriter. <u>Taking on Jim Crow, the South's entrenched regime of racial segregation, was dangerous work.</u> When Marshall made the rounds of black schools in Mississippi, documenting their shacklike buildings and paltry textbooks, the state N.A.A.C.P. president arranged to have a hearse filled with armed men follow Marshall's car for protection.

ex: early fight

Marshall = leader in ending legal racism & pers. ex. of possibs. in open society

overall point

Marshall went on to become one of the most important lawyers of the 20th century. He was the <u>architect</u> of one of America's most <u>radical trans-formations: the removal of legal racism,</u> root and branch, from the nation's leading institutions. Just as important, Marshall's personal <u>journey</u>—the <u>grandson of a slave,</u> he became the <u>first black Justice of the U.S. Supreme Court</u>—was a shining <u>example</u> of the more <u>open society he dedicated his life to achieving.</u>

ex: early success

He was <u>born in Baltimore, Md., in 1908,</u> when it was still a sleepy Southern town, and <u>he attended its segregated schools. After graduating from Howard Law School</u>—the University of Maryland's law school didn't admit blacks—Marshall hung up a shingle in his hometown and <u>did volunteer legal work for the local N.A.A.C.P.</u> One of his early cases challenged pay gaps in education—black elementary school teachers in Maryland earned $621 a year, while white janitors made $960. Marshall's mother was one of those underpaid teachers.

got rights for blacks

Successes thru NAACP + Victory of Brown v. Board of Ed

Working full time for the N.A.A.C.P., Marshall persuaded the Supreme Court to integrate Missouri's all-white law school. He also got it to strike down Texas' whites-only primary elections. And he <u>prevailed</u> on the court to stop Virginia from ordering blacks traveling through on interstate buses to move to the back of the bus. But Marshall's greatest victory was in *Brown v. Board of Education.* That landmark ruling, handed down on May 17, <u>1954,</u> held that <u>"separate but equal" public schools for blacks and whites violated the Constitution.</u> It caused <u>a firestorm as the South vowed "massive resistance"</u> to school integration. When Marshall appeared on NBC's *Youth Wants to Know,* Georgia stations replaced the show with a taped address by segregationist Governor Herman Talmadge.

extended Brown princips.

Marshall never doubted that his side would <u>prevail</u> in the end. "You can say all you want," Marshall told a black newspaper publisher not long after *Brown* was decided, "but those white crackers are going to get tired of having Negro lawyers beating them every day in court." In time <u>Marshall would persuade the court to extend the *Brown* principles to public accommodations ranging from public housing to beaches.</u>

In 1961 President Kennedy appointed Marshall to the Second Circuit Court of Appeals in New York. Four years later, President Johnson named him Solicitor General—the government's top Supreme Court lawyer—and in <u>1967 Johnson spoke of "the right thing to do, the right time to do it, the right man and the right place" and named Marshall to the Supreme Court.</u>

Imp. decisions

Role on court

Marshall penned some of the court's most important decisions, including a sweeping <u>1969</u> ruling upholding <u>people's right to possess pornography in their home</u> and a <u>1972 decision striking down the death penalty because of the inconsistent way in which it was applied</u> by judges and

*points of view
challenged
established
beliefs*

*Role on
Court*

*bitterness in
final years*

*Belief in
evolving
constitution*

juries. He brought an <u>iconoclastic perspective to the cloistered world of the high court.</u> When fellow Justices struck down racial quotas in medical-school admissions, Marshall took issue with those who said poor whites should be given the same help as blacks. "There's not a white man in this country who can say he never benefited from being white," Marshall said. He could be bitingly acerbic, falling into slave dialect and calling the other Justices "Massa." In 1980, when the University of Maryland Law School dedicated its new library to him, Marshall wouldn't attend the ceremony. The school was just "trying to salve its conscience for excluding the Negroes," he said. <u>As the court grew colder to civil rights, he did little to hide his bitterness.</u> In one of his last opinions before his retirement in 1991, Marshall complained that "power not reason is the new currency of this court's decision making." He died on Jan. 24, 1993.

The <u>Constitution,</u> Marshall once declared, was <u>"defective from the start" because it permitted slavery. But</u> he also recognized that its "true <u>miracle"</u> was not how it was conceived, but <u>how it evolved.</u> He forced the nation to evolve along with it.   8

Answer your umbrella question to state the overall point.

Here is an example of an effective umbrella question: "What made Thurgood Marshall 'the brain' of the Civil Rights movement?" Can you form a statement using your own words that answers this question and summarizes the overall point?

Make a map and write a summary.

Make your own outline or other type of map. Then write a summary of Reading 15. You can base your own map on the rough sample on page 245 and the sample marking of the reading on pages 252–254.

 Form your final thoughts.

1. From this account of Marshall's life, what do you think led him to devote so much of his energy to cases regarding discrimination in education?

2. Who do you know—personally or through the media—whose work seems to be a "calling" for them? What is that work? Why is it so important to them?

3. What kind of work can you imagine doing that would give you a great sense of purpose? Is this work that you could do for a career? Or might you do this work on a volunteer basis? Explain your answer.   ■

Chapter 9 Summary

How does Strategy 9 help you *use your reader's voice to be an active reader?*

In **writing to remember,** you map or summarize a writer's ideas to make them easier to understand and to refer back to and remember. You use your reader's voice when you restate the writer's ideas in your own words. In addition, by putting the ideas on paper you see them more clearly, so you have more to say about them.

How does the *write to remember* strategy work?

Strategy 9, **Write to Remember,** gives you two guidelines for setting down a reading's ideas on paper. The first guideline is to make a map, a visual representation that shows the relationship between the overall point and main ideas. The second guideline is to write a brief summary, a paragraph that restates the reading's main ideas in your own words. The summary is based on your map or on the ideas you marked in your book. Here are the two guidelines for Strategy 9.

STRATEGY 9: WRITE TO REMEMBER

1 Map the main ideas and overall point.

2 Write a summary based on your map or marked reading.

Are you familiar with the meaning of these terms?

box map: organization of ideas displayed with the overall point at the top and main ideas spaced horizontally below it

cluster map: organization of ideas displayed with the overall point in the center and main ideas branched around it

complete sentence: sentence that has a subject and verb and expresses a complete thought

indent: in an outline, move in from the left margin

map: a skeleton of a reading's organization of ideas

note form: shortened form of writing, such as margin notes or class notes

outline: vertical listing of ideas with the overall point at the top and main ideas below it

paraphrase: translate others' words into your own words

summary: brief—usually one-paragraph—restatement of main ideas

How is the strategy working for you so far?

Explain which parts of **writing to remember** you've found most helpful in the readings you've practiced with. Which parts have been least helpful?

TIME OUT FOR YOU

How Can You Improve Your Memory?

How much do you remember from readings or class lectures? Probably not as much as you'd like—especially when a test is coming up. But you can develop a better memory. First, get an idea of how we remember. Then learn some useful memory techniques.

Attention and Memory

Memory isn't just something you use when you want to recall a piece of information—a friend's telephone number or an important math formula. It's something you use by paying attention in the first place—when a friend gives you a phone number or a teacher writes an important math formula on the board.

What grabs our attention is what we remember. That's why you may remember the tattoos on the student sitting next to you in history class but forget what the professor was saying about the Civil War. So, if there's something you need to remember—a famous battle of the Civil War, for example—you have to find ways to focus your attention on it.

Memory Techniques

Memory techniques keep you mentally alert as you pay attention to the information. They also help you trace memory pathways in the brain. These pathways then lead you to the information when you need it. The first of the following memory techniques is the one most people are aware of using. But to improve your memory, the second and third techniques are especially helpful.

Use repetition

You've probably depended on repetition—or rote memory—for remembering details such as a telephone number, a math formula, or the spelling of a word. Repetition can work for such details, especially if you review them from time to time. But you need more than rote memory for the information in most college courses.

Make connections

To remember most information, your mind needs to be actively involved in finding meaningful connections. Often you can find meaning by connecting new material to previous knowledge. Textbook writers and your instructors use examples and explanations from everyday life to help you make these connections. For example, suppose you needed to remember the definition of "Type A" behavior for a health science test. The textbook would define the Type A person as competitive, aggressive, pressed for time, and short tempered. Your textbook might give an example of a Type A person at work, swearing, racing around the office, trying to do at least two tasks at the same time, and constantly complaining. This example would help you connect Type A behavior with behavior you're familiar with.

Your mind also becomes actively involved as you make meaningful connections among new pieces of information. Here are some guidelines:

- Look for the differences as well as similarities. (Both Type A and Type B are general types of behavior, but Type A is the opposite of Type B behavior, which is slower paced, cooperative, patient, and calm.)

- "Translate" terms into your own words. ("A Type A person has to be on top, and is hard-hitting, always in a hurry, and easily irritated.")

- Number the things you need to remember. There are four characteristics used to describe the Type A behavior. Quick—can you name them?

Use your senses

You can increase your memory of a piece of information by involving your senses. Use your sense of:

- Touch and movement (and sight). Write things down.

- Sight. Visualize things—imagine a vivid scene, make a simple drawing, or make details stand out by using a special color.

- Sound. Use rhymes ("i before e except after c"), or make up an acronym you can pronounce. An acronym is a word composed of the first letters of each word—as CAPS, for competitive, aggressive, pressed for time, and short tempered—the qualities that make up Type A behavior.

- Humor. Make your drawings or rhymes so silly they'll stand out in your mind.

CHAPTER 10

MAKE INFERENCES

You've learned several strategies for understanding and remembering ideas in a reading. Strategy 10, **Make Inferences,** gives you ways to interpret meaning when ideas are *implied*—suggested—rather than spelled out in a direct statement. Strategy 6, **Find Topics and Main Ideas,** already introduced you to unstated, that is implied, main ideas. You learned in that strategy to express an unstated main idea in a summary statement that pulled together all the important details. **Making inferences** expands your ability to grasp the meaning of implied ideas. As you increase your understanding of the writer's ideas, you gain a stronger reader's voice to respond to them.

Introduction to the New Strategy: Make Inferences

We're used to understanding implied ideas in our daily life. We see pieces of evidence, put the pieces together, and draw a logical conclusion based on that evidence. When we do this, we're **making inferences**—well-informed guesses—about what we see. For example, if you looked outside and saw everyone using an umbrella, you would make an inference—or *infer*—that it's raining, even if you couldn't see the rain. Strategy 10 shows you how to make similar kinds of inferences when you read.

STRATEGY 10: MAKE INFERENCES

1 Recognize implied ideas as well as stated ideas.

2 Make logical connections.

3 Consider word choice.

4 Make sense of metaphors.

Inferences and Implied Ideas

1 Recognize implied ideas as well as stated ideas.

The following sentences show how implied ideas are communicated from writer to reader.

- The writer *implies* an idea.

- The reader *infers* that idea, that is, **makes an inference** about it.

Here's an example of an implied idea communicated in an e-mail message. Let's say Dan wrote these words to his sister, Alicia:

> You sure were coughing a lot when you visited. Have you thought about the new nicotine patches? I think they work a lot better now.

Dan never states outright that he is worried about Alicia's smoking. Instead, he implies his worry. Alicia would get the full meaning by going beyond the stated message. She would **make an inference** by putting together his mention of her cough and his question about a nicotine patch. You probably already recognized what was on Dan's mind as he wrote to Alicia. As readers, we sometimes use the phrase "reading between the lines" when we infer ideas in this way.

Logical Connections

2 Make logical connections.

In **making inferences** we make logical connections between separate pieces of information. To any new information, we usually add our *prior knowledge*, information based on our past experience. We put all the information together to come up with a reasonable conclusion. A common expression for making these connections is "putting two and two together."

In the sample e-mail message, Alicia would make a connection between her brother's comment about her cough and his question about the nicotine patch. She might also add in her prior experience of her brother's suggesting that she give up cigarettes. Connecting all these pieces of information, she would infer that he was worried about her smoking.

You make logical connections whenever you look at a cartoon and laugh. The humor in a cartoon depends on making connections to get the implied idea. To understand what's funny, you put together the visual image and what the characters say. What prior knowledge do you draw on to understand this cartoon?

"Sorry, sir, we're filming a truck commercial up here."

by Nick Downes

Here are some things you recognize to understand the cartoon:

- the popular type of TV ad for rugged trucks on top of a mountain
- the obvious effort and danger for the mountain climber
- the ridiculousness of the TV filming crew's statement to the climber

You often use your prior knowledge to understand what's funny about a cartoon. For example, for this next cartoon, you need to think back to your knowledge of fairy tales. In those tales, a person can be turned into a frog by a witch. You also need to know something about how suspects are identified in criminal cases. You've probably seen these set-ups on TV or in the movies. This cartoon has no words, so what other parts of the picture do you need to put together to get the humor?

by Edward Frascino

Practice Exercises

Now read this passage from Reading 16, "Serving in Florida." Try "putting two and two together" to find the implied ideas. Here, the author, Barbara Ehrenreich, begins describing her first day as a waitress. (The sentences are numbered so you can refer back to them easily.)

(1) So begins my career at the Hearthside [Restaurant], where for two weeks I work from 2:00 till 10:00 P.M. for $2.43 an hour plus tips. (2) Employees are barred from using the front door, so I enter the first day through the kitchen, where a red-faced man with shoulder-length blond hair is throwing frozen steaks against the wall and yelling.... (3) "That's just Billy," explains Gail, the wiry middle-aged waitress who is assigned to train me.... (4) The cook on the morning shift had forgotten to thaw out the steaks. (5) For the next eight hours, I run after the agile Gail, absorbing bits of instruction along with fragments of personal tragedy.... (6) After [Gail's boyfriend] was gone she spent several months living in her truck, peeing in a plastic pee bottle and reading by candlelight at night, but you can't live in a truck in the summer, since you need to have the windows down, which means anything can get in, from mosquitoes on up.

In these sentences the author gives a lot of information, both stated and implied. First, note the following stated ideas. Fill in the blanks with information that is spelled out in the passage.

1. At the Hearthside Ehrenreich earned _____.

2. Ehrenreich was trained by _____.

3. When Ehrenreich came in, Billy was yelling and _____
   _____.

4. The cook on the morning shift forgot _____
   _____.

5. Gail had spent several months living _____
   _____.

Now look for implied ideas in this passage. Try "putting two and two together" about the situations and people by thinking about what the separate pieces of information add up to. The first item is done for you.

1. What does Sentence 2 imply about working conditions at the restaurant?

   Employees are prevented ("barred") from using the "front door" (where cus-
   tomers go in). This indicates they're told (not asked) what to do and are
   treated a bit like servants having to use the kitchen door.

2. What do Sentences 2, 3, and 4 imply about Billy's emotional state?

   _____

   _____

   _____

3. What do Sentences 3, and 5 imply about Gail? For example, how does she react to Billy? How experienced is she at her job?

   _____

   _____

4. What does Sentence 6 imply about Gail's financial situation?

   _____

   _____

5. What does Gail mean in Sentence 6, when she says, "anything can get in, from mosquitoes on up"?

   _____

   _____

Word Choice

3 Consider word choice.

In daily life we also infer meaning from the choice of words people use. One word can change the meaning of a whole sentence. Take these two different answers to the question, "What's Margarita doing now?"

She's talking on the phone.

She's blabbing on the phone.

The first gives a simple statement, without expressing any special meaning about the kind of talking. The meaning of the answer changes when the word "blabbing" replaces "talking." Both words have the same basic meaning, or *denotation*. "Talk" and "blab" both mean "to express in speech." But the second word has a special meaning—*connotation*—associated with it. It means "to talk idly or thoughtlessly." If we heard the word "blabbing," we would know that the speaker was making a negative comment about what Margarita was doing.

Be aware that writers often imply meaning through their choice of words. Watch for words with special connotations.

Denotation. Denotation, or *denotative meaning,* refers to a word's basic or literal meaning. As you just saw, the denotative meaning of "talk" is "to express in speech."

Connotation. Connotation, or *connotative meaning,* refers to suggestions or emotional responses a word may carry with it. These connotations add to the denotative meaning of the word. The added meaning may be positive, negative, or specialized in some way. The word "blab" has a negative connotation. It adds a cluster of negative suggestions—idle, thoughtless, and in some cases, gossipy—to its denotative meaning.

The second sentence of the sample passage gives an example of a word with a special connotation. Ehrenreich could have said, "employees were not allowed to use the front door." Those words would have had the same denotation as the words she actually chose: "barred from using the front door." But "barred" brings with it the association of a bar coming down across the door. It gives a much stronger sense of keeping someone out.

Practice Exercises

Like the word "barred," many words always have a special connotation. The meaning of "talk" is purely neutral. But in addition to "blab" there are several other words with the same denotative meaning that have special connotations. Compare these four words. What different connotations does each verb have for showing a different way of talking?

babble   mutter

converse   chat

The following pairs of words have the same denotative meaning but different connotations. Which word in the pair is either neutral or positive? Which one has a special—usually negative—meaning?

walk	stagger	grab	take
stuffy	formal	discuss	argue
news	gossip	strong	tough
rigid	firm	brainy	intelligent

Metaphors

4 *Make sense of metaphors.*

Another way writers imply meaning beyond their actual words is by using *metaphors.*

Familiar metaphors. A *metaphor* is based on a surprising and imaginative comparison that highlights a particular image or idea. The words that make up a metaphor aren't used in their *literal,* that is their ordinary or primary, meaning. Instead, the words are used to suggest a new way of imagining someone or something. There are familiar metaphors we use frequently in our everyday speech. Here are three:

My boss is a bear.

The employees are suffering from burnout.

The cashier was so green he still couldn't work the cash register.

Obviously, the word "bear" doesn't carry its ordinary or literal meaning. Instead, it is used to suggest the power and fierceness of the boss. Similarly, the word "burnout" doesn't literally mean the employees have gone up in flames. But they are so physically and mentally exhausted they feel as if they've burned up all their resources. Finally, the cashier doesn't have green-colored skin. The word "green" refers to his being inexperienced, as if he were "unripe," like green fruit.

The broader sense of metaphor. The word metaphor sometimes refers to a specific kind of surprising comparison, one that doesn't use "like" or "as." In contrast, a *simile* spells out the comparison by using "like" or "as." Notice the familiar simile underlined in this sentence: "My mother watches me like a hawk."

For the purposes of **making inferences,** think of metaphor in its bigger sense. In this broader meaning, the term metaphor covers all comparisons that point to an imaginative, nonliteral meaning. Writers use both common metaphors and new ones. To recognize new metaphors, see if the words are being used in a nonliteral way.

Practice Exercises

Underline the metaphors in the following paragraph from Reading 1, "Poppa and the Spruce Tree." You can recognize the metaphors in words or phrases that are used in a nonliteral way so that they create a surprising picture or idea in your mind.

In Paragraph 5, Mario Cuomo describes the fallen spruce tree in this way:

> The spruce [was] pulled almost totally from the ground and flung forward, its mighty nose bent in the asphalt of the street . . . . When we saw our spruce, defeated, its cheek on the canvas, our hearts sank.

Now try explaining the imaginative comparisons each metaphor makes. Or, you might try making a simple drawing that illustrates the comparison.

_____

_____

_____

Here are the three metaphors: "its mighty nose," "its cheek on the canvas," and "our hearts sank." Note the following explanations for each metaphor.

■ The "mighty nose": when it's standing, the tree's top could be compared to a person's head. So, when it fell, its pointed, nose-shaped top fell to the ground the way a person's face would, nose first.

■ The "cheek on the canvas": the tree's top is still compared to a person's face. But this time another comparison is added. When a boxer is knocked down, his cheek is literally on the canvas of the boxing ring. In this case, the tree was knocked down so hard it seemed "knocked out," the way a boxer is knocked out, with his face on the canvas.

■ "Our hearts sank": this expression is so familiar, you might not recognize it as metaphorical. Hearts don't literally sink. But disappointment can make you feel as if your heart drops lower down in your body.

Apply the New Strategy: Make Inferences

You've already looked for implied ideas in the first paragraph of "Serving in Florida." As you read about Ehrenreich's experience, **make inferences,** that is, look for implied ideas in the reading.

CHECK IN

Before reading, **check in.** Then **ask questions,** using appropriate cues, especially the notes before the reading and the first paragraph. Ask your umbrella question and predict the topics and overall point. As you read, use all appropriate strategies for understanding main ideas. Note the writer's use of examples and other supporting details that give clear pictures of her job, her customers, and her coworkers.

READING 16 ## SERVING IN FLORIDA

BARBARA EHRENREICH

This reading is an excerpt from Barbara Ehrenreich's best-seller, Nickel and Dimed: On (Not) Getting By in America *(2001). Ehrenreich is a well-known lecturer and writer on social issues. She has published 12 books and is a frequent contributor to such magazines as* Time *and* Harper's. *In the late 1990s, Ehrenreich wondered about the welfare reform promise that everyone would be better off working, no matter what the job. How do millions of Americans make do working full-time at poverty-level wages? To see for herself, she went "undercover," working at various low-wage jobs, first in Florida, then in Maine and Minnesota. Part of her title—"On (Not) Getting By"—sums up her experience. In this excerpt, she starts off in her first job: as a waitress, or "server."*

So begins my career at the Hearthside, where for two weeks I work   1
from 2:00 till 10:00 P.M. for $2.43 an hour plus tips.[1] Employees are barred from using the front door, so I enter the first day through the kitchen, where a red-faced man with shoulder-length blond hair is throwing frozen

---

[1] According to the Fair Labor Standards Act, employers are not required to pay "tipped employees," such as restaurant servers, more than $2.13 an hour in direct wages. However, if the sum of tips plus $2.13 an hour falls below the minimum wage, or $5.15 an hour, the employer is required to make up the difference. This fact was not mentioned by managers or otherwise publicized at either of the restaurants where I worked.

steaks against the wall and yelling . . . . "That's just Billy," explains Gail, the wiry middle-aged waitress who is assigned to train me . . . . The cook on the morning shift had forgotten to thaw out the steaks. For the next eight hours, I run after the <u>agile</u> Gail, absorbing bits of instruction along with fragments of personal tragedy. All food must be trayed, and the reason she's so tired today is that she woke up in a cold sweat thinking of her boyfriend, who was killed a few months ago in a scuffle in an upstate prison. No refills on lemonade. And the reason he was in prison is that a few DUIs° caught up with him, that's all, could have happened to anyone. Carry the creamers to the table in a "monkey bowl," never in your hand. And after he was gone she spent several months living in her truck, peeing in a plastic pee bottle and reading by candlelight at night, but you can't live in a truck in the summer, since you need to have the windows down, which means anything can get in, from mosquitoes on up.

At least Gail puts to rest any fears I had of appearing overqualified. From the first day on, I find that of all the things that I have left behind, such as home and identity, what I miss the most is competence. Not that I have ever felt 100 percent competent in the writing business, where one day's success <u>augurs</u> nothing at all for the next. But in my writing life, I at least have some notion of *procedure:* do the research, make the outline, rough out a draft, etc. As a server, though, I am beset by requests as if by bees: more iced tea here, catsup over there, a to-go box for table 14, and where are the high chairs, anyway? Of the twenty-seven tables, up to six are usually mine at any time, though on slow afternoons or if Gail is off, I sometimes have the whole place to myself. There is the touch-screen computer-ordering system to master, which I suppose is meant to minimize server-cook contacts but in practice requires constant verbal fine-tuning: "That's gravy on the mashed, OK? None on the meatloaf," and so forth. Plus, something I had forgotten in the years since I was eighteen: about a third of a server's job is "side work" invisible to customer—sweeping, scrubbing, slicing, refilling, and restocking. If it isn't all done, every little bit of it, you're going to face the 6:00 P.M. dinner rush defenseless and probably go down in flames. I screw up dozens of times at the beginning, sustained in my shame entirely by Gail's support—"It's OK, baby, everyone does that sometime"—because, to my total surprise and despite the scientific detachment I am doing my best to maintain, I *care.* . . .

After a few days at Hearthside, I feel the service ethic° kick in. . . . The plurality of my customers are hardworking locals—truck drivers, construction workers, even housekeepers from the attached hotel—and I want them to have the closest to a "fine dining" experience that the grubby circumstances will allow. No "you guys" for me; everyone over twelve is "sir" or

2

3

For underlined words, **Use Context Clues** and **Find the Right Definition.**

DUI: driving under the influence of alcohol

RESPOND
Imagine yourself in Ehrenreich's circumstances. How would you feel?

service ethic: sense of duty toward those one serves

Ehrenreich sees firsthand the real-world survival struggles of restaurant workers, like this waitress. What has been your experience—or that of your friends—working in a restaurant?

"ma'am." I <u>ply</u> them with iced tea and coffee refills; I return, midmeal, to inquire how everything is; I doll up their salads with chopped raw mushrooms, summer squash slices, or whatever bits of produce I can find that have survived their <u>sojourn</u> in the cold storage room mold-free.

There is Benny, for example, a short, tight-muscled sewer repairman who cannot even think of eating until he has absorbed a half hour of air-conditioning and ice water. We chat about <u>hyperthermia</u> and electrolytes° until he is ready to order some finicky combination like soup of the day, garden salad, and a side of grits. There are the German tourists who are so touched by my pidgin *"Wilkommen"* and *"Ist alles gut?"* that they actually tip. (Europeans, no doubt spoiled by their trade union–ridden, high-wage welfare states, generally do not know that they are supposed to tip. Some restaurants, the Hearthside included, allow servers to "grat" their foreign customers, or add a tip to the bill. Since this amount is added before the customers have a chance to tip or not tip, the practice amounts to an automatic penalty for imperfect English.) There are the two dirt-smudged lesbians, just off from their shift, who are impressed enough by my <u>suave</u> handling of the fly in the piña colada that they take the time to praise me to Stu, the assistant manager. There's Sam, the kindly retired cop who has to plug up his tracheotomy° hole with one finger in order to force the cigarette smoke into his lungs.

4

electrolytes: chemical compounds in the human body

tracheotomy: surgical opening in the windpipe to allow breathing

"penance . . . transgression":
self-punishment to show
sorrow for past wrongdoing

Sometimes I play with the fantasy that I am a princess who, in penance°   5
for some tiny transgression, has undertaken to feed each of her subjects by
hand. But the nonprincesses working with me are just as <u>indulgent</u>, even
when this means ignoring management rules—as to, for example, the
number of croutons that can go on a salad (six). "Put on all you want," Gail
whispers, "as long as Stu isn't looking." She dips into her own tip money
to buy biscuits and gravy for an out-of-work mechanic who's used up all
his money on dental surgery, inspiring me to pick up the tab for his pie and
milk. Maybe the same high levels of love for others can be found throughout the "hospitality industry°." I remember the poster decorating one of the
apartments I looked at, which said, "If you seek happiness for yourself you
will never find it. Only when you seek happiness for others will it come to
you," or words to that effect—an odd sentiment, it seemed to me at the
time, to find in the dank° one-room basement apartment of a bellhop at the
Best Western. At Hearthside, we utilize whatever bits of <u>autonomy</u> we have
to ply our customers with the <u>illicit</u> calories that signal our love. It is our job
as servers to assemble the salads and desserts, pour the dressings, and
squirt the whipped cream. We also control the number of butter pats our
customers get and the amount of sour cream on their baked potatoes. So if
you wonder why Americans are so obese, consider the fact that waitresses
both express their humanity and earn their tips through the <u>covert</u> distribution of fats.

"hospitality industry":
businesses such as
restaurants and hotels

dank: damp, chilly

Ten days into it, this is beginning to look like a livable lifestyle. I like   6
Gail, who is "looking at fifty," agewise, but moves so fast she can alight in
one place and then another without apparently being anywhere between. I
clown around with Lionel, the teenage Haitian busboy, though we don't
have much vocabulary in common, and loiter near the main sink to listen
to the older Haitian dishwashers' musical Creole, which sounds, in their
rich bass voices, like French on testosterone°. I bond with Timmy, the four-
teen-year-old white kid who buses at night, by telling him I don't like people putting their baby seats right on the tables: it makes the baby look too
much like a side dish. He snickers delightedly and in return, on a slow
night, starts telling me the plots of all the *Jaws* movies (which are <u>peren-
nial</u> favorites in the shark-ridden [Florida] Keys): "She looks around, and
the water-skier isn't there anymore, then SNAP! The whole boat goes. . . ."

testosterone: male hormone

I especially like Joan, the <u>svelte</u> fortyish hostess, who turns out to be a   7
militant feminist, pulling me aside one day to explain that "men run everything—we don't have a chance unless we stick together." Accordingly, she
backs me up when I get overpowered on the floor, and in return I give her a
chunk of my tips or stand guard while she sneaks off for an unauthorized
cigarette break. We all admire her for standing up to Billy [the manager]. . . .

I finish up every night at 10:00 or 10:30, depending on how much side   8
work I've been able to get done during the shift, and cruise home to the
tapes I snatched at random when I left my real home—Marianne Faithfull,
Tracy Chapman, Enigma, King Sunny Adé, Violent Femmes—just drained

cranium resonating: skull or
head vibrating

enough for the music to set my cranium resonating°, but hardly dead. Midnight snack is Wheat Thins and Monterey Jack, accompanied by cheap
white wine on ice and whatever AMC° has to offer. To bed by 1:30 or 2:00,

AMC: American Movie
Classics

up at 9:00 or 10:00, read for an hour while my uniform whirls around in the
landlord's washing machine, and then it's another eight hours spent fol-

"Mao's . . . Little Red Book":
former dictator of China, who
kept power by appealing to
the common people; his book
gave rules for living

lowing Mao's° central instruction, as laid out in the Little Red Book, which
was: Serve the people.

Follow-Up Activities   After you've finished reading, use these activities to
respond to "Serving in Florida." You may write your answers or prepare them
in your mind to discuss in class.

Grab your first impressions.

Respond with your first impressions. Say what you like and dislike; relate
your personal experiences to the reading; consider what more you want to
know.

Work with new words.

Some words in this reading may be unfamiliar to you. Use the methods
of Strategies 3 and 4 to explain what the listed words mean.

1. Use context clues.

   a. agile (Paragraph 1) (use logic clues)

   _____

   b. augurs (Paragraph 2) (use logic clues)

   _____

2. Use word parts.

   a. hyperthermia (Paragraph 4) (you know "hyper"; "thermia" means
   heat)

   _____

   b. autonomy (Paragraph 5) (remember the meaning of "auto"; the word
   means "self-rule" or "independence")

   _____

    c. illicit (Paragraph 5) (note that "il" is the spelling for "in" before a word beginning with "l"; "licit" means "legal.")

_____

    d. covert (Paragraph 5) (think of the word "cover" and use logic clues)

_____

3. Use the dictionary.

   Choose the correct definition of these words as they are used in the context of this reading.

   a. ply (Paragraph 3)

_____

   b. sojourn (Paragraph 3)

_____

   c. suave (Paragraph 4)

_____

   d. indulgent (Paragraph 5)

_____

   e. perennial (Paragraph 6)

_____

   f. svelte (Paragraph 7)

_____

Ask and answer questions.

1. What are some of the duties that keep Ehrenreich busy throughout her shift?

2. How does Ehrenreich try to give her customers a "fine dining" experience? Give some specific examples.

3. What part of the food preparation do the servers get to control? How do they take advantage of that control?

4. What does Ehrenreich do when she finishes her shift?

Inference questions.

5. Why did Ehrenreich have "fears ... of appearing overqualified"? (In answering this, consider what she was doing before this job.)

6. Notice the metaphorical expression in Paragraph 2, "I am beset by requests as if by bees." How does this word picture relate to what Ehrenreich is facing?

7. Identify the metaphor in this sentence from Paragraph 2: "If it isn't all done, every little bit of it, you're going to face the 6:00 P.M. dinner rush defenseless and probably go down in flames." What does the metaphor mean?

8. What does Ehrenreich mean when she says at the end of Paragraph 5, "So if you wonder why Americans are so obese, consider the fact that waitresses both express their humanity and earn their tips through the covert distribution of fats"?

9. How does Ehrenreich get along with her coworkers? Give examples to explain your answer.

10. What makes Ehrenreich think—ten days into the job—that it could be a livable lifestyle?

 Ask and answer your own question.

Write a question of your own. Share your question with others, and work together on an answer.

Make a map and write a summary.

What was your umbrella question for Reading 16? Try forming a statement using your own words that answers that question and summarizes the overall point. Then make an outline or other type of map using that overall point and the main ideas you found.

How close is your map to the cluster map for Reading 16 on page 276? Make necessary changes or additions to your own map. Then use your map to write a summary of the reading.

 Form your final thoughts.

1. This excerpt from Ehrenreich's book ends with her saying that her lifestyle is beginning to look livable. However, in her book, soon after this point, she faces problems and has to make changes. Based on what you've read, and on your own experiences, what sorts of problems might come up in a situation like hers?

2. By the end of her book, Ehrenreich found she could not survive on $7.00 per hour if she had to pay for living indoors. What would it be like in your

community to pay for housing, food, and other expenses on $7.00 per hour?

3. Look closely at Ehrenreich's footnote on page 269 about requirements for paying "tipped employees." In your experience (or that of someone you know), do employers generally follow them? Should they? Explain your answer.   ■

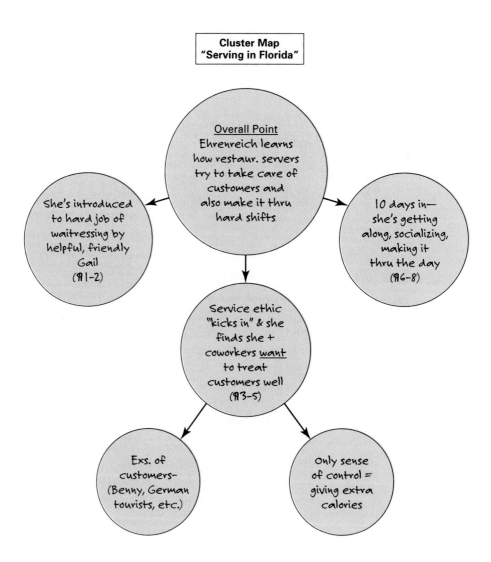

Cluster Map
"Serving in Florida"

Overall Point
Ehrenreich learns how restaur. servers try to take care of customers and also make it thru hard shifts

She's introduced to hard job of waitressing by helpful, friendly Gail (¶1–2)

10 days in— she's getting along, socializing, making it thru the day (¶6–8)

Service ethic "kicks in" & she finds she + coworkers want to treat customers well (¶3–5)

Exs. of customers— (Benny, German tourists, etc.)

Only sense of control = giving extra calories

Chapter 10 Summary

How does Strategy 10 help you *use your reader's voice to be an active reader?*

In everyday life you interpret what you see around you. You **make inferences** about what others do and say. Similarly, in reading, you **make inferences** about the writer's meaning. With this strategy you understand the meaning of implied ideas as well as ideas that are stated outright. Having a clear sense of ideas encourages your reader's voice to respond to them.

How does the *make inferences* strategy work?

This strategy helps you understand ideas that are implied rather than spelled out in a direct statement. You see pieces of evidence—often certain details or word choices—and put these pieces together in your mind. You then **make an inference**—a logical conclusion—based on that evidence. For inferring meaning from metaphors, you put together evidence to get the mental picture suggested by the words.

STRATEGY 10: MAKE INFERENCES

1 Recognize implied ideas as well as stated ideas.

2 Make logical connections.

3 Consider word choice.

4 Make sense of metaphors.

Are you familiar with the meaning of these terms?

connotation (connotative meaning): specialized associations that accompany a word

denotation (denotative meaning): basic or literal meaning of a word

implied idea: idea suggested by using certain words, details, or other evidence

infer (make inferences): make connections and draw logical conclusions based on evidence

inference: well-informed guess

literal: using the ordinary or primary meaning of a word ("bear" as a type of animal is literal; "bear" as a type of boss is metaphorical)

metaphor: (broadly defined) nonliteral comparison that points to a surprising image or idea; (narrowly defined) nonliteral comparison, not using "like" or "as" (Example: "My boss is a bear.")

prior knowledge: knowledge we have from past experience

simile: special type of nonliteral comparison, using "like" or "as" ("My boss is like a bear.")

How is the strategy working for you so far?

Explain which parts of **making inferences** you've found most helpful in the readings you've practiced with. Which parts have been least helpful?

TIME OUT FOR YOU

What Helps You Plan
Your Next Term?

When you pass the midpoint of the term, it's time to begin thinking ahead about how to get the most out of your studies next time around. To make plans for the next term, consider what has helped your performance in your courses so far. In addition, make use of campus resources that can help you choose courses and find extra support services you might need.

What Helps You Do Well in Your Courses?

What have you discovered about your study needs and preferences? For example, did a tutor or a study group improve your performance in a course? Or did finding out about your learning style help clarify the type of course that works well for you? Look over the following list. In your planning for next term, be sure to include any element that helped—or might have helped—this term.

- Work with a tutor. Find out how to sign up early next term before tutoring slots are taken.

- Meet with a study group. If study groups have helped you, think about how to set up a group next term.

- Know your learning style. Review the "Time Out for You" in Chapter 2, "What Is Your Learning Style?" Use this knowledge in choosing courses and instructors.

- Talk with a counselor or advisor. He or she can give you vital information about courses and can tell you about different instructors' teaching styles.

- Know your interests. Use this knowledge in choosing courses.

How Can You Manage Studying, Work, and Your Personal Life?

You know you need time for studying. So you'll want to arrange your courses, work schedule, and your personal life to allow for that time.

- Have a work schedule that accommodates your studying. Plan ahead with your employer to get reasonable work hours.

- Investigate good transportation. Find out transportation alternatives, such as a bus or carpool, if necessary.

- Arrange for help with family responsibilities. For example, find out about child care on or off campus.

- Be realistic about your schedule. Know how much studying and work you can take on. Remember to give yourself some time for yourself and for socializing.

How Can Campus Resources Help?

College campuses have resources that provide you with everything from information on careers to support services for helping you stay in college. Here are some of the resources you can make use of:

- Individual counseling appointments at the counseling center

- Career information center or job placement center

- Courses and tests for assessing career interests

- Career development courses (for exploration of careers in many different fields)

- Apprenticeship programs

- Tutoring services

- Financial aid programs

CHAPTER 11

ANALYZE THE INFORMATION

Throughout this book you've found ways to use your reader's voice. You've learned how to increase your understanding so you "listen" carefully to what the writer has to say. But you've also learned to voice your own response to the writer's ideas. Strategy 11, **Analyze the Information,** develops your reader's voice further. With this final strategy, you learn more ways to interpret the writer's reasons for writing and consider the soundness of his or her ideas. By gaining this broader understanding, you can respond more fully to what you've read.

Introduction to the New Strategy: Analyze the Information

Strategy 11, **Analyze the Information,** helps you expand your view of a reading. It shows you how a writer's *purpose*—the reasons for writing—affects the way his or her ideas are presented. The strategy also helps you examine how a writer uses *facts* and *opinions*. In Chapter 7 you learned that a fact can be proven, or confirmed, by going to a reliable source. On the other hand, an opinion cannot be proven or disproven, but may be valuable if backed up with evidence. **Analyzing the information** gives you a more complete sense of a reading on which to base your response.

STRATEGY 11: ANALYZE THE INFORMATION

1 Recognize the writer's purpose.

2 Understand the use of facts and opinions.

Before reading "Lost Jobs, Ragged Safety Net," Reading 17, become more familiar with Strategy 11, **Analyze the Information.**

The Writer's Purpose

1 *Recognize the writer's purpose.*

An important part of **analyzing the information** is knowing the reasons a writer had for writing. Recognizing a writer's purpose helps you know what kind of ideas and language to expect in a reading. You can recognize the writer's purpose by paying attention to the type of writing, the intended audience, and the writer's perspective.

Types of writing. Keep in mind the *type of writing* a writer uses. A type of writing is a way of presenting ideas. Each type is appropriate for a certain purpose.

For each of these types, an example of a previous reading in this book is given. Try adding other examples for each of the first three types.

Narration   *Narration* tells what happened. It is used when a writer wants to tell a story—real or imaginary—or give an account of a personal experience or historical events. Reading 3, "The Struggle to Be an All-American Girl," is one example of narration from this book. What others can you think of?

Description   *Description* shows what someone or something is like. It is used when a writer wants to give you a picture in words or appeal to one of your other senses. Reading 12, "The Men We Carry in Our Minds," contains several descriptive passages. What other readings in this book include examples of description?

Exposition   *Exposition*—or expository writing—explains something. A writer uses exposition to explain such things as why something happens or how something works. Your textbooks and most other college readings use exposition to instruct students about a field of knowledge. For example, Reading 7, "Movie Censorship: A Brief History," is an excerpt from a textbook on mass media. That reading explains how movies were censored in the past and how our present rating system works. What are some other of the fields of knowledge covered in the textbook excerpts in this book?

Argument   An *argument* is written to persuade or convince you. The writer of an argument deals with a subject that people disagree about. Reading 17, "Lost Jobs, Ragged Safety Net," is an argument. The author, Robert Reich, wants to persuade you to take his side about what should be done for low-wage workers. You have to read any argument carefully so you can think about how much you agree or disagree with the author's side.

Intended audience. You speak differently with your friends than you do with your boss, your teachers, or even your parents. In the same way, writers communicate differently depending on the readers they expect to reach—their *intended audience.*

Consider these two different readings, both on the theme of working in America. Who would be the intended audience for each reading? How would the writers' aims to reach those readers affect the ideas and language they use?

Reading 16, "Serving in Florida," is an excerpt from a best-selling paperback book.

Reading 18, "The Conditions of Work," is an excerpt from a history textbook.

Reading 16 is written to inform and entertain *general readers,* people who are not experts or students of a subject. The writer uses exposition to explain her ideas. But she relies even more on narration and description coming from her personal experiences. The vocabulary is informal and includes slang used by her coworkers. In contrast, the excerpt from the history textbook is written to instruct college students about changes that took place for nineteenth-century workers. The excerpt includes narration—stories about workers—that helps college students relate to the information. But the type of writing is mainly exposition, with the ideas based on academic research. The vocabulary is formal.

As you respond to a reading, consider how the writer's ideas and language work in terms of his or her intended audience. A textbook may provide students with information they need, but it may not entertain as much as a book for general readers.

The writer's perspective. Writers also have a certain *perspective* that influences their purpose for writing.

Your perspective on a subject is your way of looking at it, or your position on it. Your way of looking at a subject is based on your experience and beliefs. For example, what is your own perspective on the subject of gambling? Before answering, ask yourself these questions:

- What has been your experience in relation to gambling?

- Have you or friends or family had fun gambling as an occasional form of entertainment? Or is there someone close to you who has a serious gambling addiction?

- What beliefs about gambling—its entertainment value or its dangers—do you have from your family, your religion, or your friends?

Writers' different perspectives lead them to have different purposes for writing about a subject. On the subject of gambling, writers would divide according to their perspectives. Contrast the kinds of ideas two writers would include about gambling, depending on their perspective.

- One with a positive perspective might write about the economic boost that occurs when a casino comes into a community.

- One with a negative perspective might write about the ruined lives of habitual gamblers and their families.

It is helpful to know the writer's perspective before reading. That way you know the kinds of ideas to expect. The notes that appear after reading titles in magazine articles and in some textbooks—like this one—will often tell you about the writer's perspective. Look for:

- The writer's experience with the subject

- The writer's beliefs about the subject

For example, notes might describe the first writer's experience helping city governments get out of financial trouble by creating attractions that will bring in tourists. Notes might also state—or imply—his belief that gambling is harmless entertainment. Once you take into account the writer's experience and beliefs, consider what the opposite perspective might be. In this case, what is the opposite perspective? What would the second writer say in opposition to the first writer?

By noting the type of writing, the intended audience, and the writer's perspective, you understand the writer's purpose. This way of **analyzing the information** gives you a broader view of the reading.

Facts and Opinions

2 *Understand the use of facts and opinions.*

Another important way to **analyze the information** is to understand the writer's use of facts and opinions. Because you use your reader's voice, you already read with a questioning mind. You don't believe everything you see in print. But in order to question the facts and opinions a writer uses, you must be able to distinguish a fact from an opinion.

Here are some facts and opinions. Find the two statements that are not facts.

1. The country to the south of the United States is Mexico.

2. The Pilgrims landed at Plymouth Rock in 1620.

3. The fado is a type of Portuguese folk song that draws on Arabic and African, as well as Spanish and Portuguese influences.

4. Children under two years of age do less well if they are in day care instead of at home with their mothers.

5. The government needs to provide more job training for newly unemployed workers.

Facts. A *fact* can be proven or *verified* (checked for accuracy) by going to a dependable source, such as an encyclopedia or a textbook in an appropriate field. The first three statements are facts. The first is widely known and could be proven by looking at any map of North America. The second is well known and could be verified by going to an encyclopedia or history textbook. The third statement could be checked in an encyclopedia. Facts are usually used for important supporting details.

Opinions. An *opinion* cannot be proven or disproven but is open to debate or argument. Main ideas or supporting details may be opinions. In addition, the overall point of a reading may be an opinion, especially in an argument. In the list above, the fourth and fifth statements are opinions. Reasonable people might agree or disagree with each of those statements.

Analyzing facts and opinions. Facts can provide good support for main ideas or a writer's overall point. But be aware that statements that are presented as factual may be incorrect. For example, a fact may be so out-of-date that it is no longer true.

Opinions can also provide good support. But some opinions are more valuable than others. If an opinion is simply a personal preference, it doesn't carry much weight. For example, if you were someone who preferred having her toddler in day care, your preference alone wouldn't convince anyone that day care is a good option.

In contrast, opinions that are shared by many experts in a field can be as convincing as a fact. For example, experts in child psychology agree that a loving and well-run day care center can be as good for toddlers as being at home with the mother. That expert opinion, based on many years of research, would be more convincing support for backing day care than your personal preference. Indeed, quotations from experts are often used to support writers' own opinions. However, personal opinions can also be convincing when they are backed up with observations, reasons, or other evidence.

The following table summarizes how to distinguish valuable from poor support provided by both facts and opinions.

Support

	Facts: Can be proven	Opinions: Can't be proven; open to debate
Valuable Support	Facts you know to be true or that you could verify	Opinions supported by observations, reasons, or other evidence
		Opinions widely held by experts in a field, often stated as quotations
Poor Support	Incorrect "facts"	Unsupported personal beliefs or preferences

Try the New Strategy: Analyze the Information

Now that you understand Strategy 11, put it into practice with Reading 17, "Lost Jobs, Ragged Safety Net."

Before reading, **check in**. Then, **ask questions**, using appropriate cues, especially the notes before the reading. Ask your umbrella question, and predict the topics and overall point. The notes will also help

CHECK IN

you **analyze the information,** by telling you about the writer's purpose. To interpret the purpose, note:

The type of writing: _____

The intended audience: _____

The writer's perspective on the subject (think also about what the opposite perspective would be): _____

_____

As you read, **make inferences,** and use strategies for understanding main ideas. **Look for patterns of thought,** especially the pattern of cause-and-effect reasoning. **Analyze the information** by being alert to the author's use of facts and opinions. This reading was first published two months after the September 11, 2001, terrorist attacks on the World Trade Center in New York City and on the Pentagon. As you read, notice which ideas remain significant today and which ones now seem less important.

READING 17   Lost Jobs, Ragged Safety Net

Robert Reich

Currently a professor of economics at Brandeis University, Robert Reich was secretary of labor during President Bill Clinton's first term. He has published many books and articles promoting his ideas for economic and social change. He believes that government should fund more programs to help low-wage or unemployed workers. This reading first appeared on the opinion page in the New York Times on November 11, 2001. Reich tells how the attacks of September 11th caused consumers to cut their spending, and he examines the effect of this drop in spending on low-paid workers. He then argues that current government polices are inadequate for helping those workers.

The economic fallout from <u>terrorism</u> is hitting some Americans much   1
harder than others, and we need to respond. Last year, when the slowdown began, layoffs and pay cuts hit hardest at manufacturing workers, white-collar managers and professionals. But since the <u>terrorist</u> attacks, consumers have cut their spending, and now a different group is experiencing the heaviest job losses: the mostly low-paid workers in America's vast personal-service sector°.

For underlined words, **Use Context Clues** and **Find the Right Definition.**

sector: social or economic subdivision of society

With retail sales down, there's less need for sales clerks. Half-empty   2
hotels don't need nearly as many cleaners and bellmen. Vacant convention halls have no use for <u>platoons</u> of custodians and staffers. Unfilled restaurants can't keep waiters and busboys busy. And so on through all the

RESPOND

Keep in mind your own experience as a worker and consumer as you read about the economy.

workers who attend, drive, pamper, launder, polish, clean, prepare and otherwise make life more pleasant for the people who pay them.

In October [2001] 439,000 private-sector jobs were lost—the largest   3
monthly decline in more than a quarter-century. Hotels alone lost 46,000; <u>retailers</u>, 81,000; airlines, 42,000. Minority workers, with a <u>disproportionate</u> share of low-wage service jobs, have been especially hard hit. Unemployment among blacks rose to 9.7 percent last month, a full percentage point higher than in September and up 2.3 points from a year ago. Unemployment among Hispanics is 2.2 percentage points higher than it was last year at this time.

There is reason to expect that job cuts at the lower end of the wage   4
scale will get even larger and occur even faster in the months ahead. That's because so much consumer spending is <u>discretionary</u>, turning more on psychological wants than on physical needs. Consumers don't have to dine outside the home, travel, enjoy live entertainment or go on shopping binges. They can choose to spend less on these services as soon as their wallets feel even slightly pinched. And when they do, lower-wage workers feel a bigger pinch. The Fiscal° Policy Institute estimates that 48,000 of the 80,000 jobs that New York City will have lost by the end of the year pay an average of $23,000, significantly below the citywide average of about $58,000.

fiscal: related to financial matters

Another <u>vulnerability</u> of lower-income service workers is that they   5
have fewer means of cushioning the blow than they had in prior <u>recessions</u>. Most have no savings and are deeper in debt than they were last time, because their inflation-adjusted° earnings never really got off the ground in the 90's. The steady decline in higher-paying manufacturing jobs and an <u>influx</u> of low-skilled immigrants combined to keep wages down.

inflation-adjusted: showing the real buying power of earnings, since when prices go up, a dollar buys less

Government will be less helpful this time around. Safety nets are in tat-   6
ters. Welfare-to-work programs made sense when work was plentiful, but without work, those no longer eligible for welfare have nowhere else to turn. Even job losers who still qualify will find that welfare payments in most states are worth less than before.

Unemployment insurance is also harder to get. Fewer than 30 percent   7
of people who lose jobs now receive it, down from more than half several decades ago. Eligibility rules have grown steadily tighter. Since part-time workers, temps°, the self-employed and people who have moved in and out of employment often don't qualify, a large portion of the lower-wage work force is excluded. Many who don't qualify are women with young children.

temps: temporary workers

Meanwhile, federal programs for job training and low-income housing   8
have been shrunk by budget cuts. State and local governments are in no position to step in. They're already strapped by rapidly declining tax <u>revenues</u>. Rather than <u>beefing up</u> social services, they're starting to cut them.

"stimulus" plan: 2001 tax cut meant to stimulate the economy and therefore create more jobs

Why does Reich use quotation marks around "stimulus"?

reeling ... capacity: doing badly because of producing more goods than they could sell

Update on employment: from Sept. 2001 to July 2004 there was a job loss of 1.1 million.

In short, the fat years of the 90's have left us woefully unprepared for a   9
deep recession that's likely to take a particularly large toll on the poor and lower-wage workers. Given all this, a "stimulus" plan° like the one that passed last month in the House of Representatives and is being backed by the White House, which <u>confers</u> most of its benefits on large corporations and upper-income households, seems exactly the reverse of what's needed. Large corporations, already reeling° from too much capacity, won't be <u>induced</u> to add more. Wealthier households, already spending whatever they want, won't be inspired to spend more. It's the bottom half who are in trouble. They're most likely to spend whatever extra they get. And they desperately need whatever government can supply.

At a time of national crisis, when the nation must pull together, it   10
seems only logical that we do what we can to avoid pulling further apart.

Follow-Up Activities   After you've finished reading, use these activities to respond to "Lost Jobs, Ragged Safety Net." You may write your answers or prepare them in your mind to discuss in class.

Grab your first impressions.

Respond with your first impressions. Say what you like and dislike; relate your personal experiences to the reading; consider what more you want to know.

Work with new words.

Some words in this reading may be unfamiliar to you. Use the methods of Strategies 3 and 4 to explain what the listed words mean.

1. Use context clues.

    a. vulnerability (Paragraph 5) (use logic clues)

    _____

    b. revenues (Paragraph 8) (use logic clues)

    _____

    c. beefing up (Paragraph 8) (note the phrase "rather than," and use contrast clues)

    _____

    d. confers (Paragraph 9) (use logic clues)

    _____

2. Use word parts.

   a. terrorism and terrorist (Paragraph 1) (note how the two suffixes change the meaning of "terror")

   _____

   b. disproportionate (Paragraph 3) (note how the prefix and suffix change "proportion," meaning "balance")

   _____

   c. recessions (Paragraph 5) (note the prefix, this time meaning "back," and use logic clues)

   _____

   d. influx (Paragraph 5) (note the prefix, and use logic clues)

   _____

3. Use the dictionary.

Choose the correct definition of these words as they are used in the context of this reading.

   a. platoons (Paragraph 2)

   _____

   b. retailers (Paragraph 3)

   _____

   c. discretionary (Paragraph 4)

   _____

   d. induced (Paragraph 9)

   _____

Ask and answer questions.

1. When Reich wrote this piece in November 2001, consumer spending had gone down significantly because of the 9/11 terrorist attacks. What were some specific effects of this cut in spending on low-paid, personal-service workers?

2. What is "discretionary spending"? How does the fact that so much of consumer spending is "discretionary" affect lower-wage workers?

3. In Paragraphs 5 and 6, Reich gives reasons for saying that lower-income service workers will have a harder time during the 2001 economic downturn than in previous recessions. What are his reasons for saying this?

4. Why does Reich say that unemployment insurance is harder to get now than it used to be several decades ago?

Inference questions.

5. In Paragraph 6, Reich refers to a commonly used metaphor, "safety nets." He says, "Safety nets are in tatters," which points back to the title, "Lost Jobs, Ragged Safety Net." What are safety nets? Why does he say they are "ragged" or "in tatters"?

6. Identify and explain the metaphor in this sentence: "In short, the fat years . . . left us woefully unprepared for a deep recession."

7. Reich puts quotation marks around "stimulus" in Paragraph 9. Why? How is the stimulus plan referred to in that paragraph supposed to work? Why does Reich say it won't?

8. In the last sentence, Reich says, "When the nation must pull together, it seems only logical that we do what we can to avoid pulling further apart." What does he mean by "pull together"? What does he mean by "pull apart"?

Questions involving analysis.

9. Write a sentence explaining Reich's purpose in writing "Lost Jobs, Ragged Safety Net." Before writing your sentence, consider Reich's perspective on the subject of the safety net for low-wage workers. What would be an opposite perspective from Reich's?

   _____

   _____

   _____

   _____

   _____

10. Analyze facts and opinions in the reading. Which of these statements are facts (F), and which are opinions (O)? If the statement is an opinion, say briefly what evidence Reich uses to back it up. The first item is done for you.

    a. __*O*__ Large corporations, already reeling from too much capacity, won't be induced to add more. (Paragraph 9) *Statement can't be proven, but opinion is backed up by the idea that corporations have more goods—or the capacity to produce more goods—than they can sell.*

b. _____ The economic fallout from terrorism is hitting some Americans much harder than others, and we need to respond. (Paragraph 1)_____

_____

_____

c. _____ Last year, when the slowdown began, layoffs and pay cuts hit hardest at manufacturing workers, white-collar managers and professionals. (Paragraph 1)_____

_____

_____

d. _____ In October 439,000 private-sector jobs were lost—the largest monthly decline in more than a quarter-century. (Paragraph 3)_____

_____

_____

e. _____ Fewer than 30 percent of people who lose jobs now receive [unemployment insurance], down from more than half several decades ago. (Paragraph 7) _____

_____

_____

f. _____ Wealthier households, already spending whatever they want, won't be inspired to spend more. (Paragraph 9)_____

_____

_____

 Ask and answer your own question.

Write a question of your own. Share your question with others, and work together on an answer.

Make a map or write a summary.

What was your umbrella question for Reading 17? What is the overall point that answers that question? Show the overall point and the reading's main ideas in the format that works best for you: an outline or another type of map or a written summary.

 Form your final thoughts.

1. Those who disagree with Reich believe that, instead of providing welfare and unemployment payments to the poor and unemployed, government

should try to create more jobs by giving tax benefits to corporations and the wealthy. What are some criticisms they would make of Reich's argument?

2. Look at Reich's ideas from the context of the current economy and your present financial situation. Which ideas do you, personally, find significant? Which ideas are not relevant to your present situation?   ■

Apply the New Strategy: Analyze the Information

Reading 18, "The Conditions of Work," will give you more practice with Strategy 11.

CHECK IN

Before reading, **check in.** Then, **ask questions,** using appropriate cues, especially the notes before the reading, the introduction, and the illustration on page 297. Ask your umbrella question, and predict the topics and overall point. The notes will also help you **analyze the information,** by telling you about the writer's purpose. To interpret the purpose, note:

The type of writing: _____

The intended audience: _____

The writers' perspective on the subject:_____

_____

As you read, **make inferences,** and use strategies for understanding main ideas. **Look for patterns of thought,** especially the pattern of cause-and-effect reasoning. You may think of history as containing only facts. But historians rely on opinions, too. As you read **analyze the information** by noting the difference between the facts and opinions.

READING 18   THE CONDITIONS OF WORK

JAMES KIRBY MARTIN, RANDY ROBERTS, STEVEN MINTZ,
LINDA O. McMURRY, AND JAMES H. JONES

James Martin and the four other writers of the history textbook America and Its Peoples: A Mosaic in the Making *(2001) are all university professors of history, each with a special interest in a certain area of American history. This reading is an excerpt from the chapter about the American economy during the late nineteenth and early twentieth centuries. It tells how workers' lives were changed by industrialization, the process through which industry replaced agriculture as the source of income for most people in the working class°.*

working class: class of
people who work for wages,
often at physical labor

laborer: worker doing physical labor

"adjusted . . . price level": reflecting real buying power of earnings in that time period

For underlined words, **Use Context Clues** and **Find the Right Definition.**

Was it worth it? Was the price paid of industrialization worth the bene- 1
fits native-born and immigrant labor received? This is not a simple question to answer. In fact, each laborer° might have answered it differently,
since wages played an important role in a laborer's attitude. In general,
wages rose and prices fell during the late nineteenth and early twentieth
centuries. Exactly how much is a question of heated historical debate. One
economic historian estimated that when adjusted° for changes in the price
level, real annual earnings increased from approximately $300 in 1860
to more than $425 in 1890. Other historians believe those estimates are
overly optimistic, underline{contending} that wages tended to underline{stagnate}, especially in
the large textile industries. All, however, admit that the pace of wages
and earnings lagged well behind the spectacular growth in the American
economy.

Even with modest improvements in wages, laborers continually bat- 2
tled poverty. More often than not, the prosperity of a family depended on
how many members of that family worked. Carroll D. Wright, chief of the
Massachusetts Bureau of the Statistics of Labor, expressed the matter
plainly in 1882: "A family of workers can always live well, but the man with
a family of small children to support, unless his wife works also, has a
small chance of living properly." The material quality of life often depended
more on circumstances than on occupation or wages.

Take, for example, two hard-working union coal miners who earned 3
$1.50 a day and were studied in 1883 by the Illinois Bureau of Labor Statis-
tics. The first worked only 30 weeks in 1883, and his total income was $250.
He lived with his wife and five children in a $6-per-month, two-room,
crowded but neat underline{tenement} apartment. During the year, he spent only $80
on food, mainly bread, salted meat, and coffee. His income was barely
enough to allow his family to maintain a minimal standard of living. His
existence was underline{precarious}: strikes, layoffs, sickness, or injury could easily
throw him and his family into underline{abject} poverty.

The second miner worked full time in 1883 and earned $420. He had a 4
wife and four children, three of whom were also miners, and who brought
home an additional $1000. They all lived comfortably in their own six-room
house perched on an acre of land. They ate well, spending $900 a year on
food—steak, butter, potatoes, bacon, and coffee comprised a typical break-
fast. They bought books and enjoyed a full leisure life.

In many working-class families, fathers and sons, mothers and daugh- 5
ters, and often aunts, uncles, and grandparents—all contributed to the family economy. Carroll D. Wright in the United States Census of 1880 warned,
"the factory system necessitates the employment of women and children
to an injurious extent, and consequently its tendency is to destroy family

life and ties and domestic habits, and ultimately the home." In truth, however, the opposite was probably true. Economically, families worked as a single entity; the desires of any individual often had to be sacrificed for the good of the family. Far from destroying the family, working for the family economy often strengthened it.

During the first decade of the twentieth century, social workers conducted numerous studies to determine how much money was needed to sustain a typical working-class existence for a year. Estimates for New York City ranged between $800 and $876 for a family of four, $505 for a single man, and $466 for a working woman. Many of New York's laborers fell painfully below the recommended minimum, and single women lived particularly difficult lives. In New York women earned about half as much as men—the majority made less than $300 per year. One woman worker described her <u>meager</u> existence: "I didn't live, I simply existed. I couldn't live that [which] you could call living. . . . It took me months and months to save up money to buy a dress or a pair of shoes. . . . I had the hardest struggle I ever had in my life."

Conditions for African Americans, Asians, and Mexicans in America were even worse. They were given the most exhausting and dangerous work, paid the least, and were fired first during hard economic times. For a black sharecropper° farming a patch of worked-over soil in Mississippi, or a Chinese miner carrying nitroglycerin° down a hole in a Colorado mountain, or a Mexican working on a Texas ranch, $300 per year would have seemed a kingly sum.

There were clear divisions among workers. At the top were the highly skilled laborers. Mostly English-speaking, generally Protestant, and almost exclusively white, they were paid well, had good job security, and considered themselves elite craftsmen. Below them were the semiskilled and unskilled workers, most of whom were immigrants from southern and eastern Europe, spoke halting if any English, and were Catholics or Jews. They lacked job security and had to struggle for a decent existence. At the bottom were the nonwhite and women workers, usually semi- and unskilled, for whom even a decent existence was normally out of reach.

Hours of work varied widely. Long hours were not new—farm workers and <u>artisans</u> often labored from sunup to sundown. The tempo° and quality of their labor was different, however. During summer months and harvest season, the work was intense, but it slowed down during the shorter days of winter. There was always time for fishing, horse racing, visiting, and tavern-going. Preindustrial workshops similarly mixed work with fellowship. If the workdays were long, they were also sociable. As they worked, laborers talked, joked, laughed, and even drank.

sharecropper: tenant farmer (especially in the South), works land for a share of profits from the crops

nitroglycerin: explosive, poisonous liquid

tempo: rate of speed

Nor was time measured out in teaspoons. <u>Punctuality</u> was not the   10
golden virtue it became during industrialization. In the early nineteenth
century, household clocks were rare and many of them possessed only a
single hand. Cheap, mass-produced pocket watches did not become readily available until the Civil War. Certainly the idea of punching a time clock
was alien to the preindustrial worker, who might think in terms of hours
but not minutes.

Preindustrial labor, then, was done in a more relaxed atmosphere. This   11
is not meant to romanticize it. Farm work and shop labor could be hard and
dangerous, but there were not sharp lines between labor and leisure. Gambling, storytelling, singing, debating, and drinking formed a crucial part of
the workday. Thrift, regularity, <u>sobriety</u>, orderliness, punctuality—hall-
marks of an industrial society—were virtues not rigorously observed.

The new concept of time changed not only how people worked but   12
also how they regarded the worker. The most <u>prominent</u> feature of nine-
teenth- and early twentieth-century New England mill towns was the giant
factory bell towers. Before clocks and watches, the bell towers served a
<u>utilitarian</u> function. They told the laborers when to get out of bed, be at
work, eat lunch, and go home. The importance of time was literally drilled
home in a brochure prepared by the International Harvester Corporation to
teach Polish laborers the English language. "Lesson One" read:

I hear the whistle. I must hurry.   13
I hear the five minute whistle.
It is time to go into the shop.
I take my check from the gate board and hang it on the department
board.
I change my clothes and get ready to work.
The starting whistle blows.
I eat my lunch.
It is forbidden to eat until then.
The whistle blows at five minutes of starting time.
I get ready to go to work.
I work until the whistle blows to quit.
I leave my place nice and clean.
I put all my clothes in the locker.
I must go home.

The lesson also perfectly describes the ideal industrial worker: punc-   14
tual, hardworking, clean, and sober.

Given this new standard of work and time demanded by factory own-   15
ers, laborers were reluctant to work the preindustrial dawn-to-dusk workday. In 1889 hundreds of trade unionists paraded through the streets of

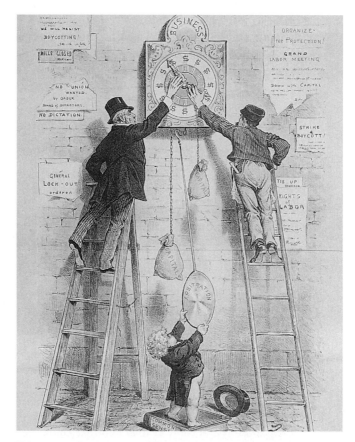

This cartoon from the period shows the conflict between management and workers over the eight-hour workday. Note that dollar signs replace numbers on the clock face.

Worcester, Massachusetts, behind a banner that stated their goal. "Eight Hours for Work, Eight Hours for Rest, Eight Hours for What We Will." A popular song of the day captured the ideal.

naught: nothing

> We mean to make things over;
> We're tired of toil for naught°;
> We may have enough to live on,
> But never an hour for thought.
> We want to feel the sunshine,
> We want to smell the flowers;
> We are sure that God has willed it,
> And we mean to have eight hours.

16

The reality, however, fell far short of this ideal. It is difficult to generalize about hours since they varied considerably from occupation to occupation.

17

In 1890, for example, bakers averaged over 65 hours a week, steelworkers over 66, and canners nearly 77. Even as late as 1920, skilled workers still averaged 50.4 hours a week and the unskilled 53.7 hours. Before the 1930s, workers regarded an 8-hour day or even a 10-hour day as an <u>unattainable</u> dream.

Follow-Up Activities   After you've finished reading, use these activities to respond to "The Conditions of Work." You may write your answers or prepare them in your mind to discuss in class.

Grab your first impressions.

Respond with your first impressions. Say what you like and dislike; relate your personal experiences to the reading; consider what more you want to know.

Work with new words.

Some words in this reading may be unfamiliar to you. Use the methods of Strategies 3 and 4 to explain what the listed words mean.

1. Use context clues.

   a. contending (Paragraph 1) (use logic clues)

   _____

   b. stagnate (Paragraph 1) (use contrast clues; note the contrasting sentences about estimates of earnings)

   _____

   c. precarious (Paragraph 3) (use example clues)

   _____

   d. meager (Paragraph 6) (use example clues)

   _____

   e. punctuality (Paragraph 10) (use logic clues)

   _____

2. Use word parts.

   a. sobriety (Paragraph 11) (notice the word "sober" in this word)

   _____

   b. prominent (Paragraph 12) (note the prefix "pro-" and use logic clues)

   _____

    c. utilitarian (Paragraph 12) (relate this word to "utilize")

    _____

    d. unattainable (Paragraph 17) (note how the prefix and suffix change "attain," meaning "reach")

    _____

3. Use the dictionary.

   Choose the correct definition of these words as they are used in the context of this reading.

   a. tenement (Paragraph 3)

   _____

   b. abject (Paragraph 3)

   _____

   c. artisans (Paragraph 9)

   _____

Ask and answer questions.

1. Note the main idea statement at the end of Paragraph 2: "The material quality of life often depended more on circumstances than on occupation or wages." The next two paragraphs contrast the lives of two miners. What are some important differences between these miners that support that main idea?

2. What effects did gender or race or ethnicity have on the amount of money workers could earn or the kind of work they could do? Give some specific examples of these effects.

3. What was the main difference between the workday for preindustrial workers and the workday for industrial workers?

4. How did laborers respond to these changes in their workday?

Inference questions.

5. What is the "heated historical debate" referred to in Paragraph 1? What do historians on both sides of the debate agree on?

6. In Paragraph 10, the authors say, "Nor was time measured out in teaspoons." What do they mean by that statement?

7. How did the "new concept of time," referred to in Paragraph 12, change "not only how people worked but also how they regarded the worker"?

Questions involving analysis.

8. Write a sentence explaining the authors' purpose in writing "Conditions of Work." Before writing, answer the following questions:

   a. What is the type of writing? _____

   b. Who is the intended audience? _____

   c. Do the authors have a particular perspective on their subject? Or do they attempt to present different perspectives?

   _____

   _____

   _____

9. Analyze facts and opinions in the reading. Which of these statements are facts (F), and which are opinions (O)? If the statement is an opinion, say briefly what evidence the authors use to back it up.

   a. _____ One economic historian estimated that when adjusted for changes in the price level, real annual earnings increased from approximately $300 in 1860 to more than $425 in 1890. (Paragraph 1)

   _____

   _____

   b. _____ Far from destroying the family, working for the family economy often strengthened it. (Paragraph 5)

   _____

   _____

   c. _____ In New York women earned about half as much as men—the majority made less than $300 per year. (Paragraph 6)

   _____

   _____

   d. _____ If the workdays were long, they were also sociable. (Paragraph 9)

   _____

   _____

   e. _____ Cheap, mass-produced pocket watches did not become readily available until the Civil War. (Paragraph 10)

   _____

   _____

f. _____ In 1889 hundreds of trade unionists paraded through the streets of Worcester, Massachusetts, behind a banner that stated their goal. (Paragraph 15)

_____

_____

10. What are some examples the authors include to make their subject come to life?

 Ask and answer your own question.

Write a question of your own. Share your question with others, and work together on an answer.

Make a map or write a summary.

What was your umbrella question for Reading 18? What is the overall point that answers that question? Show the overall point and the reading's main ideas in the format that works best for you: an outline or another type of map or a written summary.

Form your final thoughts.

1. Think about your own family history in relation to the working conditions described in this reading. What was work life like for your great-grandparents or your great-great-grandparents? Were they living in this country? If not, what would they have faced if they had arrived in the United States at that period in history?

 2. This textbook excerpt shows how historians use various sources to give an accurate picture of a historical period. What examples can you find of the following: statistics, personal stories, and quotations, as well as a brochure, a popular song, and a cartoon of the period? Which sources are used mainly as facts, and which are used mainly as opinions?

3. The late nineteenth century saw dramatic changes in the kind of work most workers did. Today, we, too, are facing some dramatic changes in work life. For example, well-paying manufacturing jobs are being lost, and weekly work hours are increasing. How have you or your family or friends been affected by these or other changes?   ■

Chapter 11 Summary

How does Strategy 11 help you *use your reader's voice to be an active reader?*

Analyzing information encourages you to step back and get a broader view of the writer's ideas. By considering the writer's purpose and understanding the way facts and opinions are used, you are more prepared to voice your own ideas about what the writer says.

How does the *ask questions* strategy work?

With Strategy 11, **Analyze the Information,** you look for elements that demonstrate a writer's purpose: the type of writing, the intended audience, and the writer's perspective on the subject. You also investigate how well the writer's facts and opinions support the ideas and overall point in a reading. Here are the two guidelines for Strategy 11.

STRATEGY 11: ANALYZE THE INFORMATION

1 Recognize the writer's purpose.

2 Understand the use of facts and opinions.

Are you familiar with the meaning of these terms?

argument: writing that persuades you to believe something or do something

description: writing that shows what someone or something is like

exposition: writing that explains something or instructs

fact: statement that can be proven or confirmed

general reader: someone who is not an expert or student of a subject

intended audience: the readers a writer expects to reach

narration: writing that tells what happened, or tells a story

opinion: statement that cannot be proven or disproven, but may be valuable if backed up with evidence

perspective: way of looking at a subject; position on a subject

purpose: the writer's reasons for writing

type of writing: a way of presenting ideas; each type is appropriate for a certain purpose

verify: check for accuracy

How is the strategy working for you so far?

Explain which parts of **analyze the information** you've found most helpful in the readings you've practiced with. Which parts have been least helpful?

TIME OUT FOR YOU

WHAT HAS WORKED WELL FOR YOU IN THIS COURSE?

A final exam gives a picture of what you learned in a college course, but it's not the complete picture. It doesn't show what you discovered about your learning and studying preferences. Now, at the end of this course, try analyzing what worked well for you and what worked less well. An analysis of this course—and your other courses, too—will increase your awareness of what will work best for you in your future study.

Your Preferences for Readings

Glance back over the readings you've read in this book. Answer the following questions about them. See if you can find any general ideas about what made you prefer some readings over others.

1. What three or four readings were your favorites?

   _____

   _____

   _____

   _____

2. What three or four readings were your least favorites?

   _____

   _____

   _____

   _____

3. What general ideas did you discover about your reading preferences from looking back at the readings? For example, did you usually like the same kind of reading—magazine article or personal story or textbook excerpt? Or did you like readings with the same type of subject matter?

_____

_____

_____

_____

4. Did you find that you came to like some readings you did not like at first? If so, what changed your mind?

_____

_____

_____

_____

Learning In and Out of the Classroom

You need to take into account the time and effort you put into each aspect of the work you did in and out of the classroom. But while acknowledging your own responsibility, try to see which kinds of classroom environments and types of studying worked best for you. Jot down the pluses and minuses of each of the following aspects to use for future reference.

■ Group work_____

_____

■ Instructor-led discussion or lecture_____

_____

■ Use of media _____

_____

■ Special projects _____

_____

■ Writing about readings _____

_____

■ Quizzes and tests _____

_____

■ Other _____

_____

How Has the Course Changed Your Ideas?

Ask this question at the end of any course: "How has the course changed my ideas about the field of study?" Answering this question helps you summarize for yourself the most important idea (or ideas) you will take away from the course. Because students differ in their learning preferences, experience, knowledge, and motivation, you are likely to answer the question somewhat differently from other students.

How has this course changed your ideas about reading? Think what your answer shows about you as well as about the course. Discuss your answer with others.

_____

_____

_____

_____

_____

_____

PART IV

ADDITIONAL READINGS ON
WORKING IN AMERICA

The readings that follow will give you further practice in using the strategies you've learned throughout this book, with a variety of readings on the theme of working in America.

READING IV-A SATISFACTION NOT GUARANTEED, BUT YOU CAN FIND MEANING IN YOUR WORK

SONDRA FARRELL BAZROD

Sondra Farrell Bazrod wrote this article for the Los Angeles Times, *September 9, 2001. For her article, Bazrod consulted professors in business management and in psychology. She also interviewed workers doing a variety of types of jobs.*

CHECK IN

*Before reading, **check in**. Then, **ask questions,** using appropriate cues. Note that this reading, like many newspaper articles, organizes ideas into many short paragraphs. Keep that organization in mind as you ask your umbrella question and predict the topics and overall point. As you read, use all appropriate strategies for understanding main ideas and interpreting ideas. Recognize the writer's purpose, and **analyze the information.***

RESPOND

Relate these ideas to jobs you've had and to your hopes for the future.

Most Americans grow up with the idea that they will have a satisfying career, yet for many the reality is that work is anything but fulfilling.   1

Experts say, however, that anyone, whether they work on a loading dock or in a corner office, can find satisfaction in their job—or at least find another job that is satisfying. The key is not expecting the job to make you happy.   2

A person needs to find meaning in a job to find satisfaction, said Samuel Culbert, a professor at UCLA's Anderson Graduate School of Management, and they often have to create that meaning for themselves.   3

For underlined words, **Use Context Clues** and **Find the Right Definition.**

"I think happiness comes after some things that are far more fundamental," Culbert said. "For example, a job has to be personally meaningful, and some jobs are not. People make them personally meaningful. A job needs to give a person a sense of purpose that he or she is not just a <u>cog</u> in the machinery. Jobs aren't created with the individual in mind."   4

Knowing that he's creating a future for his family provides that meaning for Guillermo Perez, 32, a loading dock foreman.   5

307

"This company has given me the opportunity of my life to do more and keep succeeding," said Perez, who lives in Covina and works at U.S. Growers Cold Storage in Vernon. At his previous job at an auto parts warehouse, he said he was working only for a paycheck. 6

"I had mid-level jobs before," he said. "Now it's been a challenge to keep succeeding. I have a good life and my wonderful wife and three children understand that I work many hours, but our living comes from this job. We have our first house and now we live in a decent neighborhood. [My family] feels more confident about me and their future lives." 7

Three things can influence your job satisfaction, said Anita Blanchard, an assistant professor of psychology at the University of North Carolina at Charlotte: How significant your job is to other people, how much freedom you have to make decisions, and how many different things you get to do at work. 8

"People who are negative tend to be more dissatisfied, but one way they can improve their outlook and job satisfaction is to think about the positives of the job and think how it is helping people," Blanchard said. 9

And job fit is important. 10

"Everybody has their own unique interest and it's most important to find the job that fills your needs," Blanchard said. 11

Finding that job doesn't necessarily mean making huge changes in a career. 12

For Katrina Elias, 34, now a saleswoman at Beverly Hills Ford, switching from one sales job to another made all the difference in her satisfaction with work. 13

"I sold radio time to small businesses, but I really believed it didn't benefit them," said Elias of North Hollywood. "If you're a salesperson and don't believe in the product, it's a very depressing job. I certainly didn't think I was helping the small businesses. I thought I was ripping them off." 14

As a car saleswoman, Elias said, she "really takes pleasure when a family is excited by the purchase when they drive off. It's a challenge getting people financed who have special needs, but my job was created to help people buy a car. The magic is believing in your product." 15

Seeing your job as a way to help someone is a key way of finding satisfaction, said Sidney Walter, a former UCLA psychology professor who now works as a forensic psychologist for the Department of Health and Human Services. 16

"Unfortunately, many people don't realize this," said Walter, who lives in Chico. "I've asked thousands of people, 'What's the purpose of your job?' and most will answer, 'To make money.' This is true of all types of workers, from lawyers to janitors." 17

Walter recommends that people discover and accept the purpose of   18
their jobs.

"It is not for you to earn money," he said. "It is to serve others. All   19
occupations have the same end purpose—helping others. The teacher to
educate, the baseball player to entertain, the shoe clerk to assist, the jailer,
vendor, seamstress and spouse to help, assist, to aid others. The basic purpose of all is to help. Until this is recognized and accepted you cannot be
happy at your job."

And if you're having trouble finding that purpose?   20

"Know all you possibly can about your occupation," Walter said.   21
"What it does, what happens after you are through with your part. During
World War II, when the airplane <u>riveters</u> found out what their little contribution did toward the end result, and saw the airplane flying in newsreels,
their output increased significantly."

Learning on the job—not just about the job—is another way to create a   22
more meaningful work life, said UCLA's Culbert.

"A lot of people don't learn because they fear that if they put them-   23
selves in a learning mode, they will do something that's a mistake and
they'll be criticized or punished for it," Culbert said. "It's self protection. We
get defensive even if we want to learn because we're scared, but if you
want to have meaning on the job you have to feel it's OK to learn."

Meaning, happiness and <u>productivity</u> go beyond pay, Culbert said.   24

Yet the relationship between work and home cannot be isolated, said   25
Blanchard of the University of North Carolina.

Los Angeles resident Milton Moreno, 27, said he realizes the need for   26
balance in his life.

"When I come home I can't bring my problems from the job so I have   27
to be two people on the same day with two personalities," said Moreno, 24,
who has been a cashier and delivery person at Owens Market in West Los
Angeles for nine years. "I also can't mix my problems at home with my job
or I'll end up with nothing in the long run. I try to take one day at a time."

And at a time when workers are being asked to do more, doing less   28
may be one of the quickest ways to job satisfaction.

"When I was working at one of my first jobs in a large corporation,   29
I noticed that the people who did the most work and stayed overtime
were asked to do even more and became increasingly unhappy," Walter
said. "Those who did just enough and did it well were accepted as good
workers."

Being a workaholic is the only addiction that's applauded, said   30
Jonathon Lazear, author of "The Man Who Mistook His Job for a Life,"
which <u>chronicles</u> his life as a <u>workaholic</u>.

"Statistics indicate that productivity actually decreases the more over-   31
time one is actively working," Lazear said. "But we tell ourselves otherwise."

"There's more to life than your job," he said. "Finding balance outside   32
of work will make you a better worker, someone who can bring a fresher
perspective to the job."

Follow-Up Activities   After you've finished reading, use these activities to
respond to "Satisfaction Not Guaranteed, But You Can Find Meaning in a Job."
You may write your answers or prepare them in your mind to discuss in class.

Grab your first impressions.

Respond with your first impressions. Say what you like and dislike; relate
your personal experiences to the reading; consider what more you want to
know.

Work with new words.

A few of the words in this reading may be unfamiliar to you. Use the
methods of Strategies 3 and 4 to explain what the listed words mean.

1. Use context clues.

   a. cog (Paragraph 4) (use logic clues)

   _____

   b. chronicles (Paragraph 30) (use logic clues)

   _____

2. Use word parts.

   a. productivity (Paragraph 24) (note how the suffixes "-ive" and "-ity"
      change the meaning of product)

   _____

   b. workaholic (Paragraph 30) (note the combination of the words "work"
      and "alcoholic")

   _____

3. Choose the correct definition of these words as they are used in the context of this reading.

   a. forensic (Paragraph 16)

   _____

b. riveters (Paragraph 21)

_____

Ask and answer questions.

1. What gives Guillermo Perez's present job meaning? How is his present situation different from his previous job?

2. According to Katrina Elias, what does a salesperson require in order to feel satisfaction with work? Why was Elias unsatisfied at her previous job?

3. Both Anita Blanchard and Sidney Walter present the same key way for people to improve their outlook and job satisfaction. What is that way?

4. When Walter worked at one of his first jobs, what did he discover about the people who did the most work and stayed overtime? What did he discover about the workers who did "just enough"?

Inference questions.

5. "Cog in the machinery" is a commonly used metaphor. Explain how it is used in Paragraph 4. How can a person be a "cog"?

6. What does Jonathon Lazear mean by saying that "being a workaholic is the only addiction applauded"? Who applauds and why?

7. Why do the experts Bazrod consulted say "the key [to finding job satisfaction] is not expecting the job to make you happy"?

Questions involving analysis.

8. Write a sentence explaining Bazrod's purpose in writing. Before writing your sentence, consider that the writer is a newspaper reporter. She reports what she learned from several "experts" as well as ordinary workers.

   _____

   _____

   _____

9. There are few facts used to support opinions in this reading. Instead, Bazrod reports experts' opinions and workers' opinions. State an opinion of one of these three experts: Samuel Culbert, Anita Blanchard, or Sidney Walter. How is that opinion supported by the opinion—based on experience—of one of the workers?

10. Two of the following statements are presented as facts, and one is an opinion. Identify the facts (F). Identify the opinion (O), and say what evidence is used to back it up.

a. _____ Statistics indicate that productivity actually decreases the more overtime one is actively working. (Paragraph 31)

_____

_____

b. _____ During World War II, when the airplane riveters found out what their little contribution did toward the end result, and saw the airplane flying in newsreels, their output increased significantly. (Paragraph 21)

_____

_____

c. _____ Seeing your job as a way to help someone is a key way of finding satisfaction. (Paragraph 16)

_____

_____

 Ask and answer your own question.

Write a question of your own. Share your question with others, and work together on an answer.

Make a map or write a summary.

What was your umbrella question for Reading IV-A? What is the overall point that answers that question? Show the overall point and the reading's main ideas in the format that works best for you: an outline or another type of map or a written summary.

 Form your final thoughts.

1. Based on your own work experience, what do you think of the opinions expressed in Bazrod's article? Are there changes you could make that would give you more job satisfaction? Why or why not?

2. Compare the ideas in this reading with one of the other readings in Part IV. Consider especially Reading 14, "The Effects of Work on Motivation," Reading 16, "Serving in Florida," or Reading 18, "The Conditions of Work." What do you think the writers would agree on? What might they disagree about?   ■

READING IV-B ONE AIRLINE'S MAGIC: HOW DOES SOUTHWEST SOAR?'

SALLY B. DONNELLY

Southwest Airlines employees are known for working extra hard and having fun doing it, as the photograph on page 315 shows. In this reading from Time *magazine, October 28, 2002, Sally B. Donnelly explores Southwest's success, a success due in large part to the way the airline treats its employees.*

CHECK IN

Before reading, **check in.** *Then,* **ask questions,** *using appropriate cues, especially the notes before the reading, the introduction, and the photograph on page 315. Ask your umbrella question, and predict the topics and overall point. As you read, use all appropriate strategies for understanding main ideas and interpreting ideas. Recognize the writer's purpose, and* **analyze the information.**

RESPOND

Relate your own experience of working and your hopes for the future to these ideas.

For underlined words, **Use Context Clues** and **Find the Right Definition.**

LOOK FOR PATTERNS OF THOUGHT

Bomaster's story is used as an illustration; note also cause-and-effect reasoning, and comparison and contrast.

Most folks know Buffalo, N.Y., for its chicken wings, but in the airline business it's famous for <u>ferocious</u> winter storms that bring air travel—and sometimes all travel—to a frozen halt. That's what happened last December when Buffalo was buried under a record 7 ft. of snow. Southwest Airlines, with its lean scheduling system, was hit harder than most. One of its planes got stuck so long it came due for a routine maintenance check. Without it, the plane wouldn't be allowed to fly—and that would cost Southwest tens of thousands of dollars in lost <u>revenue</u>. What to do? 1

Johnny Bomaster, 38, had an idea. A <u>certified</u> maintenance-check mechanic for Southwest, he lived just seven miles from the Buffalo airport but couldn't reach it over roads clotted with snow. So he tossed his toolbox onto the back of a snowmobile and zoomed through the drifts to the stranded plane. By next morning, when the runways and roads had been plowed and passengers were streaming through the terminal, Bomaster had thoroughly checked the plane and allowed it to take off fully loaded. (A new storm then stranded him at the airport for an additional 24 hours.) 2

Bomaster and workers like him are a big part of the reason that amid record losses by its competitors, Southwest last week reported $75 million in earnings for the third quarter and stands as the only profitable U.S. airline among the top eight. . . . 3

How does Southwest do it? The answer starts with lower costs. The Air Transport Association reports that other major airlines (American, United, Delta, Northwest, Continental, U.S. Airways, America West and Alaska) had unit costs—measured in cost per seat for each mile flown—nearly 100% higher than Southwest. . . . The airline "has long-term, <u>systemic</u> advantages the other carriers° can likely never match," says Vaughn Cordle, an airline pilot who heads his own consulting firm, AirlineForecasts. 4

carriers: airlines

Although starting pay for some positions at Southwest lags behind that of other carriers, Southwest has traditionally made up that <u>deficit</u> with 5

profit sharing: system in which employees receive part of company profits

stock options: the right to buy shares of a stock at a lower price than is offered to the public

shares: shares of stock; each share is a small portion of ownership in a company

generous profit sharing° and stock options°—based on shares° that have dropped 24% so far this year, after almost doubling in value over the past five years. The company is valued at $10.8 billion, more than the other major U.S. airlines combined. And employees own more than 10% of Southwest's outstanding shares. Southwest also offers something even scarcer than a valuable stock: job security. While the other majors are shrinking their service and laying off workers, Southwest is adding routes and flights, accelerating delivery of planes, hiring workers—and scooping up market share from its rivals.

To be sure, Southwest in the third quarter earned only about half as much as it did in the same period in 2001. Its top executives aren't certain whether the airline will be able to stay profitable for the final three months of 2002. And Southwest's pay advantage° is shrinking. In recent months, as workers at other airlines have been forced to make pay <u>concessions</u>, Southwest unions have been signing new contracts for pay hikes.   6

pay advantage: lower pay for employees is a pay advantage for the company

But Southwest's core advantage isn't that its employees get paid less for their work; rather, it's that they work more for their pay. They work more productively, more flexibly and more creatively—like Johnny Bomaster. Southwest pilots routinely fly nearly 80 hours a month; United pilots fly just over 50 hours, even in a busy month. Southwest pilots are paid for each trip, not each hour, so they have a strong interest in keeping flights on schedule. And because a big chunk of their <u>compensation</u> comes in the form of stock options, they tend to watch costs like bean counters. Air-traffic controllers say Southwest pilots are constantly pushing to get quicker routings to their destinations. On occasion pilots have even pitched in to help ground crews move luggage—a step <u>virtually</u> unheard of at Southwest's bigger rivals.   7

Flight attendants at Southwest work as many as 150 hours a month, compared with 80 hours at many other airlines, says union president Thom McDaniel. Southwest attendants are required by contract to "make a reasonable effort to tidy the airplane" between flights, a chore that other major airlines pay contractors to do. According to an airline labor expert, senior flight attendants at United get as many as 52 vacation days (compared with 35 days for veterans at Southwest). And they never have to clean up after the passengers.   8

NASCAR: National Association for Stock Car Racing

Operating like a NASCAR° pit crew, Southwest's mechanics pride themselves on changing airplane tires faster than their <u>counterparts</u> at other airlines. And mechanics at Southwest don't use the standard $500 tool to remove the magnetic device that detects metal chips in engine oil, as other mechanics do; they simply and quickly use their hand to pop it out. "Those tools are a waste," says a mechanic.   9

Although Southwest has a higher proportion of union members among its employees than any other major airline, the 30-year-old carrier has never suffered a layoff or strike. Unlike any other CEO° in the business, Jim Parker, 55, who joined Southwest in 1986 and took over the top spot from founder Herb Kelleher last year, personally leads most <u>negotiations</u> from Day One. "The biggest complaint in the industry is that management doesn't listen to employees," observes Southwest pilot Brad Bartholomew. "But you can't say that at Southwest. The top guy is in the room." After sometimes <u>acrimonious</u> talks with the mechanics union, Parker took both sides out to dinner. He insists, however, that the company must defend the flexibility over work rules and pay that has helped it prosper. "We cannot afford not to° take a strike if a labor demand threatens Southwest."

CEO: chief executive officer, head decision-making authority

"cannot afford not to": note the meaning of the two negatives

10

When the union that represents Southwest's pilots told members to reject the company's contract offer, Southwest pilots rebelled. "The industry—and the economy—is going to hell, and I'm supposed to vote against?" scoffed veteran pilot Tracy Price. "The union was out of touch. I took the raise." Two-thirds of the pilots voted in September to accept management's

11

The exceptional job performance of Southwest Airlines employees is due in part to management's encouragement of their creativity and sense of humor—something this employee is demonstrating.

offer. They voted the union leadership out of office last week, in large part because of its unrealistic stance on wages.

More than other airlines, Southwest <u>compensates</u> its workers in ways   12
other than base pay. It contributes 15% of its pre-tax income to a profit-sharing plan. Immediately after Sept. 11, 2001°, Southwest management assured its workers and unions that no one would be laid off. . . .

Sept. 11, 2001: day of the terrorist attacks on the World Trade Center in New York City and on the Pentagon.

Management is working to maintain the airline's trademark high   13
<u>morale</u> and good customer service, in large part through careful recruitment and training. The airline received 200,000 resumes last year but hired only 6,000 workers—making it more selective than Harvard. "Attitude is critical; skills are not," says Lorraine Grubbs-West, director at the People Department. (Southwest doesn't use the word employee.) Byron Woods, 22, a customer-service-agent trainee at Southwest, isn't much bothered that he is getting only half the $18 an hour he once made at United. That airline, he says, "trained me for eight hours on how to use the computer, then just threw me into the job." At Southwest, Woods is spending several days doing funny skits about government rules and playing games with his peers. Says Woods: "I feel lucky to be here."

point-to-point: air traffic flies directly from one airport to another

hub-and-spoke: one major airport is a central transfer point to and from other airports

Southwest has other advantages beyond its work force. It flies point-   14
to-point° domestic routes, as opposed to the complex and expensive hub-and-spoke° international networks operated by other major airlines. There are no meals served onboard, no bulky drinks carts and no entertainment. Where it makes sense, as at Oakland International Airport in California and Midway Airport in Chicago, Southwest uses less expensive, less crowded secondary airports. It flies only one type of aircraft—the Boeing 737—to reduce maintenance costs and turnaround time, and it contracts out its most intensive maintenance work. That allows the airline to employ only 1,478 mechanics for its 366 airplanes, while United needs 12,611 mechanics for 557 planes. That sounds like a lot of extra work for the folks at Southwest. But remember: one of them is Johnny Bomaster.

Follow-Up Activities   After you've finished reading, use these activities to respond to "One Airline's Magic: How Does Southwest Soar?" You may write your answers or prepare them in your mind to discuss in class.

Grab your first impressions.

Respond with your first impressions. Say what you like and dislike; relate your personal experiences to the reading; consider what more you want to know.

Work with new words.

Some words in this reading may be unfamiliar to you. Use the methods of Strategies 3 and 4 to explain what the listed words mean.

1. Use context clues.

    a. ferocious (Paragraph 1) (use logic clues)

    _____

    b. revenue (Paragraph 1) (use logic clues)

    _____

    c. deficit (Paragraph 5) (use logic clues)

    _____

    d. compensation, compensates (Paragraph 7; Paragraph 12) (use logic clues)

    _____

    e. acrimonious (Paragraph 10) (use logic clues)

    _____

2. Use word parts.

    a. systemic (Paragraph 4) (note the base word "system" and use logic clues)

    _____

    b. counterparts (Paragraph 9) (note the prefix "counter")

    _____

3. Choose the correct definition of these words as they are used in the context of this reading.

    a. certified (Paragraph 2)

    _____

    b. concessions (Paragraph 6)

    _____

    c. virtually (Paragraph 7)

    _____

    d. negotiations (Paragraph 10)

    _____

e. morale (Paragraph 13)

_____

Ask and answer questions.

1. What did Johnny Bomaster do to check out a plane so that it could take off when it was supposed to? What was unusual about his actions?

2. Aside from the example of Bomaster, what are some examples of Southwest employees working harder for their pay than their counterparts in other airlines?

3. Southwest employees' base pay often doesn't match that of employees at other airlines. What are two financial advantages mentioned in the reading that make up for Southwest workers' lower base pay?

4. How is management at Southwest trying to maintain high employee morale and good customer service?

Inference questions.

5. "Like bean counters" is a commonly used metaphorical expression (a simile in this case). Explain how it is used in Paragraph 7. Why are the pilots compared to "bean counters"?

6. Why did Southwest's pilots reject the union's recommendation and instead go with the management offer?

7. Why is it important to employees that the CEO of the company—"the top guy"—is "in the room" during negotiations between management and the union?

8. Why should activities such as "doing funny skits" and playing games with his peers make Byron Woods feels lucky to be at Southwest even though he now makes half of his United Airlines pay? What does Woods's example indicate about what keeps employee morale high at Southwest?

Questions involving analysis.

9. Write a sentence explaining Donnelly's purpose in writing.

_____

_____

_____

_____

10. Donnelly uses many facts to explain Southwest's success. But only two of the following statements are presented as facts; the other statement is an opinion. Identify the facts (F). Identify the opinion (O), and say what evidence is used to back it up.

   a. _____ The biggest complaint in the industry is that management doesn't listen to employees . . . . But you can't say that at Southwest. (Paragraph 10)

   _____

   _____

   b. _____ The 30-year-old carrier has never suffered a layoff or strike. (Paragraph 10)

   _____

   _____

   c. _____ [Southwest] flies point-to-point domestic routes, as opposed to the complex and expensive hub-and-spoke international networks operated by other major airlines. (Paragraph 10)

   _____

   _____

 Ask and answer your own question.

Write a question of your own. Share your question with others, and work together on an answer.

Make a map or write a summary.

What was your umbrella question for Reading IV-B? What is the overall point that answers that question? Show the overall point and the reading's main ideas in the format that works best for you: an outline or another type of map or a written summary.

 Form your final thoughts.

1. Southwest is remarkably successful in recruiting workers. In your opinion, what would be major reasons people might want to work at such a company? Would you want to work there? Why or why not?

2. How much does work satisfaction depend on the attitude and effort the individual worker brings to a job? How much does this satisfaction depend on working conditions created by the employer? In discussing this question, consider what other readings in Part IV have to say. ■

READING IV-C THE BRIDGE

DANIEL OROZCO

"The Bridge" is a short story by Daniel Orozco, who teaches fiction writing at Stanford University. Because this reading is a work of fiction, it is different from the other readings in this book. A story gives you an experience rather than factual information. Though fictional, the experience of the workers in "The Bridge" seems real. As you read about the challenges these bridge workers face on the job, think about some of the same questions introduced in other readings in Part IV: What gives us a sense of purpose in our work? How can we get through tough times at work? What makes people work well together?

CHECK IN

*Some reading strategies you've learned work just as well for reading stories as for reading nonfiction. Before reading, you get a sense of what the story will be like by **checking in** and **asking questions** to get an overview. But use only the notes before the reading and the first paragraph or so. Don't read the ending, because you don't want to ruin any surprises in the story!*

MAKE INFERENCES

*As you read, **make inferences** as you observe the characters and follow the action, or plot, that moves events along. Finally, **make inferences** at the climax, the point where you know how things will end.*

*Other strategies—**respond** and **ask questions**—work well during and after reading a story.*

It was tradition on the bridge for each member of the paint crew to get   1
a nickname. It was tradition that the name be pulled out of the air, and not really mean anything. It was just what you go by at work. But Baby's name was different. Baby's name was a special case.

Union Hall had sent him up when W.C. retired last summer. Although   2
he'd been working high steel a few years, Baby was young, about twenty-

Imagine the view—and the stories—of those who work on the highest parts of a bridge.

five, but looked younger. He was long and skinny, with wide hands that dangled by thin wrists from his too-short sleeves. He had a buzz-top haircut that made his ears stick out. His face got blotchy and pink in the sun. He was the youngest in Bulldog's crew by twenty years. His first day, when Bulldog brought him to the crew shack inside the south tower and introduced him around, you could see this boy sizing up the old-timers, calculating the age difference in his head and grinning about it. He tossed his gear into W.C.'s old locker and flopped on the bench next to it. He pulled out a Walkman and started fiddling with the earphones. And while the crew was getting down to first things first, discussing a nickname for him, he let out a phlegmy little snort and muttered, Well geez°, just don't call me Kid. Then he turned on his Walkman, opened his mouth, and shut his eyes. Bulldog and the crew regarded him for a moment, this skinny, open-mouthed boy stretched out on W.C.'s bench, his big booted feet bouncing fitfully to the tinny scratching of music coming from his ears. The painters then returned to the matter at hand. They would not call him Kid. They would not call him Sonny or Junior, either. They would go one better. And with little discussion, they decided to veer from tradition just this once. And Baby's name was born.

For underlined words, Use Context Clues and Find the Right Definition.

Well geez . . . Kid: there are no quotation marks when characters speak in this story. Here "muttered" and the words themselves show Baby is speaking.

Being new to bridge painting, Baby is still getting the hang of things, with his partner Whale telling him to check his harness, to yank on it at least a hundred times a day to make sure it's fast; to check that his boots are laced up because there's no tripping allowed, not up here, the first step is a killer; and to always attach his safety line, to clip it onto anything and everything. Baby listens, but under duress, rolling his eyes and muttering, Yeah, yeah, yeah, I got it, I got it, which sets Whale off. But Bulldog and the rest of them tell him to take it easy. They are old hands at this, they remind him. They are cautious and patient men, and Baby's just young, that's all. He'll learn to slow down, as each of them learned; he'll learn to get used to the steady and deliberate pace of their work, what Bulldog calls the Art of Painting a Bridge: degreasing a section of steel first; sandblasting and inspecting for corrosion; and after the iron crew's done replacing the corroded plates or rivets or whatever, blasting again; sealing the steel with primer one, and primer two the next day; then top coat one the day after that, and top coat two the day after that.   3

Note the extra space between paragraphs here and at other points. See how they break up events in the story.

Note how you can tell what the characters say to each other without having actual quotations from them.

Whale doesn't like working with Baby, but he's partnered with him. So the two of them are under the roadbed, up inside the latticework. They go from the joists° down, moving east-west along a row of crossbeams on the San Francisco side of the south tower. Whale is blasting rust out of a tight   4

joists: beams ranged parallel from wall to wall to support a floor or ceiling

spot behind a tie brace, and Baby moves in to spray primer one, when suddenly his paint gun sputters and dies. He yanks off his noise helmet, shouts at Whale over the wind, and unclips his safety line to go look for the kink in his paint hose. Pissed off, Whale yells, Goddammit, but it's muffled under his helmet. Baby clunks down the platform in his big spattered boots. His line trails behind him, the steel carabiner clip° skittering along the platform grating.

He spots the trouble right away, at the east end, just over his head—a   5
section of hose hung up between the power line and the scaffold° cable. He reaches up, stands on his toes, and leans out a little, his hips high against the railing. He grasps the hose, snaps it once, twice, three times until it clears. And just as he's turning around to give Whale the thumbs-up, a woman appears before him, inches from his face. She passes into and out of his view in less than two seconds. But in Baby's memory, she would be a woman floating, suspended in the flat light and the gray swirling mist.

The witnesses said she dived off the bridge headfirst. They said she   6
was walking along when she suddenly dropped her book bag and scrambled onto the guardrail, balancing on the top rail for a moment, arms over her head, then bouncing once from bended knees and disappearing over the side. It happened so fast, according to one witness. It was a perfect dive, according to another.

But her <u>trajectory</u> was poor. Too close to the bridge, her foot smashed   7
against a beam, spinning her around and pointing her feet and legs downward. She was looking at Baby as she went past him, apparently just as surprised to see him as he was to see her. She was looking into his face, into his eyes, her arms upstretched, drawing him to her as she dropped away.

And wondering how you decide to remember what you remember,   8
wondering why you retain the memory of one detail and not another, Baby would remember, running those two seconds over and over in his head, her hands reaching toward him, fingers splayed, and her left hand balling into a fist just before the fog swallowed her. He would remember a thick, dark green pullover sweater, and the rush of her fall bunching the green under her breasts, revealing a thin pale waist, and a fluttering white shirttail. He would remember bleached blue jeans with rips flapping at both knees, and basketball shoes—those red high-tops that kids wear—and the redness of them arcing around, her legs and torso following as she twisted at the hips and straightened out, knifing into the bed of fog below. But what he could not remember was her face. Although he got a good look at her—at one point just about nose to nose, no more than six inches away—it was not a clear sustained image of her face that stayed with him, but a flashing one, shutter-clicking on and off, on and off in his head. He could not remember a single detail. Her eyes locked with his as she went past and down, and Baby

carabiner clip: oblong metal ring with one spring-hinged side, used to hold a rope

scaffold: movable platform for working high up

RESPOND

Imagine yourself in Baby's place; think how you'd respond.

could not—for the life of him, and however hard he tried—remember what color they were.

But he would remember hearing, in spite of the wind whistling in his ears, in spite of the roar of traffic, the locomotive clatter of tires over the expansion gaps° in the roadbed above, in spite of the hysterical thunking° of the air compressor° in the machine shed directly over him—Baby would remember hearing, as she went past, a tiny sound, an *oof* or an *oops,* probably her reaction to her ankle shattering against the beam above less than a second before. It was a small muted grunt, a sound of minor exertion, of a small effort completed, the kind of sound that Baby had associated—before today—with plopping a heavy bag of groceries on the kitchen table, or getting up, woozy, after having squatted on his knees to zip up his boy's jacket.

Whale drops his gun and goes clomping down the platform after Baby, who stands frozen, leaning out and staring down, saying, Man oh man, man oh man oh man. He gets to Baby just as his knees buckle, and hooks his safety line first thing. He pulls him to his feet, pries his gloved fingers from around the railing, and walks him to the other end of the platform. He hangs on to Baby as he reels the scaffold back under the tower, too fast. The wet cables slip and squeal through their pulleys, and the platform travels in jolts and shudders until it slams finally into the deck with a reassuring clang. He unhooks their safety lines—Baby's first, then his own—and reaches out to clip them onto the ladder. He grabs a fistful of Baby's harness and eases him—limp and obedient—over the eighteen inch gap between the scaffold gate and the ladder platform. He puts Baby's hands on the first rung. They brace themselves as they swing out; the gusts are always meaner on the west side of the bridge. The shifting winds grab at their parkas and yank at their safety lines, the yellow cords billowing out in twin arcs, then whipping at their backs and legs. They go one rung at a time, turtling up the ladder in an intimate embrace—Whale on top of Baby, belly to back, his mouth warm in Baby's ear, whispering, Nice and easy, Baby, over and over, That's it, Baby, nice and easy, nice and easy. Halfway up, they can hear the Coast Guard cutter below them, its engines revving and churning as it goes past, following the current out to sea.

They knock off a little early. In the parking lot, Baby leans against his car, smoking another cigarette, telling Whale and Bulldog and Gomer that he's okay, that he'll be driving home in a minute, just let him finish his cigarette, all right? Whale looks over at Gomer, then takes Baby's car keys and drives him home. Gomer follows in his car and gives Whale a ride back to the lot.

9

10

11

expansion gaps: gaps put in a bridge because metal in a bridge roadbed expands and contracts

thunking: similar to "thumping"

air compressor: machine that uses air pressure to spray paint

Suiting up in the crew shack the next morning, they ask him how he's   12
doing, did he get any sleep, and he says, Yeah, he's okay. So they take this
time, before morning shift starts, to talk about it a little bit, all of them
needing to talk it out for a few minutes, each of them having encountered
jumpers, with C.B. seeing two in one day once—just an hour apart—from

bosun's platform: platform (usually on a ship) where someone can survey the work of a crew

his bosun's platform° halfway up the north tower, first one speck, then
another, going over the side and into the water, and C.B. not being able to
do anything about it. And Whale taking hours to talk one out of it once, and
her calling him a week later to thank him, then jumping a week after that.
And Bulldog having rescued four different jumpers from up on the pedes-
trian walkway, but also losing three up there, one of them an old guy who
stood shivering on the five-inch-wide ledge just outside the rail and seven
feet below the walkway, shivering there all morning in his bathrobe and
slippers, looking like he'd taken a wrong turn on a midnight run to the toi-
let, and after standing there thinking about it, changing his mind; and
reaching through the guardrail for Bulldog's outstretched arm, brushing
the tips of Bulldog's fingers before losing his footing.

But that's how it goes, Bulldog says, and he slaps his thighs and tells   13
everybody to get a move on, it's time to paint a bridge.

At lunch, Baby is looking through the paper. He tells Gomer and C.B.   14
and the rest of them how he hates the way they keep numbering jumpers.
She was the 975th, and he wished they'd stop doing that. And when
they're reeling in the scaffold for afternoon break, he turns to Whale and
tells him—without Whale's asking—the worst thing about it was that he
was the last person, the last living human being she saw before she died,
and he couldn't even remember what she looked like, and he didn't need
that, he really didn't.

And that's when Baby loses his noise helmet. It slips out from the   15
crook of his arm, hits the scaffold railing, and <u>lobs</u> over the side. It being a
clear day, they both follow the helmet all the way down, not saying anything, just leaning out and watching it, squinting their eyes from the sun

cowl: fabric hood attached to the helmet

reflecting off the surface of the bay, and hearing it fall, the cowl° fluttering
and snapping behind the headpiece, until the helmet hits with a loud sharp
crack, like a gunshot. Not the sound of something hitting water at all.

At break, Baby's pretty upset. But Bulldog tells him not to sweat it, the   16
first helmet's free. Yeah, Red says, but after that it costs you, and Red
should know, having lost three helmets in his nineteen years. But Baby
can't shut up about it. He goes on about the sound it made when it hit the
water, about how amazing it is that from 220 feet up you can single out one
f****** sound. He's worked up now. His voice is cracking, his face is red-
der than usual. They all look at him, then at each other, and Bulldog sits

him down while the rest of them go out to work. Baby tells him he's sorry about the f****** helmet, he really is, and that it won't happen again. And that's when Bulldog tells him to go on home. Go home, he says, and kiss your wife. Take the rest of the day, Bulldog says, I'll clear it with the bridge captain, no sweat.

Everybody's suiting up for morning shift. It's a cold one today, with the   17
only heat coming from the work lights strung across a low beam overhead. They climb quickly into long johns° and wool shirts and sweaters and parkas. They drink their coffee, fingers of steam rising from open thermoses, curling up past the lights. They wolf down donuts that Red brought. Whale is picking through the box looking for an old-fashioned glaze, and C.B. is complaining to Red why he never gets those frosted sprinkled ones anymore, when Baby, who hasn't said a word since coming back, asks nobody in particular if he could maybe get a new nickname.

long johns: long underwear

The painters all look at each other. Tradition says you don't change the   18
nickname of a painter on the bridge. You just never do that. But on the other hand, it seems important to the boy. And sometimes you have to accommodate the members of your crew, because that's what keeps a paint crew together. They watch him sitting there, concentrating on relacing his boots, tying and untying them, saying, It's no big deal, really, it's just that I never liked the name you gave me, and I was just wondering.

So they take these few minutes before the morning shift to weigh this   19
decision. Whale chews slowly on the last old-fashioned glaze. Bulldog pours himself another half-cup, and C.B. and Red both sit hunched over, coiling and uncoiling safety line. Gomer tips his chair back, dances it on its hind legs, and stares up past the work lights. The boy clears his throat, but Bulldog reaches over, touches his knee with two fingers, shakes his head. The boy falls silent. He looks over at Gomer rocking his chair with his head thrown back. He follows his gaze. Squinting past the lights, peering up into the dark, he listens to the gusts outside whistling through the tower above them.

Follow-Up Activities   After you've finished reading, use these activities to respond to "The Bridge." You may write your answers or prepare them in your mind to discuss in class.

Grab your first impressions.

Respond with your first impressions. Say what you like and dislike; relate your personal experiences to the reading; consider what more you want to know.

Work with new words.

Some words in this reading may be unfamiliar to you. Use the methods of Strategies 3 and 4 to explain what the listed words mean.

1. Use context clues.

   a. veer (Paragraph 2)

   _____

   b. fast (Paragraph 3) (use logic clues)

   _____

   c. duress (Paragraph 3) (use logic clues)

   _____

2. Choose the correct definition of these words as they are used in the context of this reading.

   a. phlegmy (Paragraph 2)

   _____

   b. corrosion and corroded (Paragraph 3)

   _____

   c. rivets (Paragraph 3)

   _____

   d. trajectory (Paragraph 7)

   _____

   e. lobs (Paragraph 15)

   _____

Ask and answer questions.

1. What was the tradition for giving crew members a nickname? How did Baby's name break that tradition?

2. What was the trouble with the paint hose? What did Baby do to fix it?

3. How did Baby see the woman fall? What happened during her fall that made her face right side up as she fell past him?

4. What were some of the examples of jumpers that members of the crew had tried to help in the past?

Inference questions.

Making inferences is essential for understanding and enjoying stories. These questions explore some important aspects of the story, but continue asking your own inference questions after answering these.

5. Why doesn't Whale like working with Baby? How do the other crew members help Whale accept being Baby's partner?

6. Why is Baby so bothered by the fact that he remembers details about the woman's fall, including the way she was dressed, but he can't remember her face?

7. Notice the metaphorical expression "knifing" in this sentence from Paragraph 8: "He would remember bleached blue jeans with rips flapping at both knees, and basketball shoes—those red high-tops that kids wear—and the redness of them arcing around, her legs and torso following as she twisted at the hips and straightened out, <u>knifing</u> into the bed of fog below." How does this metaphorical expression contribute to the picture of the way the woman falls through the fog?

8. Notice the metaphorical expression "turtling" in Paragraph 10: "They go one rung at a time, <u>turtling</u> up the ladder in an intimate embrace—Whale on top of Baby, belly to back, his mouth warm in Baby's ear, whispering, "Nice and easy, Baby, over and over, That's it, Baby, nice and easy, nice and easy." What makes Baby and Whale seem like a turtle going up the ladder?

9. What are some important details about the way Whale gets Baby back up to the safety of the bridge? What do these details show about Whale?

10. Why does Whale take the keys from Baby? What does it show about Whale and Gomer that they drive Baby home?

11. Why is Baby so upset when he loses his noise helmet? How does the rest of the crew react? Why does Bulldog tell Baby to take the rest of the day off and "Go home . . . and kiss your wife"?

12. Orozco gives many details to show what Baby sees and hears. Choose some details that show images or sounds. How do these details help you understand what's happening to Baby?

 Ask and answer your own questions.

Write questions of your own. Share your questions with others, and work together on answers.

Form your final thoughts.

1. What was your favorite piece of description in the story? Explain to others what you liked about it.

2. Read the final paragraph (paragraph 19) carefully. What does Bulldog do to indicate that the crew members will not change Baby's nickname? How important is this decision to the meaning of the story? Discuss what difference it would make to the story if the crew had decided instead to make the change.

3. What does this story show about finding purpose in work or about getting through tough times at work? Can you relate the experience of these workers to any work situation you've been in? Why or why not?   ■

READING IV-D WHO BURNS FOR THE PERFECTION OF PAPER

MARTÍN ESPADA

CHECK IN

This poem is by Martín Espada. Espada is now a professor of English at the University of Massachusetts and author of several books of poetry, but formerly he was a lawyer working for tenants' rights.

At sixteen, I worked after high school hours
at a printing plant
that manufactured legal pads:
Yellow paper
stacked seven feet high   5
and leaning
as I slipped cardboard
between the pages,
then brushed red glue
up and down the stack.   10
No gloves: fingertips required
for the perfection of paper,
smoothing the exact rectangle.
sluggish: slow-moving   Sluggish° by 9 PM, the hands
would slide along suddenly sharp paper,   15
crevices: narrow openings   and gather slits thinner than the crevices°
of the skin, hidden.
The glue would sting,
hands oozing

till both palms burned   20
at the punch clock.

Ten years later, in law school,
I knew that every legal pad
was glued with the sting of hidden cuts,
that every open law book   25
was a pair of hands
upturned and burning.

Follow-Up Activities   After you've finished reading, use these activities to respond to "Who Burns for the Perfection of Paper." You may write your answers or prepare them in your mind to discuss in class.

Grab your first impressions.

Respond with your first impressions. Say what you like and dislike; relate your personal experiences to the reading; consider what more you want to know.

Ask and answer inference questions.

To understand and enjoy poems, you need to **make inferences**. For example, the experience described in this poem is quite clear. But the following questions explore the important implied meaning in the poem. Continue asking your own inference questions after answering these.

1. What details in lines 2–6 give you an image of the worker on the job? What is the size of the job in comparison to the worker?

2. Why couldn't workers use gloves? Why were "fingertips required"?

3. Why is the speaker in the poem "sluggish by 9 PM"? What had he been doing until that time?

4. Why would being sluggish make the hands "slide along suddenly sharp paper"?

5. The palms would burn doing other activities, but why is it important to the poem to show them burning "at the punch clock"?

6. What kinds of things might the speaker of the poem have done during the ten years between working in the printing plant and going to law school?

7. In lines 22–24, the poet uses a metaphor to describe how the legal pad was made. What is that metaphor? What is its meaning?

8. The final lines of the poem are made up of another metaphor. What does the poet mean by saying, "every open law book/was a pair of hands/upturned and burning"?

 Ask and answer your own questions.

Write questions of your own. Share your questions with others, and work together on answers.

 Form your final thoughts.

1. Remember that a poem often implies more than one meaning. What meaning do you get from the title of this poem? Discuss the possible meanings with others.

2. How does this poem relate to you as a worker or as someone who uses what other workers have made?   ■

PART IV REVIEW
REMEMBERING AND INTERPRETING

You've completed Part IV. Now take some time to look back at both the theme and the strategies introduced in this part.

Theme: Working in America

The theme of Part IV is the place of work in our personal lives and in the social and economic life of the nation. Write down or discuss with others in class the ideas you found most interesting on this theme. Which were your favorite readings? Why?

_____

_____

_____

_____

_____

Strategies: Write to Remember, Make Inferences, and Analyze the Information

In Part IV you saw how mapping—making an outline or another type of map—and summarizing can help you clarify and remember ideas. You also learned to deepen your interpretation of a reading by understanding implied ideas and by analyzing the writer's purpose and use of facts and opinions. Look at the chart on page 332 to remind yourself when you use the three new strategies, **Write to Remember, Make Inferences,** and **Analyze the Information.** The new strategies are in white.

PART IV REVIEW

Using Strategies Throughout the Reading Process

GET STARTED   Begin with strategies that help you think about the subject and find out about what the writer will say.

- Check in
- Ask questions

READ   Use strategies that help you read with greater understanding, interpret the language, and respond with your own questions and ideas.

- Use context clues
- Find the right meaning
- Ask questions
- Find main ideas
- Look for support
- Look for patterns of thought
- Make inferences
- Analyze the information
- Write to remember
- Respond

FOLLOW UP   End with strategies that help you look more closely at the language and ideas in the reading, assess your understanding, and respond in a thoughtful way.

- Find the right meaning
- Ask questions
- Find main ideas
- Look for support
- Look for patterns of thought
- Write to remember
- Make inferences
- Analyze the information
- Respond

How Are the Strategies Working for You?

Here is your last chance in this book to evaluate the strategies you've learned. But you'll keep using these strategies as you read for your college courses. Continue thinking about how to get the best use from them.

First, answer the following questions to help you evaluate Strategies 9 through 11. Finally, compare notes with other students, and ask your instructor for ideas on how to get more out of all the reading strategies.

1. How much time are these strategies taking?

   _____

   _____

   _____

2. Overall, how helpful have these strategies been in increasing your ability to understand and enjoy what you read?

   _____

   _____

   _____

3. Think about the courses you're likely to take next term. Which strategies do you think will be most useful for the types of reading in those courses?

   _____

   _____

   _____

GLOSSARY

active reading: reading that keeps you involved, as you respond with your own questions and ideas to what the writer says

annotations: notes you write in margins to go along with underlining

argument: writing that persuades you to believe something or do something

box map: organization of ideas displayed with the overall point at the top and main ideas spaced horizontally below it

cluster map: organization of ideas displayed with the overall point in the center and main ideas branched around it

complete sentence: sentence that has a subject and verb and expresses a complete thought

connotation (connotative meaning): specialized associations that accompany a word

context: the surroundings in which you find a word

context clues: clues from surrounding words and ideas that suggest the meaning of a new word

contrast clues: clues that suggest that the meaning of a new word is the opposite of a word you already know

cues: parts of a reading that lead you to important ideas

definition clues: words or punctuation marks that show you a new word is being defined for you

denotation (denotative meaning): basic or literal meaning of a word

description: writing that shows what someone or something is like

descriptions: details that tell how someone or something looks, sounds, or feels

etymology: origin and history of a word

example clues: clues that use examples or instances to suggest the meaning of a new word

examples: instances that give specific situations or cases to demonstrate a general idea

explanations: clarifications or reasons given to support an idea exposition: writing that explains something or instructs

fact: statement that can be proven or confirmed

general: refers to a large category (for example, fruit)

general reader: someone who is not an expert or student of a subject

headings: words or phrases that act as titles for each section of a reading

implied idea: idea suggested by using certain words, details, or other evidence

indent: in an outline, move in from the left margin

infer (make inferences): make connections and draw logical conclusions based on evidence

inference: well-informed guess

intended audience: the readers a writer expects to reach

journal or reading log: a place for writing down your ideas about a reading

literal: using the ordinary or primary meaning of a word ("bear" as a type of animal is literal; "bear" as a type of boss is metaphorical)

logic clues: clues about the meaning of a word that come from the logic of the rest of the sentence

main idea: general or overall idea about a main topic; it helps explain the overall point

major detail: detail that directly supports the main idea

map: a skeleton of a reading's organization of ideas

margin notes: words, phrases, or symbols written in the margin next to a sentence or sentences you want to respond to or annotate

metaphor: (broadly defined) nonliteral comparison that points to a surprising image or idea; (narrowly defined) nonliteral comparison, not using "like" or "as" (Example: "My boss is a bear.")

minor detail: more specific detail that supports a major detail

narration: writing that tells what happened, or tells a story

note form: shortened form of writing, such as margin notes or class notes

notes before a reading: notes about the author and the reading

on-line dictionary: dictionary on the Internet

opinion: statement that cannot be proven or disproven, but may be valuable if backed up with evidence

outline: vertical listing of ideas with the overall point at the top and main ideas below it

overall point: the writer's most important message that covers—or includes—all of the other ideas in a reading

overview: an overall sense of the entire subject, indicating what is important in a reading

paraphrase: translate others' words into your own words

patterns of thought: structures our minds use as we think, talk, read, or write

perspective: way of looking at a subject; position on a subject

predict: use all the cues in a reading to see what to expect

prefix: a word part that comes at the beginning of a word; it indicates such information as direction (in, out, under) and number

prior knowledge: knowledge we have from past experience

purpose: the writer's reasons for writing

quotation: the exact words used by another writer or speaker

reader's voice: the voice in your mind that responds as you read what the writer is saying

reading strategy: a clear plan or method for approaching a reading assignment

review: go over again to study and remember

root: a word part that gives a word its core meaning; it may come at the beginning, middle, or end of a word

simile: special type of nonliteral comparison, using "like" or "as" ("My boss is like a bear.")

specific: refers to a particular type or part within a larger category (for example, type of fruit, including bananas, grapes, apples)

stated main idea: idea expressed directly in a sentence or two in the reading

subheading: heading that names a subtopic

subject: what the reading is about; the focus for all the ideas

subtopic: a specific topic that supports a more general topic suffix: a word part that comes at the end of a word; it shows how the word is used in the sentence (noun, verb, adjective, or adverb)

summary: brief—usually one-paragraph—restatement of main ideas

support: various ways of explaining, demonstrating, or backing up a main idea

supporting detail: specific detail used to support a more general idea

synonyms: two words or phrases that have the same meaning

testing a main idea sentence: examining the sentence to see if it covers all the supporting details

topic: what a part of a reading is about

topic sentence: the stated main idea of a paragraph

transition: a word or phrase that serves as a bridge or link from one thought to the next

type of writing: a way of presenting ideas; each type is appropriate for a certain purpose

umbrella question: question based on the title and other cues from your overview

underlining: using pencil or pen to draw a line under important phrases or sentences

unstated main idea: idea understood without its appearing in one sentence; can be given as a summary statement of important details

verify: check for accuracy

word part: element of a word that has a constant meaning

ADDITIONAL QUESTIONS FOR
THE READER'S VOICE

This section of the book gives you and your instructor additional ways to make sure you've understood a reading and learned some of the new words the author used. For each reading you'll find five multiple-choice comprehension questions. Starting with Reading 7, after you've been introduced to Strategy 3, **Use Context Clues,** and Strategy 4, **Find the Right Definition,** you'll also find five multiple-choice vocabulary questions for each reading.

Chapter 1

Reading 1: Poppa and the Spruce Tree: A Lesson from My Father

Comprehension Questions

Choose the answer that best completes each statement.

_____ 1. At the beginning of the reading, Cuomo was very discouraged about his

    a. writing career.

    b. teaching career.

    c. father's health.

    d. political campaign.

_____ 2. Cuomo's father was a

    a. gardener.

    b. grocer.

    c. governor of New York.

    d. printer.

_____ 3. Cuomo got his sons to help him rescue the tree by

    a. pulling up the tree with a rope and pruning the dead branches.

    b. digging it up and replanting it.

    c. pulling up the tree with a rope and digging a wider hole for it.

    d. covering it to protect it from frost.

_____ 4. The main lesson Cuomo learned from the way his father dealt with the tree was

    a. how skilled at gardening his father was.

    b. when to cover a tree in cold weather.

    c. he could get someone else to help him with a problem.

    d. he could overcome obstacles that seemed overwhelming.

_____ 5. Remembering the lesson helped Cuomo

    a. get excited again about his political campaign.

    b. get interested in gardening again.

    c. deal with losing the campaign for governor.

    d. overcome his writer's block.

Reading 2: A Role Model of Resiliency: Bouncing Back from Disaster

Comprehension Questions

Choose the answer that best completes each statement.

_____ 1. As a high school student Thomas had been a

    a. top high school athlete.

    b. grade-A student.

    c. drug dealer.

    d. composer.

_____ 2. As part of Thomas's "starting over from scratch" he had to relearn how to

    a. see.

    b. speak.

    c. hear.

    d. feed himself.

_____ 3. A main way Thomas finds spiritual strength is through

    a. special skiing for the blind.

    b. silent meditation.

    c. fasting.

    d. music.

_____ 4. When coaching youthful basketball players, Thomas

  a. has his sighted assistant show them moves.

  b. gets out on the floor and shows them moves.

  c. uses a video to demonstrate the moves.

  d. requires the players to take notes about the moves.

_____ 5. An important technique Thomas uses in his inspirational presentations is to have his audience

  a. chant positive sayings about their ability to change.

  b. discuss his ideas in small groups.

  c. visualize things with their eyes shut.

  d. draw visual representations of what they hear.

Chapter 2

Reading 3: The Struggle to Be an All-American Girl

Comprehension Questions

Choose the answer that best completes each statement.

_____ 1. After school every day, her mother wanted her to go to Chinese school, but Wong herself wanted to play with her friends or

  a. watch her favorite TV programs.

  b. take care of her neighbor's animals.

  c. hunt ghosts and animal bones.

  d. read books her American teacher gave her to read.

_____ 2. One of the things Wong hated about the Chinese school was

  a. the hard seats on the chairs.

  b. the old, dirty pictures on the walls.

  c. the way it smelled.

  d. the fact that it had no windows.

_____ 3. To Wong, the Chinese language sounded like

  a. French.

  b. confused, nonsensical speech.

  c. chop suey.

  d. strange, pleasant-sounding music.

_____ 4. When Wong was able to stop going to Chinese school, she says, "At last, I was one of you; I wasn't one of them." By "them" she means

　　a. people from mainstream American culture.

　　b. a local troop of American Girl Scouts.

　　c. her Mexican-American friends.

　　d. people from her Chinese-American culture.

_____ 5. Wong's last sentence is "Sadly, I still am." By this she means she regrets

　　a. losing contact with her Chinese background.

　　b. being angry with her brother.

　　c. not being able to be as American as she would like.

　　d. eating Mexican food rather than Chinese food.

Reading 4: Self-Esteem

Comprehension Questions

Choose the answer that best completes each statement.

_____ 1. As a young girl Elizabeth Wong had negative feelings about her Chinese background. "Self-Esteem," Reading 4, suggests that Wong's feelings would contribute to her

　　a. positive self-esteem.

　　b. low self-esteem.

　　c. resentment of her brother's self-esteem.

　　d. suicidal tendencies.

_____ 2. "Drivers" as defined in the Building Communication Skills box are beliefs that

　　a. substitute for formal religion.

　　b. allow you to drive a car or other vehicle.

　　c. force you to do things you shouldn't do.

　　d. motivate you to act in certain ways.

_____ 3. One step for eliminating self-defeating drivers is to

　　a. take on more realistic and self-affirming beliefs.

　　b. try harder next time.

　　c. recognize what you need to do to please other people.

　　d. take on a stronger drive to be perfect.

_____ 4. Saying "I'm open to new ideas," "I'm responsible," and "I'm goal directed" are all examples of

   a. self-importance.

   b. self-consciousness.

   c. self-affirmation.

   d. self-denial.

_____ 5. Exercise seemed to contribute to the self-esteem of adults aged 60 to 75 because

   a. they lost weight, which made them look better.

   b. their increased strength gave them more control over their environment.

   c. they met fellow exercisers at the gym and formed new friendships.

   d. they began winning sports competitions for their age group.

Chapter 3

Reading 5: Sounds of Home: An 8,690-Mile Echo

Comprehension Questions

Choose the answer that best completes each statement.

_____ 1. After the Cambodian monks blessed the river and the colorful dragon boats were launched, there was Cambodian music and dance alternating with

   a. young women singing well-known American folk songs.

   b. children making flower wreathes and throwing them into the river.

   c. rowers in the dragon boats having short races on the river.

   d. young women singing the songs of Whitney Houston and Celine Dion.

_____ 2. The Khmer Rouge was responsible for

   a. the deaths of at least one million Cambodians.

   b. the overthrow of the Communist regime in Cambodia.

   c. the invasion of Vietnam.

   d. the Southeast Asian Water Festival.

_____ 3. When three leaders of Seasia went back to Cambodia with Arn Chorn-Pond they performed with traditional musicians and

  a. appeared on Cambodian television.

  b. learned to play the traditional Cambodian instruments.

  c. studied Cambodian music at the university in Phnom Penh.

  d. taught American folk and popular songs to children in village schools.

_____ 4. The moment Tony Roun and the other Seasia band members decided they could put a Cambodian band together was when they

  a. arrived in Lowell and met one another.

  b. heard a West Coast Cambodian group perform.

  c. heard a Latin group perform.

  d. had mastered the traditional Cambodian music.

_____ 5. Seasia's song "Hero in My Eyes" helps to sum up the whole reading because it

  a. honors Arn Chorn-Pond for taking them back to Cambodia.

  b. makes a bridge between the respect for traditional Cambodian music and the new American hip-hop music.

  c. shows the group's expertise in playing the traditional music their Cambodian master has taught them.

  d. demonstrates their rebellion against their traditional Cambodian culture.

Chapter 4

Reading 6: American Youth Slang: From Flappers 2 Rappers

Comprehension Questions

Choose the answer that best completes each statement.

_____ 1. Throughout the twentieth century, American youth slang has been most heavily influenced by African-American

  a. folk and gospel singers.

  b. opera and musical comedy singers.

  c. jazz musicians and rappers.

  d. television and movie comedians.

_____ 2. One theory says that young people use slang to hide the meaning of what they say from adults who are in authority; Dalzell disagrees with this theory because he says most young people

    a. are afraid of getting in trouble with adults.

    b. don't use slang unless they're angry.

    c. have learned a better vocabulary and don't need to use slang.

    d. don't use slang in front of adults.

_____ 3. According to Dalzell, slang is a way for young people to defy authority; in other words, they use slang to

    a. keep secrets from adult authority figures.

    b. rebel against the language and manners of adult authority figures.

    c. sound impressive to adult authority figures.

    d. learn the language and manners of adult authority figures.

_____ 4. "Groovy" is an example of a cyclical slang word—one that was forgotten and then came back to popularity; another example Dalzell gives of a slang word that cycled back into use is

    a. trip.

    b. drag.

    c. freak.

    d. mellow.

_____ 5. Dalzell says that slang gives established greetings and farewells for young people to use with each other; one thing these greetings and farewells do is help young people avoid

    a. risking embarrassing themselves.

    b. talking to people they don't want to talk to.

    c. having to make any physical contact.

    d. saying the same thing over and over.

Chapter 5

Reading 7: Movie Censorship: A Brief History

Vocabulary Questions

Using the methods of Strategy 3, **Use Context Clues,** and Strategy 4, **Find the Right Definition,** choose the correct definition of each underlined word as it is used in the context of this reading.

_____ 1. devised a five-step rating system (Paragraph 1):

    a. developed   c. denied

    b. began   d. thought about

_____ 2. a prominent Republican (Paragraph 2):

    a. well-known   c. determined

    b. conservative   d. primary

_____ 3. some chapters boycotted theaters (Paragraph 5):

    a. supported   c. stayed away from

    b. concealed   d. burned down

_____ 4. banned as a sacrilege (Paragraph 6):

    a. lack of knowledge about religious beliefs

    b. lack of sacrifice for religious beliefs

    c. lack of courage to defend religious beliefs

    d. lack of respect for religious beliefs

_____ 5. film-makers became a bit more venturesome (Paragraph 6):

    a. timid   c. handsome

    b. daring   d. thoughtful

Comprehension Questions

Choose the answer that best completes each statement.

_____ 1. The Motion Picture Production Code of 1930 prevented movie-goers from seeing naughty language, sexually suggestive material, and

    a. unpatriotic material.

    b. bad guys going unpunished.

    c. religious material.

    d. on-screen murders.

_____ 2. A major reason the 1930s movie theater owners decided not to show movies that didn't meet the code was because of

a. a decision of the Supreme Court.

b. people's lack of money during the Depression.

c. actions organized by the Legion of Decency.

d. a protest by the movie theater owners themselves against immoral movies.

_____ 3. The 1953 movie *The Moon Is Blue* was important for understanding the history of movie censorship because it

a. was the first movie to be boycotted throughout the entire nation.

b. was the first movie since before the code to show nudity.

c. became a First Amendment issue and a victory for free expression.

d. was a box-office hit even though it failed to receive code approval.

_____ 4. In the current movie code, movies are

a. not banned, but rated so parents can judge which movies to let their children see.

b. banned unless they meet current standards of taste.

c. banned for sexual content but not for violence.

d. not banned, but if movies have sexual content, there must be edited versions made for children.

_____ 5. An R rating for a movie means that an adult must accompany anyone under the age of

a. 13.

b. 16.

c. 17.

d. 18.

Reading 8: The Day Athletics Won Out Over Politics

Vocabulary Questions

Using the methods of Strategy 3, **Use Context Clues,** and Strategy 4, **Find the Right Definition,** choose the correct definition of each underlined word as it is used in the context of this reading.

_____ 1. inexplicably, he had trouble (Paragraph 1):

     a. rarely   c. nervously

     b. strangely   d. understandably

_____ 2. silently berating himself (Paragraph 2):

     a. analyzing   c. criticizing

     b. cheering   d. readying

_____ 3. feat of winning four gold medals (Paragraph 5):

     a. accomplishment   c. defeat

     b. reward   d. dream

_____ 4. patron of the Games (Paragraph 7):

     a. dictator   c. addict

     b. boss   d. sponsor

_____ 5. tawdry international politics (Paragraph 9):

     a. risky and underhanded

     b. cheap and sleazy

     c. opinionated and biased

     d. concealed and sneaky

Comprehension Questions

Choose the answer that best completes each statement.

_____ 1. Before he started having trouble qualifying for the long jump, Jesse Owens had

     a. already won the 100 meters race.

     b. a history of psychological problems.

     c. lost the 200 meters race.

     d. been snubbed by Hitler.

_____ 2. Long's advice to Owens was to

   a. use a mark a few inches beyond the takeoff board.

   b. calm himself down by taking deep breaths.

   c. use a mark a few inches in front of the takeoff board.

   d. close his eyes as he was about to take off.

_____ 3. Hitler was troubled by the success of Owens and the other African-Americans on the U.S. track team because they

   a. represented a threat to the Nazi army.

   b. backed up Hitler's ideas about racial superiority.

   c. undercut the Nazi myths about racial superiority.

   d. would become too friendly with some of the German athletes, such as Luz Long.

_____ 4. We can see evidence of the lasting friendship between Owens and Long in the fact that they

   a. each won Olympic medals.

   b. fought in the same unit in Italy.

   c. continued to write each other letters.

   d. saw each other many times after the Berlin Games.

_____ 5. Their friendship was important for the history of the Olympic Games because it showed that

   a. athletes can communicate with each other in spite of their language differences.

   b. the spirit of open and honest competition between athletes can overcome offensive political beliefs.

   c. athletes have a superior ability to cooperate and make friends.

   d. the spirit of the Games can help make people rise above materialistic economic interests.

Chapter 6

Reading 9: Money Fights Can Ruin a Marriage

Vocabulary Questions

Using the methods of Strategy 3, **Use Context Clues,** and Strategy 4, **Find the Right Definition,** choose the correct definition of each underlined word as it is used in the context of this reading.

_____ 1. two steady incomes or one that's <u>erratic</u> (Paragraph 1):

    a. changeable   c. incorrect

    b. reliable   d. sizable

_____ 2. you do have to <u>delve</u> beyond the dollars-and-cents dilemmas (Paragraph 3):

    a. shoot   c. glance

    b. develop   d. investigate

_____ 3. money is a <u>metaphor</u> for power (Paragraph 3):

    a. method   c. warning

    b. symbol   d. poem

_____ 4. making <u>snide</u> remarks (Paragraph 5):

    a. stuck-up and conceited

    b. shocking and alarming

    c. polite and courteous

    d. mean and insulting

_____ 5. made a list of all their <u>assets</u> (Paragraph 26):

    a. problems and responsibilities

    b. antiques and works of art

    c. possessions and resources

    d. suitcases and bags

Comprehension Questions

Choose the answer that best completes each statement.

_____ 1. Hales says men define manhood in terms of money, sex, and

    a. companionship.   c. family.

    b. power.   d. muscles.

_____ 2. Jake and Lucy, in "Whose Money Is It Anyway?" resolved their differences about money by

    a. setting up three separate bank accounts.

    b. setting up two separate bank accounts.

    c. putting Jake in charge of their joint bank account.

    d. putting Lucy in charge of their joint bank account.

_____ 3. Arlene Modica Matthews, a psychologist referred to by the author, says that before having a child, a lot of working couples

    a. return to old family patterns.

    b. eat out all the time.

    c. live like financial roommates.

    d. spend more than they make.

_____ 4. When Jason and Molly, in "Why Can't We Get Out of Debt?" stopped using credit cards and only used cash, they found ways to boost their spirits without spending money; they also learned how to

    a. make extra money for special purchases.

    b. get a new credit card for emergencies.

    c. forgive each other if they spent more than they'd agreed on.

    d. express their feelings directly.

_____ 5. Hales says that money is a source of conflict for most couples because of what it represents for us: power and freedom, as well as

    a. self-esteem and love.

    b. desire and greed.

    c. security and charity.

    d. responsibility and success.

Reading 10: The Influence of Sports on Male Identity

Vocabulary Questions

Using the methods of Strategy 3, **Use Context Clues,** and Strategy 4, **Find the Right Definition,** choose the correct definition of each underlined word as it is used in the context of this reading.

_____ 1. some sports <u>exalt</u> the "male values" (Paragraph 1):

    a. teach   c. put off

    b. put down   d. glorify

_____ 2. rough physical contact, <u>akin</u> to violence (Paragraph 1):

    a. family   c. identical

    b. similar   d. next

_____ 3. men . . . follow sports in order to <u>affirm</u> male cultural values (Paragraph 1):

    a. support   c. weaken

    b. tolerate   d. deny

_____ 4. in the manner of a priestly <u>benediction</u> (Paragraph 7):

    a. permission   c. ring

    b. blessing   d. rejection

_____ 5. boys . . . develop instrumental relationships [and] such an <u>orientation</u> . . . brings problems (Paragraph 8):

    a. following a compass

    b. way of thinking

    c. method of accounting

    d. introduction before instruction

Comprehension Questions

Choose the answer that best completes each statement.

_____ 1. According to the author, certain sports

    a. promote cooperation.

    b. encourage male values.

    c. discourage violence.

    d. teach responsibility.

_____ 2. The professional football player said he was most anxious to prove himself to his

    a. mother and father.

    b. coach and teammates.

    c. brothers and father.

    d. TV fans.

_____ 3. The coaches at the summer basketball camp let the boys know how well they had played by having the older boys

    a. applaud more loudly or softly depending on how well the boys played.

    b. pick the best players for their team.

    c. boo the players with the poorest ability.

    d. take a secret vote to decide on the top players.

_____ 4. "Instrumental relationships" are relationships that are

    a. formed through interacting with others on a team.

    b. based on the feelings you have for another person.

    c. developed through band practice.

    d. based on how useful the relationship is.

_____ 5. According to the sociologist Michael Messner, males are likely to construct their identities on being successful in competition, and females are likely to construct their identities

    a. on finding a mate.

    b. on self-exploration.

    c. on meaningful relationships.

    d. on being physically attractive.

Chapter 7

Reading 11: How Men and Women Communicate in Relationships

Vocabulary Questions

Using the methods of Strategy 3, **Use Context Clues,** and Strategy 4, **Find the Right Definition,** choose the correct definition of each underlined word as it is used in the context of this reading.

_____ 1. recent research <u>validates</u> (Paragraph 2):

    a. remains   c. ignores

    b. confirms   d. contradicts

_____ 2. he <u>divulges</u> his innermost thoughts (Paragraph 2):

    a. reveals   c. hides

    b. forgets   d. records

_____ 3. <u>inhibited</u> the expression of their emotions (Paragraph 4):

    a. called attention to   c. held back

    b. overlooked   d. put forward

_____ 4. make clear what is <u>relevant</u> (Paragraph 6):

    a. revealed   c. required

    b. related   d. responsible

_____ 5. say <u>inflammatory</u> things (Paragraph 6):

    a. preventing fire   c. awakening romance

    b. causing fire   d. stirring up anger

Comprehension Questions

Choose the answer that best completes each statement.

_____ 1. Women tend to be more interested in developing and taking care of relationships, whereas men are usually more interested in

    a. avoiding competitive situations.

    b. developing their physical strength.

    c. maintaining social status or power.

    d. exploring their own innermost thoughts.

_____ 2. The author refers to a study in which men and women were both shown scenes of people in distress; the study suggests that men

a. don't feel emotions as strongly as women do.

b. are able to control their heart rate and blood pressure better than women.

c. are less able than women to recognize when another person is in distress.

d. feel emotions as much as women but have difficulty expressing them.

_____ 3. Men tend to turn their anger outward and see something or someone else as the cause of their anger, and women

a. only feel anger toward the person they are closest to.

b. turn their anger toward physical objects rather than people.

c. don't feel anger as often as men do.

d. see themselves as the cause of anger.

_____ 4. The four techniques for improving communication between couples are: editing, documenting, validating, and

a. leveling.

b. respecting.

c. accusing.

d. clearing.

_____ 5. According to the author, an important reason for the difficulties men and women have in communicating with each other comes from

a. women's difficulties in taking part in competitive activities.

b. different socialization processes experienced by men and women.

c. inborn personality differences seen between girl and boy babies.

d. men's difficulties in feeling or expressing emotions.

Reading 12: The Men We Carry in Our Minds

Vocabulary Questions

Using the methods of Strategy 3, **Use Context Clues,** and Strategy 4, **Find the Right Definition,** choose the correct definition of each underlined word as it is used in the context of this reading.

_____ 1. the brute <u>toiling</u> animal (Paragraph 1):

      a. starving   c. wandering

      b. dangerous   d. laboring

_____ 2. bodies . . . were twisted and <u>maimed</u> (Paragraph 3):

      a. seriously wounded   c. wrapped around

      b. close to death   d. upside down

_____ 3. I was <u>baffled</u> (Paragraph 7):

      a. upset   c. excited

      b. puzzled   d. offended

_____ 4. deep <u>grievances</u> of women (Paragraph 8):

      a. good looks   c. complaints

      b. advantages   d. illnesses

_____ 5. I was an <u>ally</u> (Paragraph 11):

      a. enemy   c. stranger

      b. equal   d. supporter

Comprehension Questions

Choose the answer that best completes each statement.

_____ 1. In Sanders' earliest memories, two groups of men came to represent the "laborer" and the "boss"; these two groups were

    a. prisoners and guards.

    b. farmers and store owners.

    c. ordinary soldiers and army officers.

    d. steelworkers and factory owners.

_____ 2. Sanders sometimes dreaded growing up because all the men he knew

    a. beat their wives and children.

    b. had been in prison for some period of time.

    c. had to train as soldiers to kill or be killed.

    d. had been hurt physically and mentally by their labor.

_____ 3. As a child, the women Sanders knew

    a. were rarely allowed out of the house.

    b. worked outside the home and also had to take care of the household.

    c. had more time to enjoy life than men did.

    d. had nonstop household chores that kept them from enjoying life as much as men.

_____ 4. The college women Sanders met complained that men had unfair advantages in life because the men they had grown up with

    a. didn't have to worry about losing their looks as they aged.

    b. kept their wives from having careers.

    c. had all the powerful positions, such as banker, physician, or stockbroker.

    d. were so wealthy they didn't have to work.

_____ 5. Sanders believed he and the college women had similar desires, including

    a. becoming wealthy enough to retire early.

    b. finding jobs that made use of their abilities.

    c. meeting the right mate.

    d. getting scholarships for studying abroad.

Chapter 8

Reading 13: When Not Asking for Directions Is Dangerous to Your Health

Vocabulary Questions

Using the methods of Strategy 3, **Use Context Clues,** and Strategy 4, **Find the Right Definition,** choose the correct definition of each underlined word as it is used in the context of this reading.

_____ 1. crystallize the frustration (Paragraph 2):

    a. make sparkle   c. cause to flake

    b. take apart   d. give form to

_____ 2. repeated this anecdote (Paragraph 5):

    a. story   c. remedy

    b. plan   d. lie

_____ 3. did not want to humiliate himself (Paragraph 5):

    a. harm   c. disgrace

    b. glorify   d. spoil

_____ 4. moral of the story (Paragraph 6):

    a. message   c. will

    b. goodness   d. sketch

_____ 5. repercussions for co-workers (Paragraph 6):

    a. effects   c. causes

    b. benefits   d. dangers

Comprehension Questions

Choose the answer that best completes each statement.

_____ 1. Tannen's explanation for why men don't like to stop and ask for directions is that asking for any kind of help

    a. shows that a person has limited intelligence and low self-esteem.

    b. puts a person in a one-down position.

    c. requires a person to know how to ask the right questions.

    d. means the person has to trust someone else to have the right answers.

_____ 2. Men told Tannen that it makes sense not to ask for directions because finding your own way

a. proves that you never need to ask for help.

b. prevents you from getting confusing directions from other people.

c. shows that you can rely on your own sense of direction.

d. teaches you about a neighborhood and navigation.

_____ 3. The amateur pilot Tannen talked to got back into his plane immediately after he landed because he realized

a. he had enough gas after all.

b. he had stumbled upon a business he was not supposed to be aware of.

c. he was still not ready to ask for help.

d. he saw that he had landed in a cow pasture, not a landing field.

_____ 4. This same pilot said he thought some small-plane crashes occur because some amateur pilots

a. don't want to admit they're lost.

b. try to do all their own maintenance on their planes.

c. don't want to get enough help from their instructor in how to land a plane.

d. don't realize how far away they are from their home airports.

_____ 5. When Tannen says "the moral is flexibility" she means

a. women should become more self-reliant and practice their map-reading skills.

b. men should stop being embarrassed about asking for directions when they're lost.

c. we should realize that sticking to our habits might get us into dangerous situations.

d. we should practice our habitual way of acting so we know how to react in dangerous situations.

Chapter 9

Reading 14: The Effects of Work on Motivation

Vocabulary Questions

Using the methods of Strategy 3, **Use Context Clues,** and Strategy 4, **Find the Right Definition,** choose the correct definition of each underlined word as it is used in the context of this reading.

_____ 1. consistent rules (Paragraph 2):

    a. harsh and demanding   c. constant and regular

    b. smooth and even   d. fair and equitable

_____ 2. feelings of competence (Paragraph 4):

    a. self-esteem   c. fondness

    b. rivalry   d. capability

_____ 3. proportion of men and women (Paragraph 6):

    a. percentage   c. opposition

    b. section   d. attraction

_____ 4. stifle many people's aspirations (Paragraph 6):

    a. hold back   c. urge on

    b. wipe out   d. make stronger

_____ 5. feeling apathetic (Paragraph 9):

    a. hardhearted   c. sensitive

    b. uninterested   d. pitiable

Comprehension Questions

Choose the answer that best completes each statement.

_____ 1. In companies that provide opportunities for creativity and flexibility in their daily work, employees

    a. work better on their own, but less well with others.

    b. are more satisfied but somewhat less productive.

    c. demand even more control over their work.

    d. are more satisfied and productive.

_____ 2. "Incentive pay" is a term for

    a. a bonus given upon completion of a goal.

    b. a promise of a future pay raise.

    c. a pay cut given as a penalty for unfinished work.

    d. an automatic raise given to motivate workers.

_____ 3. One important working condition that promotes a worker's motivation to achieve is

    a. making less money than fellow workers.

    b. having the opportunity to achieve.

    c. fear of losing one's job.

    d. segregation of occupations by gender.

_____ 4. Many people form gender stereotypes of the requirements of certain careers; in such thinking, "male" jobs require

    a. motivation and self-interest.

    b. kindness and nurturance.

    c. strength and intelligence.

    d. strength and aggression.

_____ 5. We can assume that a company with a "glass ceiling" will have some women and ethnic minorities who

    a. see more opportunities for advancement.

    b. have made it up the corporate ladder.

    c. have lost much of their motivation to achieve.

    d. have sued the company for personal injury.

Reading 15: Thurgood Marshall: The Brain of the Civil Rights Movement

Vocabulary Questions

Using the methods of Strategy 3, **Use Context Clues,** and Strategy 4, **Find the Right Definition,** choose the correct definition of each underlined word as it is used in the context of this reading.

_____ 1. regime of racial segregation (Paragraph 1):

    a. kingdom   c. regulation

    b. system   d. remedy

_____ 2. <u>prevail</u> in the end (Paragraph 5):

    a. command   c. weaken

    b. appear   d. succeed

_____ 3. <u>defective</u> from the start (Paragraph 8):

    a. hidden   c. faulty

    b. blocked   d. delicate

_____ 4. how it was <u>conceived</u> (Paragraph 8):

    a. dreamed up   c. thought over

    b. concerned about   d. put up with

_____ 5. how it <u>evolved</u> (Paragraph 8):

    a. explained   c. exaggerated

    b. developed   d. lengthened

Comprehension Questions

Choose the answer that best completes each statement.

_____ 1. Marshall's work taking on Jim Crow laws in pre–Civil Rights Mississippi was so dangerous the N.A.A.C.P.

    a. refused to go with him to certain small towns where blacks were in particular danger.

    b. alerted the sheriffs' departments of all the small towns he was visiting.

    c. arranged to have armed men follow him for his protection.

    d. advised him to return home for his own safety.

_____ 2. Marshall became the first black Justice of the U.S. Supreme Court, yet he started from lowly beginnings as

    a. the first child in his family to attend a nonsegregated school.

    b. the grandson of a slave.

    c. a typist typing on a manual typewriter in his car.

    d. an orphan in a segregated school in Baltimore, Maryland.

_____ 3. In one of Marshall's earliest victories working for the N.A.A.C.P, he

    a. challenged the practice of paying black elementary teachers less than white janitors.

    b. ended segregation at the University of Maryland.

    c. struck down racial quotas in medical-school admissions.

    d. upheld the right of people to possess pornography in their homes.

_____ 4. Marshall's greatest victory, *Brown v. Board of Education,* said that "separate but equal" schools for blacks and whites

    a. violated the Constitution.

    b. was required by the Constitution.

    c. required an Act of Congress.

    d. required a Constitutional amendment.

_____ 5. Marshall dedicated his life to

    a. improving facilities at both black and white institutions.

    b. removing racism from the Supreme Court.

    c. bringing his independent and rebellious views to the Supreme Court.

    d. ending legal segregation in the nation's leading institutions.

Chapter 10

Reading 16: Serving in Florida

Vocabulary Questions

Using the methods of Strategy 3, **Use Context Clues,** and Strategy 4, **Find the Right Definition,** choose the correct definition of each underlined word as it is used in the context of this reading.

_____ 1. run after the agile Gail (Paragraph 1):

    a. hostile and irritated

    b. wounded and abused

    c. lively and quick

    d. alert and observant

_____ 2. just as <u>indulgent</u> (Paragraph 5):

    a. resentful   c. grateful

    b. generous   d. severe

_____ 3. whatever bits of <u>autonomy</u> (Paragraph 5):

    a. openness   c. routine

    b. independence   d. quickness

_____ 4. <u>illicit</u> calories (Paragraph 5):

    a. outlawed   c. appetizing

    b. prohibited   d. dishonest

_____ 5. <u>perennial</u> favorites (Paragraph 6):

    a. trustworthy   c. occasional

    b. yearly   d. continuing

Comprehension Questions

Choose the answer that best completes each statement.

_____ 1. Ehrenreich finds out that about a third of a server's job is "side work" that includes

    a. washing and ironing.

    b. sweeping and scrubbing.

    c. making coffee and tea.

    d. greeting and seating customers.

_____ 2. Ehrenreich tries to give her customers a "fine dining experience" by doing such things as

    a. giving extra butter pats and more sour cream.

    b. providing them with real linen napkins she ironed herself.

    c. paying for the meals of out-of-work customers.

    d. helping customers avoid eating high-calorie foods.

_____ 3. Ten days into her job as a server, Ehrenreich

    a. realizes she can't live on what she's making.

    b. asks Gail if the two of them could share an apartment.

    c. begins to feel like the expert waitress she used to be.

    d. thinks she has found a livable lifestyle.

_____ 4. When Ehrenreich finishes her shift she

    a. starts her other job as a housekeeper at the nearby motel.

    b. goes to sleep in her truck where she has set up a bed.

    c. goes with her coworkers to listen to music in the next-door bar.

    d. goes home and listens to music tapes.

_____ 5. Ehrenreich has "fears . . . of appearing overqualified" for being a waitress because she

    a. has years of experience as a waitress.

    b. is a restaurant critic who knows a great deal about restaurants.

    c. has a successful career as a well-known writer.

    d. has several advanced degrees from different universities.

Chapter 11

Reading 17: Lost Jobs, Ragged Safety Net

Vocabulary Questions

Using the methods of Strategy 3, **Use Context Clues,** and Strategy 4, **Find the Right Definition,** choose the correct definition of each underlined word as it is used in the context of this reading.

_____ 1. much consumer spending is discretionary (Paragraph 4):

    a. unfair   c. essential

    b. voluntary   d. planned

_____ 2. another vulnerability (Paragraph 5):

    a. weakness   c. force

    b. honesty   d. error

_____ 3. prior recessions (Paragraph 5):

    a. downturns   c. crashes

    b. recoveries   d. detours

_____ 4. influx of . . . immigrants (Paragraph 5):

    a. overflow   c. growth

    b. attack   d. arrival

_____ 5. <u>induced</u> to add more (Paragraph 9):

    a. struggled   c. persuaded

    b. started   d. forced

Comprehension Questions

Choose the answer that best completes each statement.

_____ 1. When consumers reduced their spending as a result of the 9/11 terrorist attacks, the result was

    a. more jobs for service workers such as counselors and financial advisors.

    b. more people put their money in savings accounts instead of the stock market.

    c. fewer jobs for service workers such as restaurant workers and hotel housekeepers.

    d. more jobs for accountants, doctors, and lawyers.

_____ 2. Reich says that minority workers had a disproportionate share of low-wage service jobs, so

    a. they have faced especially high unemployment.

    b. they have been able to take on extra jobs in order to make ends meet.

    c. they were no worse off than before.

    d. they were encouraged to take jobs in the manufacturing area.

_____ 3. One of Reich's reasons for saying that lower-income service workers will have a harder time during the 2001 downturn than in previous recessions is that

    a. corporations are demanding more education from their workers.

    b. workers will be forced into welfare-to-work programs.

    c. more money is going to welfare than to unemployment.

    d. unemployment insurance is harder to get.

_____ 4. As federal programs for job training and low-income housing are being shrunk by budget cuts, state and local governments are

    a. going bankrupt.

    b. also cutting social services.

    c. filling in for the federal government.

    d. increasing their tax revenues.

_____ 5. One reason Reich says the stimulus plan passed by the House of Representatives will not work is that large corporations

   a. are unprepared to make use of financial help because they are still reeling from all the corporate scandals.

   b. don't provide enough Americans with jobs because they are sending all their manufacturing overseas.

   c. don't need more money because they are already producing more goods than they can sell.

   d. need more money so they can buy the raw materials to produce more goods.

Reading 18: The Conditions of Work

Vocabulary Questions

Using the methods of Strategy 3, **Use Context Clues,** and Strategy 4, **Find the Right Definition,** choose the correct definition of each underlined word as it is used in the context of this reading.

_____ 1. wages tended to stagnate (Paragraph 1):

   a. fall sharply   c. move ahead

   b. stumble   d. stand still

_____ 2. existence was precarious (Paragraph 3):

   a. blissful   c. challenging

   b. insecure   d. daring

_____ 3. meager existence (Paragraph 6):

   a. rare   c. exceptional

   b. tiny   d. inadequate

_____ 4. prominent feature (Paragraph 12):

   a. best   c. outstanding

   b. opening   d. basic

_____ 5. served a utilitarian function (Paragraph 12):

   a. practical   c. factual

   b. honest   d. successful

Comprehension Questions

Choose the answer that best completes each statement.

_____ 1. The authors contrast the quality of life of two miners; one reason the first miner had a much poorer quality of life than the second was that he

a. had to work with an injured arm.

b. spent much of his income on alcohol.

c. worked only part-time.

d. lived mainly on steak, potatoes, and bacon.

_____ 2. In New York City in the late nineteenth century, women

a. earned about the same amount as men.

b. earned about half as much as men.

c. were not allowed to work outside of the home.

d. earned even less than African Americans, Asians, and Mexicans in America.

_____ 3. One important way preindustrial work differed from industrial work was that

a. workers had to work harder for more hours.

b. the work never varied from one season to the next.

c. workdays were shorter, but less sociable.

d. work was often combined with pleasure.

_____ 4. For factory owners of the late nineteenth century, the ideal industrial worker was

a. strong, healthy, and sociable.

b. punctual, hardworking, orderly, and sober.

c. creative, flexible, educated, and responsible.

d. respectful, polite, energetic, and thrifty.

_____ 5. The reading begins with a historical debate between different historians; the debate is about

   a. whether or not wages and earnings for laborers lagged behind the general growth in the American economy.

   b. whether historians should take an optimistic or pessimistic view of economic change during the late nineteenth century.

   c. whether the price of industrialization was worth the benefits native-born and immigrant labor received.

   d. whether native-born or immigrant laborers benefited more from the nineteenth-century industrialization.

Part I Additional Readings

Reading I-A: Learning to Write

Comprehension Questions

Choose the answer that best completes each statement.

_____ 1. Until his third year in high school, Baker was bored and confused by English grammar, but

   a. he loved writing compositions.

   b. he loved reading the classics.

   c. he did think once in a while of becoming a writer.

   d. he wrote clear and inspiring paragraphs his teachers enjoyed reading.

_____ 2. Baker uses details to show Mr. Fleagle's prim behavior. He mentions his eyeglasses, wavy hair, vested suits, starched white shirts, and his manner of

   a. walking.   c. eating.

   b. sitting.   d. speaking.

_____ 3. The class burst out laughing when Mr. Fleagle

   a. read the words of Lady Macbeth.

   b. acted out a sword fighting scene from *Macbeth.*

   c. put on Lady Macbeth's costume.

   d. forgot his lines while acting his part in *Macbeth.*

_____ 4. Baker discovered that he wanted to write for himself—not just for a school assignment—when he

    a. thought about the money he would earn as a professional writer.

    b. wanted to hold on to the pleasure of an evening with his relatives.

    c. wanted to understand why his aunts and uncles disapproved of him.

    d. discovered how much he wanted to tell people about the benefits of eating spaghetti.

_____ 5. When Baker realized that his words had the power to make people laugh, he

    a. decided to become a stand-up comedian.

    b. discovered he wanted to become a writer.

    c. was upset that people were laughing at him.

    d. accepted Mr. Fleagle's advice for improving the humor in his essay.

Reading I-B: Pandora's Box: Hope and the Power of Positive Thinking

Comprehension Questions

Choose the answer that best completes each statement.

_____ 1. The study discussed at the beginning of the reading tells what students would do if they received a D grade. Students with high levels of hope said they would

    a. hope for the best and think positive thoughts about the next test.

    b. work harder and think of different things they could do to improve their grade.

    c. be less hopeful about the next test, since their hopes were disappointed.

    d. be so sure they had performed better on the test that they would challenge the grade.

_____ 2. The psychologist C. R. Snyder shows that hope is a better predictor of first-semester grades than

    a. SAT scores.   c. teacher recommendations.

    b. high school grades.   d. fear.

_____ 3. According to Snyder, having hope

    a. is basically the same as making wishes.

    b. prevents you from taking action to change your situation.

    c. means waiting patiently for things to turn out all right.

    d. means believing you have both the will and the way to accomplish your goals.

_____ 4. People with high levels of hope have many traits, or characteristics, in common. Which one of the following is *not* one of these traits:

    a. being able to motivate yourself

    b. when you're in a bad situation, reassuring yourself that things will get better

    c. being firm and inflexible in following a single path toward a goal

    d. knowing how to break a big task down into smaller steps

_____ 5. When people with low levels of hope face difficult challenges, they are likely to

    a. reach out to others for help.

    b. develop greater emotional intelligence.

    c. face up to the difficulties and try to overcome them.

    d. give in to overpowering anxiety, a negative attitude, or depression.

Reading I-C: I May, I Might, I Must

Comprehension Questions

Choose the answer that best completes each statement.

_____ 1. A fen would be "impassable" because of the

    a. water and mud.   c. high wall.

    b. steep cliff.   d. jungle growth.

_____ 2. If someone tells her it's impossible to get across the fen, the poet will

    a. agree that getting across is impossible.

    b. say how easy it will be to get across.

    c. give reasons for why she wants to get across.

    d. explain why she can get across if she tries.

_____ 3. The words "I must" in the title suggest that the poet is

    a. wild and badly behaved.

    b. hesitant and unsure.

    c. firm and determined.

    d. respectful and obedient.

_____ 4. The words "why," "I," and "try" in the poem all rhyme with one another. The rhyme helps to emphasize the poet's

    a. sense of self-importance.

    b. lack of self-confidence.

    c. sense of purpose and willpower.

    d. feelings of anxiety.

_____ 5. When the poet says, "I then will tell you why I think that I can get across it if I try," she means that she

    a. can't really cross the fen, but can only think what it would be like.

    b. has thought about what to do and will try as hard as she can to succeed.

    c. doesn't know what to do to overcome the obstacles in her life.

    d. believes people can overcome challenges by pretending they don't exist.

Part II Additional Readings

Reading II-A: But Weight!

Vocabulary Questions

Using the methods of Strategy 3, **Use Context Clues,** and Strategy 4, **Find the Right Definition,** choose the correct definition of each underlined word as it is used in the context of this reading.

_____ 1. our ancestors survived adversity (Paragraph 2):

    a. poverty   c. change

    b. hardship   d. combat

_____ 2. [a] mechanism can be altered (Paragraph 3):

    a. developed   c. destroyed

    b. changed   d. misused

_____ 3. exercise <u>obsessively</u> (Paragraph 7):

    a. rarely   c. excessively

    b. regularly   d. nervously

_____ 4. <u>rupturing</u> the stomach (Paragraph 8):

    a. bursting   c. nourishing

    b. healing   d. smashing

_____ 5. <u>psychotherapy</u> may be required (Paragraph 8):

    a. shock treatment

    b. mind reading

    c. treatment of the insane

    d. treatment of mental problems

Comprehension Questions

Choose the answer that best completes each statement.

_____ 1. After a person loses the first pounds in a weight-loss program

    a. the remaining excess weight comes off more easily.

    b. the body is more vulnerable to diseases.

    c. the remaining excess weight is redistributed throughout the body.

    d. the body seems to resist losing any more.

_____ 2. Wallace says an unexpected benefit of exercise is that

    a. it temporarily causes more calories to be burned per unit time.

    b. it improves muscle tone, so you appear to have lost weight.

    c. it reduces your appetite for high-calorie foods, such as sugars and fats.

    d. it allows you to meet new people when you go to the gym.

_____ 3. The possible causes of anorexia nervosa in young women are

    a. lack of love from parents and fear of abuse.

    b. overconfidence and feelings of superiority.

    c. self-doubt and feelings of insecurity.

    d. overeating and lack of exercise.

_____ 4. A person with bulimia can ruin his or her health by constant

a. steam baths   c. exercise

b. vomiting   d. starvation diets.

_____ 5. Most nutritionists agree that successful weight-loss programs involve some behavior modification in order to

a. lose weight slowly and keep it off for the long term.

b. engage in a brief period of intense exercise and low-calorie dieting.

c. make significant changes in your genetic body type.

d. stop dieting and accept your body as it is.

Reading II-B: New Advertising Hits Consumers Everywhere

Vocabulary Questions

Using the methods of Strategy 3, **Use Context Clues,** and Strategy 4, **Find the Right Definition,** choose the correct definition of each underlined word as it is used in the context of this reading.

_____ 1. invades consumers' consciousness (Paragraph 3):

a. common sense

b. awareness

c. sense of right and wrong

d. direction

_____ 2. advocates like to call it (Paragraph 3):

a. promoters   c. lawyers

b. opponents   d. manufacturers

_____ 3. embracing its potential (Paragraph 4):

a. power   c. possibility

b. risk   d. certainty

_____ 4. wary of its . . . impact (Paragraph 10):

a. enthusiastic   c. thoughtless

b. panicky   d. cautious

_____ 5. its advertised allure (Paragraph 26):

a. distraction   c. opposition;

b. assurance   d. attraction

Comprehension Questions

Choose the answer that best completes each statement.

_____ 1. One new way the author gives for advertising to reach consumers is through

    a. billboards.

    b. gym towels.

    c. gas pumps.

    d. elevator music.

_____ 2. Advertisers have a harder time reaching audiences than they did a generation ago because

    a. magazines like *Life* or *Reader's Digest* are no longer as popular.

    b. schools have taught people to be more skeptical about advertising.

    c. young people have less disposable income.

    d. audiences have become fragmented.

_____ 3. The author says critics are concerned about our constant exposure to advertising; one critic worries because children

    a. pay attention to TV commercials instead of constructive programs.

    b. learn bad language and incorrect grammar from advertising.

    c. ignore some of the useful information found in ads.

    d. face commercial messages at home and school.

_____ 4. One way to fight against advertising's steady increase is to

    a. tear up or cross out advertisements found in unexpected places.

    b. complain to the owners of businesses using new types of advertising.

    c. buy only products advertised in traditional ways.

    d. avoid places where new types of advertising are found.

_____ 5. The critic Susan Douglas says, "the more advertising people are bombarded by, the less advertising they remember"; by this she means people

    a. develop headaches from feeling as if they have been hit by a bomb.

    b. don't understand or remember loud or confusing advertising.

    c. need to see the same message over and over in order to remember it.

    d. stop taking notice when they are faced with too much of the same type of messages.

Reading II-C: runnin

Comprehension Questions

Choose the answer that best completes each statement.

_____ 1. The most likely reason for the poet to not use capital letters and to use unconventional spelling is that the poet

    a. needs to use certain spellings in order to create the rhymes she wants.

    b. wants to pretend to be a hip-hop star.

    c. wants to speak to young people using their own informal language.

    d. went to a school that did not teach proper grammar or spelling.

_____ 2. In the time between "yesterday," at the beginning of the poem, and "this day," near the end of the poem, the poet describes herself

    a. coming to a complete stop.

    b. speeding up.

    c. slowing down.

    d. winning the race.

_____ 3. Choose the most likely meaning of the underlined phrases from these lines (21–26):

was goin

so fast

head tryin ta

catch my tail

<u>tongue tryin ta</u>

<u>catch my mind</u>

   a. What I was telling other people was different from what I was really thinking.

   b. I was remembering favorite childhood foods I wanted to taste again.

   c. My speech became blurred and rambling when I got very drunk.

   d. My confused thoughts seemed to race through my mind, so it was hard to put them into words.

_____ 4. One way the poem gives a sense of speed—of running—is by

   a. using only one word per line.

   b. the repetition of words like "runnin" and "goin so fast".

   c. leaving off the endings of words, such as the "g" in "running".

   d. including the words "7 miles/back" and "3 revolutions ago."

_____ 5. One important message from the poem is that you

   a. find more meaning in life when you stop running from your fears.

   b. must slow down in order to stand up to the people trying to hurt you.

   c. can overcome any difficulties if you move steadily and swiftly enough.

   d. change direction and ask for forgiveness from your parents and others you have hurt.

Part III Additional Readings

Reading III-A: Teaching Sex Roles

Vocabulary Questions

Using the methods of Strategy 3, **Use Context Clues,** and Strategy 4, **Find the Right Definition,** choose the correct definition of each underlined word as it is used in the context of this reading.

_____ 1. language shapes perceptions (Paragraph 2):

    a. reading skills   c. daydreams

    b. mental pictures   d. manners

_____ 2. exerts control over another (Paragraph 9):

    a. applies   c. prevents

    b. loses   d. seizes

_____ 3. sex equity (Paragraph 9):

    a. value   c. evenhandedness

    b. favoritism   d. similarity

_____ 4. dilutes the message (Paragraph 10):

    a. makes wet   c. wipes out

    b. concentrates   d. weakens

_____ 5. a stereotype that has been with us (Paragraph 14):

    a. oversimplified mental picture

    b. plate cast from a printing surface

    c. unoriginal idea

    d. unjust punishment

Comprehension Questions

Choose the answer that best completes each statement.

_____ 1. In order to show children that society's jobs are open to either sex, it is important to

    a. explain that a term like "fireman" can apply to both men and women.

    b. adopt non-gender-specific terms from other languages.

    c. tell them that a girl can be a "policewoman" or "chairwoman."

    d. use non-gender-specific terms, such as "police officer," or "firefighter."

_____ 2. Studies of "conversational politics" show that interruption is a way for one person to take control over the other in a conversation; these studies show that

    a. women tend to interrupt men more than the reverse.

    b. men tend to interrupt women more than the reverse.

    c. neither sex interrupts more often than the other.

    d. children interrupt their parents more than they interrupt other adults.

_____ 3. The authors say that female parents and teachers can help empower girls by teaching them to

    a. use ultrapolite language.

    b. use assertive language.

    c. be more physically aggressive.

    d. demand that boys leave their muddy shoes by the door.

_____ 4. In 1986, when researchers analyzed books for kindergartners, they found that the main character was male

    a. over 70 percent of the time.

    b. 50 percent of the time.

    c. about 40 percent of the time.

    d. almost 100 percent of the time.

_____ 5. Mothers and fathers can give their children an expanded view of roles for males and females by

    a. making sure their children attend a school with male as well as female teachers.

    b. giving dolls to boys and trucks to girls.

    c. sharing household tasks.

    d. reading books with strong female characters.

Reading III-B: Horrors! Girls with Gavels! What a Difference a Day Makes!

Vocabulary Questions

Using the methods of Strategy 3, **Use Context Clues,** and Strategy 4, **Find the Right Definition,** choose the correct definition of each underlined word as it is used in the context of this reading.

_____ 1. from its <u>inception</u> (Paragraph 3):

       a. warning   c. beginning

       b. base   d. conclusion

_____ 2. it was gender-<u>biased</u> (Paragraph 3):

       a. unearned   c. prejudiced

       b. neutral   d. specific

_____ 3. improved <u>access</u> for women (Paragraph 5):

       a. right of privacy   c. financial status

       b. legal rights   d. right of entry

_____ 4. <u>balks</u> at a female surgeon (Paragraph 6):

       a. stares in an inappropriate way

       b. shies away from

       c. criticizes harshly

       d. meets head-on

_____ 5. <u>scant</u> investment (Paragraph 7):

       a. little   c. safe

       b. rare   d. weak

Comprehension Questions

Choose the answer that best completes each statement.

_____ 1. In using the term "pyramid configuration," Quindlen refers to the way women in corporations

       a. help one another make it to the top levels of the corporate ladder.

       b. obey corporate fashion rules that emphasize an A-line style for suits and dresses.

       c. hold many low-level jobs and numerous mid-level jobs, but few high-level jobs.

       d. stay in low-level jobs, while men move into mid-level and high-level jobs.

_____ 2. One major complaint made by opponents of Take Our Daughters to Work Day was that

    a. the idea of the day was just an imitation of Take Our Sons to Work Day.

    b. it sent a bad message about females as victims.

    c. many parents have poor jobs they don't want their daughters to see.

    d. teachers will give bad grades to girls who miss their classes.

_____ 3. One piece of evidence Quindlen gives for saying that Take Our Daughters to Work Day is *not* unfair to boys is

    a. a survey showing that 61 percent of respondents believe men and women are treated differently in the workplace.

    b. the fact that the United States Senate still has no females.

    c. fathers now assume their daughters are as likely to go to college as their sons.

    d. research showing that only a small percentage of men help with the tasks in their own homes.

_____ 4. The photograph of Quindlen's daughter and the judge is significant because it demonstrates that

    a. a judge can rule effectively in court even when wearing a feminine piece of clothing instead of a robe.

    b. the judge will write a recommendation for Quindlen's daughter to get into law school.

    c. today there are 199 women judges in the federal system.

    d. women of today can do far more important jobs than when Quindlen was a girl.

_____ 5. At the end of the reading Quindlen reminds us that a generation ago the idea that people would be judged not by their gender but by their ability seemed

    a. a principle that had already been established.

    b. a dangerous error in judgment.

    c. a goal that would soon be reached.

    d. an ideal that was impossible to achieve.

Reading III-C: Only Daughter

Vocabulary Questions

Using the methods of Strategy 3, **Use Context Clues,** and Strategy 4, **Find the Right Definition,** choose the correct definition of each underlined word as it is used in the context of this reading.

_____ 1. in <u>retrospect</u> (Paragraph 5):

     a. display of wealth   c. high opinion

     b. a quick summary   d. review of past events

_____ 2. tragedy and <u>trauma</u> (Paragraph 7):

     a. comedy   c. suffering

     b. problems   d. reality

_____ 3. trying to <u>woo</u> (Paragraph 8):

     a. attract   c. flee

     b. hypnotize   d. ignore

_____ 4. bouts of <u>nostalgia</u> (Paragraph 9):

     a. longing for things past

     b. feelings of emptiness

     c. dreams for the future

     d. fantasies of greatness

_____ 5. <u>stubbed</u> by a history of hammer and nails (Paragraph 13):

     a. ignored   c. honored

     b. bashed   d. bounced

Comprehension Questions

Choose the answer that best completes each statement.

_____ 1. Several years ago Cisneros wrote that she was "the only daughter in a family of six sons"; now one detail she would like to add is that

     a. her mother and father divorced when she was a teenager.

     b. she is the only daughter of a working-class family of nine.

     c. she was born and grew up in Mexico.

     d. she had two half-sisters.

_____ 2. The fact that Cisneros' brothers didn't want to "play with a girl" became an advantage for her because

 a. she learned how to play like a boy.

 b. her parents gave her extra attention.

 c. her mother taught her how to care for a house and family.

 d. she had more time to read and develop her imagination.

_____ 3. Cisneros' father thought college would be good for her because she would

 a. have an easier time making it up the corporate ladder.

 b. find a husband.

 c. learn more about her people's history.

 d. become a better writer.

_____ 4. Cisneros understood that her father appreciated her story when he

 a. read it very slowly.

 b. hugged and congratulated her.

 c. asked for copies for his relatives.

 d. cried when he read it.

_____ 5. Cisneros says her father represents the "public majority" she wants to woo because like this public, her father is

 a. uninterested in reading.

 b. an enthusiastic reader.

 c. a working-class immigrant.

 d. suspicious of women writers.

Part IV Additional Readings

Reading IV-A: Satisfaction Not Guaranteed, but You Can Find Meaning in Your Work

Vocabulary Questions

Using the methods of Strategy 3, **Use Context Clues,** and Strategy 4, **Find the Right Definition,** choose the correct definition of each underlined word as it is used in the context of this reading.

_____ 1. not just a <u>cog</u> in the machinery (Paragraph 4):

 a. mechanism   c. driver

 b. part   d. robot

_____ 2. <u>forensic</u> psychologist (Paragraph 16):

     a. employed in schools

     b. expert in drug addiction

     c. specializing in dream analysis

     d. involved with legal investigations

_____ 3. airplane <u>riveters</u> found out (Paragraph 21):

     a. workers who clean the entire airplane

     b. airplane engine mechanics

     c. workers who fasten pieces of metal with a metallic pin

     d. assistants to pilots who fly only in emergencies

_____ 4. <u>chronicles</u> his life (Paragraph 30):

     a. reports   c. honors

     b. insults   d. constructs

_____ 5. life as a <u>workaholic</u> (Paragraph 30):

     a. worker who takes a lot of time off

     b. worker with a poor work history

     c. worker who needs to work all the time

     d. worker with alcohol problems

Comprehension Questions

Choose the answer that best completes each statement.

_____ 1. The first example in the reading is Guillermo Perez, who finds meaning in his new job because

     a. he is now making more money than in his last job.

     b. he enjoys being a professor of psychology.

     c. the company has given him new opportunities.

     d. he never had a mid-level job before.

_____ 2. Katrina Elias, now a saleswoman at Beverly Hills Ford, says that to be happy a salesperson needs to

     a. find a business that sells actual products, not just radio or television time.

     b. sell products cheaply so people with special needs can afford them.

     c. beat the sales records of the other salespeople in the business.

     d. believe the product you're selling will benefit the buyer.

_____ 3. When the psychologist Sidney Walter asks people what the purpose of their job is, most answer

    a. they want to make a difference to others.

    b. they don't know.

    c. to make money.

    d. to have a better job than their parents did.

_____ 4. When Walter worked at one of his first jobs in a corporation, he discovered that the people who did the most work and stayed overtime

    a. were rewarded with better jobs and became more and more satisfied;

    b. were asked to do more and became increasingly unhappy.

    c. burned out quickly and had to quit after a year or so.

    d. found such satisfaction in their work that they soon learned to relax and enjoy life more.

_____ 5. The experts the author consulted say "the key [to finding job satisfaction] is not expecting the job to make you happy" because

    a. you have to find or create your own meaning in the work you do.

    b. work is naturally difficult, so you can't expect any job to make you happy.

    c. most bosses are difficult and have unreasonable expectations.

    d. in order to get ahead in a job, you have to put aside your desires for happiness.

Reading IV-B: One Airline's Magic: How Does Southwest Soar?

Vocabulary Questions

Using the methods of Strategy 3, **Use Context Clues,** and Strategy 4, **Find the Right Definition,** choose the correct definition of each underlined word as it is used in the context of this reading.

_____ 1. ferocious winter storms (Paragraph 1):

    a. fierce   c. freezing

    b. howling   d. hateful

_____ 2. made up that deficit (Paragraph 5):

    a. shortfall   c. duty

    b. need   d. dues

_____ 3. make pay <u>concessions</u> (Paragraph 6):

    a. preferences   c. contributions

    b. compromises   d. conflicts

_____ 4. chunk of their <u>compensation</u> (Paragraph 7):

    a. advantage   c. payment

    b. improvement   d. weakness

_____ 5. high <u>morale</u> (Paragraph 13):

    a. drive   c. meaning

    b. faith   d. spirits

Comprehension Questions

Choose the answer that best completes each statement.

_____ 1. At the beginning of the reading, the author tells about Johnny Bomaster, a Southwest mechanic; what Bomaster did was unusual because he

    a. was snowed in at home but called in detailed instructions to another Southwest mechanic so planes could take off.

    b. tunneled through snowdrifts from the airport parking lot to the hangar to get to the planes.

    c. worked for 24 hours straight during the snowstorm in order to allow planes to take off.

    d. drove his snowmobile through high snowdrifts in order to get to work.

_____ 2. Another example of the way Southwest employees go out of their way to get things done is when

    a. flight attendants occasionally change airplane tires.

    b. pilots occasionally help ground crews move luggage.

    c. flight attendants occasionally get passengers to help them tidy up the plane between flights.

    d. pilots occasionally take over for air traffic controllers.

_____ 3. One financial advantage that helps make up for Southwest workers' lower base pay than other airlines is

    a. free travel for all family members.

    b. shorter work hours.

    c. more job security.

    d. more opportunities for moving up in the company.

_____ 4. Management tries to maintain the airline's high employee morale and good customer service mainly through

   a. careful recruitment and training.

   b. competitive pay and benefits packages.

   c. workshops featuring games and funny skits.

   d. choosing point-to-point domestic routes.

_____ 5. Southwest's pilots rejected the union's recommendations and agreed instead to the management offer because

   a. the union's recommendation did not offer a high enough raise.

   b. the airline industry and the economy were in terrible shape.

   c. management refused to negotiate on wages.

   d. the pilots wanted to retain their flexibility over work rules.

Reading IV-C: The Bridge

Vocabulary Questions

Using the methods of Strategy 3, **Use Context Clues,** and Strategy 4, **Find the Right Definition,** choose the correct definition of each underlined word as it is used in the context of this reading.

_____ 1. veer from tradition (Paragraph 2):

   a. circle around   c. break out

   b. learn something   d. turn away

_____ 2. make sure it's fast (Paragraph 3):

   a. sharp   c. quick

   b. tight   d. smart

_____ 3. under duress (Paragraph 3):

   a. weight   c. pressure

   b. load   d. problem

_____ 4. corroded plates (Paragraph 3):

   a. dull   c. rusty

   b. stained   d. damaged

_____ 5. <u>trajectory</u> was poor (Paragraph 7):

    a. path of a moving object through space

    b. shortest distance between two points

    c. free-falling motion

    d. sense of direction

Comprehension Questions

Choose the answer that best completes each statement.

_____ 1. Baby's nickname broke the bridge crew's tradition, because nicknames

    a. were usually picked at random.

    b. were rarely given to newcomers.

    c. usually matched the crew member's personality more closely.

    d. usually came from the boss's list of favorites.

_____ 2. Baby unclips his safety line and goes down the platform because

    a. his noise helmet fell over the side of the bridge.

    b. he looked up and saw someone about to jump.

    c. he was upset that Whale kept getting mad at him.

    d. he had to look for a kink in the paint hose.

_____ 3. When Baby saw the woman, her face was

    a. turned away from him.

    b. several feet away from his face.

    c. inches away from his face.

    d. distorted by the wind.

_____ 4. Whale helps Baby back up the ladder

    a. by putting his hands on the first rung and encouraging him to make it on his own.

    b. by staying with his belly to Baby's back, so they move up each rung together.

    c. but Baby finally tells him he can go up the last rungs by himself.

    d. while he whispers to Baby how stupid he was to unclip his safety line.

_____ 5. When Baby's noise helmet falls over the side of the bridge, Bulldog tells Baby to take the rest of the day off and "Go home . . . and kiss your wife" because Bulldog

    a. realizes Baby is still shocked and distressed from seeing the jumper.

    b. has been told that Baby's wife became hysterical when she heard about the jumper.

    c. wouldn't allow his crew members to work without a noise helmet.

    d. was upset because Baby's experience reminded him of his own failures to stop jumpers.

Reading IV-D: Who Burns for the Perfection of Paper

Comprehension Questions

Choose the answer that best completes each statement.

_____ 1. The paper Espada refers to in the poem is for

    a. wallpaper.

    b. newspapers.

    c. legal pads.

    d. stationery.

_____ 2. Workers couldn't use gloves because

    a. the red glue would stain gloves.

    b. gloves for workers were too costly.

    c. workers needed to develop a thick skin on their hands.

    d. bare fingertips were more accurate.

_____ 3. Being sluggish would make the hands "slide along suddenly sharp paper" because

    a. experience made the hands manage the paper more easily.

    b. fatigue causes one to be less careful.

    c. the night manager forced workers to speed up their work.

    d. a different grade of paper was used on the night shift.

_____ 4. Choose the lines that give an example of a metaphor in the poem.

   a. lines 1–2: "At sixteen, I worked after high school hours/at a printing plant"

   b. lines 23–24: ". . . every legal pad/was glued with the sting of hidden cuts"

   c. lines 4–6: "Yellow paper/stacked seven feet high/and leaning"

   d. lines 11–12: "No gloves: fingertips required/for the perfection of paper"

_____ 5. Choose the most likely interpretation of the final lines of the poem:

. . . every open law book
was a pair of hands
upturned and burning.

   a. two hands placed together in the shape of an open book represent the suffering of those who made the physical book

   b. two hands with palms pressed together represent a prayer for those who suffered making the book

   c. the open and burning hands represent the burning desire of law students to help others

   d. one hand represents the suffering of the writer of the book; the other hand represents the suffering of the maker of the physical book

BIBLIOGRAPHY

American Heritage On-Line Dictionary. www.yourdictionary.com

Baker, Russell. *Growing Up.* New York: Congdon & Weed, 1982.

Bazrod, Sondra Farrell. "Satisfaction Not Guaranteed, but You Can Find Meaning in Your Work." *Los Angeles Times*, Sept. 9, 2001.

Blum, Deborah. "Finding Strength: How to Overcome Anything." *Psychology Today,* May–June 1998.

Cisneros, Sandra. "Only Daughter." In *Latina: Women's Voices from the Borderlands,* edited by Lillian Castillo-Speed. New York: Simon and Schuster, 1995.

Cohen, Adam. "Thurgood Marshall: The Brain of the Civil Rights Movement." *Time,* June 14, 1999.

Cuomo, Mario. *Diaries of Mario M. Cuomo: The Campaign for Governor.* New York: Random House, 1984.

Dalzell, Tom. *Flappers 2 Rappers: American Youth Slang.* Springfield, MA: Merriam-Webster, 1996.

DeVito, Joseph A. *Human Communication: The Basic Course.* 8th ed. New York: Addison Wesley Longman, 2000.

Donatelle, Rebecca J. *Access to Health.* 7th ed. San Francisco: Benjamin Cummings, 2002.

Donnelly, Sally B. "One Airline's Magic: How Does Southwest Soar?" *Time,* October 28, 2002.

Ehrenreich, Barbara. *Nickel and Dimed: On (Not) Getting By in America.* New York: Henry Holt and Company, 2001.

Espada, Martín. "Who Burns for the Perfection of Paper." *City of Coughing and Dead Radiators.* New York: W. W. Norton, 1993.

Fimrite, Ron. "The Day Athletics Won Out Over Politics." *Sports Illustrated,* July 29, 1996.

Frazier, Ian. "Dearly Disconnected." *Mother Jones,* January–February 2001.

Goleman, Daniel. *Emotional Intelligence.* New York: Bantam Books, 1995.

Gonzalez-Mena, Janet, and Janet Emerita. *The Child in the Family and the Community.* 3rd ed. Upper Saddle River, NJ: Merrill Prentice Hall, 2002.

Hales, Dianne. "Money Fights Can Ruin a Marriage." *Woman's Day,* April 1, 1992.

Henderson, Nan. "The Resiliency Route to Authentic Self-Esteem and Life Success." www.resiliency.com

Henslin, James M. *Essentials of Sociology.* 4th ed. Boston: Allyn and Bacon, 2002.

Martin, James Kirby, Randy Roberts, Steven Mintz, Linda O. McMurry, and James H. Jones. *America and Its Peoples: A Mosaic in the Making.* 4th ed. New York: Addison Wesley Longman, 2001.

Medina, Tony, and Louis Reyes Rivera, editors. *bum rush the page: a def poetry jam.* New York: Three Rivers Press, 2001.

Moore, Marianne. "I May, I Might, I Must" (as "Progress"). *Tipyn O'Bob* (Bryn Mawr literary magazine), 1909.

Orozco, Daniel. "The Bridge." *Story,* Autumn 1995.

Quindlen, Anna. "Horrors! Girls With Gavels! What a Difference a Day Makes!" *Newsweek,* April 15, 2002.

Reich, Robert. "Lost Jobs, Ragged Safety Net." *New York Times,* November 12, 2001.

Rimer, Sara. "Sounds of Home: An 8,690-Mile Echo." *New York Times,* August 23, 2002.

Rozhon, Tracie. "The Race to Think Like a Teenager." *New York Times,* November 12, 2001.

Sanders, Scott Russell. *The Paradise of Bombs.* Athens, GA: University of Georgia Press, 1984.

Talaski, Karen. "Ambient Advertising Invades Consumers." *Detroit News,* October 21, 2001.

Tannen, Deborah. *Talking from 9 to 5: Women and Men in the Workplace.* New York: William Morrow & Co., 1994.

Vivian, John. *The Media of Mass Communication.* 6th ed. Boston: Allyn and Bacon, 2003.

Wade, Carole, and Carol Tavris. *Invitation to Psychology*. 2nd ed. Upper Saddle River, NJ: Prentice Hall, 2002.

Wallace, Robert A. *Biology: The World of Life*. 7th ed. Menlo Park, CA: Addison Wesley Longman, 1997.

Wanamaker, Tom. "A Role Model of Resiliency: Bouncing Back from Disaster." *Indian Country Today*, March 20, 2002.

Wong, Elizabeth. "The Struggle to Be an All-American Girl." *Los Angeles Times*, 1994.

CREDITS

Photo Credits

INDEX